Econfina Creek

Maid

Bunkers Cove

Redfish Point

Smack Bayou

Tyndall A.F.B.

Island

N
W · E
S

Bay Fêtes

A Tour of Celebrations Along the Gulf Coast

The Junior Service League of Panama City

People's First Community Bank

People's First Community Bank, sponsor of the front cover, has been pleased to help support the work of the Junior Service League of Panama City by participating as an underwriter of this cookbook. The bank, which was established in 1983, is committed to serving communities as an outstanding corporate citizen, both through involvement by its employees in charitable activities and through the financial support of laudable organizations like the Junior Service League.

Bay Fêtes

A Tour of Celebrations Along the Gulf Coast

The Junior Service League of Panama City

Bay Fêtes

A Tour of Celebrations Along the Gulf Coast

Published by The Junior Service League of Panama City, Inc.

Photography: Chip Lloyd
Artist: Jann Wyckoff Daughdrill

This cookbook is a collection of favorite recipes, which are not necessarily original recipes.

Library of Congress Catalog Number: 2002113170
ISBN: 0-9615014-2-1

Edited, Designed, and Manufactured by
Favorite Recipes® Press
an imprint of

P.O. Box 305142
Nashville, Tennessee 37230
800-358-0560

Art Director: Steve Newman
Book Design: Jim Scott
Project Manager: Jane Hinshaw
Editor: Debbie Van Mol, RD
Production Design: Sara Anglin
Copy Editor: Anne Gillem

Manufactured in the United States of America
First Printing: 2003
20,000 copies

Professional Credits

Photographer Chip Lloyd

For more than twenty years, Chip and Sherri Lloyd have been capturing important moments in the lives of Florida's Emerald Coast residents with fine-quality portrait photography. A business that began as a hobby and a dream has evolved into the area's preeminent family portrait studio. Their work can be viewed on line at www.lloydsphotography.com.

Artist Jann Wyckoff Daughdrill

Jann Wyckoff Daughdrill is an accomplished and successful portraitist, one of the few to work in watercolor as well as in oil. Since 1981, she has been accepting commission work, which has supplied creative freedom through a consistent and satisfying livelihood.

Coldwell Banker Residential Real Estate, Inc.,

formerly Arvida Realty Services
Steve Counts

Coldwell Banker, sponsor of the back cover, has been in business since the early 1900s. Coldwell Banker has its own charitable foundation, the Cares Program, which services a vast array of charities.

Preface

It is in the spirit of celebration that the Junior Service League of Panama City undertook the monumental task of creating and publishing *Bay Fêtes*, its first-ever entertainment cookbook. As the name suggests, *Bay Fêtes* (pronounced "fetts") is all about celebrations, whether they be holidays, special occasions, or simply good times with family and friends.

The ensuing pages are filled with carefully tested recipes, entertainment menus, and party ideas. *Bay Fêtes* endeavors to be more than just a great entertainment cookbook, however. It is also meant to be a celebration of life in Bay County, both past and present. From downtown Panama City with all of its history, to the white-sand beaches, to the rustic northern hunting lodges, each chapter of *Bay Fêtes* takes its reader on a multifaceted tour through a different part of the county. Each stop along the tour highlights the special people, places, events, and traditions that have made Bay County the place that it is today.

While its recipes are set in the context of purely local traditions and celebrations, all of the recipes presented in *Bay Fêtes* can be easily adapted to celebrations wherever they may be held. Indeed, the French word "fête," literally meaning "party," is not characterized by a particular place, but rather by a spirit of festivity and merrymaking.

1999–2000 Junior Service League Board

President: Cathie Hanson
President-Elect: Carolyn Carroll
Treasurer: Cindy Reimers
Assistant Treasurer: Pamm Chapman
Recording Secretary: Sherri Schaler
Corresponding Secretary: Ashby Hunnicutt

2000–2001 Junior Service League Board

President: Carolyn Carroll
President-Elect: Kim Harders
Treasurer: Pamm Chapman
Assistant Treasurer: Mary Millett
Recording Secretary: Claire Sherman
Corresponding Secretary: Kim Carroll

2001–2002 Junior Service League Board

President: Kim Harders
President-Elect: Pamm Chapman
Treasurer: Mary Millett
Assistant Treasurer: Marianne Rudolph
Recording Secretary: Sealy Ledman
Corresponding Secretary: Sandy Wing

2002–2003 Junior Service League Board

President: Pamm Chapman
President-Elect: Claire Sherman
Treasurer: Marianne Rudolph
Assistant Treasurer: Kay Judah
Recording Secretary: Mary Millett
Corresponding Secretary: Barri Sapoznikoff Noll

There is an emanation from the heart in genuine hospitality
which cannot be described, but is immediately felt, and
puts the stranger at once at his ease.

—Washington Irving

Contents

Junior League Prayer

We pray that we will never be so blind
That our small world is all we see,
Or so supremely satisfied,
that what we are
Is all we ever hope to be.
Grant us the job of filling
someone's need.
Make us gracious followers;
Make gracious those who lead
And more than all we pray
That through the years,
we will remember
There are always new frontiers.

Introduction

In January of 2002, the Junior Service League of Panama City celebrated its 50th anniversary by throwing a gala "Charity Ball." More than 400 guests attended the party, including the League's first president, twenty Founding Members, and the Mayor of Panama City. That so many members and guests came to pay tribute to the League and celebrate with its members attests to the far-reaching impact that the Junior Service League has had and continues to have in the lives of Bay County residents.

Since its founding in 1951, the League has raised nearly $2,000,000 and has provided countless volunteer hours to the community through programs such as "Kids On the Block," the After School Assistance Program, the Mentorship Program, Teen Court, and the Domestic Violence Shelter Assistance Program. Nowhere are the League's fundraising and volunteer efforts more evident than at the Child Service Center and Happy Hanger programs. With an annual budget of over $50,000, these two programs provide new clothing to over 1,000 Bay County schoolchildren each year, with a grand total of nearly 20,000 children clothed.

The many successes of the Junior Service League are directly attributable to the dedication of its past and present members, as well as to the support and generosity of the local community. The League's annual "Holly Fair," which began over a decade ago as a typically local event, now attracts merchants and visitors from across the South and generates more than $120,000 in revenue for the League. The League redistributes 100 percent of this money to the community in the form of direct charitable donations. In addition to its extensive public service involvement, the Junior Service League has, since 1975, owned and operated its own publications marketing business called Bay Publications ("Bay Pub"). Bay Pub oversees the nationwide marketing and sales of the League's two existing cookbooks, *Bay Leaves* and *Beyond the Bay*, as well as a pictorial history of Bay County titled *Along the Bay*. Both cookbooks have been selected for numerous awards, including *Southern Living*'s Cookbook Hall of Fame. *Along the Bay* is in its third printing since its initial publication in 1994.

As the Junior Service League of Panama City embarks upon its second fifty years, it indeed has good reason to pause and celebrate its successful history. Even in the midst of celebration, however, the League is always forging ahead in anticipation of the future by looking into the community to identify new areas of need, and looking within its own organization for ways to insure that these needs are met. In this manner, the Junior Service League of Panama City strives continuously year after year to follow the Junior League prayer.

Acknowledgments

The Junior Service League of Panama City, Florida, appreciates the generosity of our members and friends in our community who helped to take Bay Fêtes *from a dream to a reality. We are truly indebted to the following people and wish to extend our heartfelt thanks for their time, talent, energy, and resources.*

A very special thanks goes to . . .

Chip Lloyd, Photography
Jann Daughdrill, Artwork

For the use of their beautiful homes . . .

Kerrie and Carl Beasley
Toni and Allen Bense
Amy and Steve Counts
Georgia Dake
Barbara and John Daniel
Judy and Grover Davis
Gloria and George Goodreau
Frankie and Don Gowdy
Cathie and Mike Hanson
Sandy and Jim Hundley
Sealy and Tom Ledman
The McKenzie House Foundation
Tina and Chip Nichols
John Henry Sherman
Beth and Roger Spencer
Cumi and Gary Walsingham
Melanie and George Walters

For the use of the artwork on the "Puttin' on the Ritz" menu . . .

Katrina and Elbert Fisher

For their generosity and culinary expertise . . .

Chef Paul Albrecht
Jeremy Bazata
Chef Dee Brown
Gloria Goodreau
Hannelore Holland
Michelle Holland
Chef Paul's at Carillon
Ree Pollman
Somethin's Cooking
St. Andrew Bay Yacht Club
Tebble's Table
The Treasure Ship
Penny H. Vause
Chef John Wilbert

For their generosity and valuable resources . . .

The Antique Cottage
The Fashion Corner
Reba and Dick Lovejoy
Pam McElreath
Panama City Magazine
Paper Moon
Sandpiper–Beacon Beach Resort
Something Blue
Somethin's Cooking

Set in Sterling

Ruby Remembers

A View of Grand Lagoon

Puttin' on the Ritz

Menu

Ruby Remembers

When entertaining calls for a special occasion, bring out your finest china, sterling, and crystal, like those featured from Miss Ruby's Cove Hotel. Set the table ahead of time to enjoy the splendor before the party begins. Freshly cut flowers from the garden add an old-fashioned elegance to your table.

American Cocktail

1 teaspoon bourbon
$^1/_2$ teaspoon sugar
1 dash of bitters
$^1/_2$ cup Champagne, chilled
fresh peach slice

Combine the bourbon, sugar and bitters in a Champagne flute and stir to dissolve the sugar. Fill the flute with the chilled Champagne. Garnish the rim of the flute with a peach slice.
   Serves 1

Kir Royale

1 teaspoon crème de cassis
$^3/_4$ cup Champagne, chilled
1 fresh raspberry

Pour the crème de cassis into a Champagne flute. Add the Champagne and mix gently. Garnish with a raspberry.
   Serves 1

The Cove Hotel

Any visitor to Panama City who has ever driven through the Cove is sure to recall an image of a place reminiscent of the past—an image of towering live oak trees draped with Spanish moss that form canopies across winding roads to soften the light while gentle breezes float in from the bay to provide relief from the stillness of midsummer.

It was here that the Cove Hotel, headed by Mrs. Ruby Harris, once welcomed its guests with true southern hospitality. Celebrities, honeymooners, and families alike came to stay at the Cove Hotel, which was located directly on St. Andrew Bay. Guests of the hotel enjoyed sweeping views of the open bay, their own private beach, beautiful manicured grounds, and sumptuous gourmet meals.

The Cove Hotel graced the bay from 1926 until it was tragically destroyed by fire in 1976. Its legacy lives on, however, through stories, pictures, paintings, and, not least of all, the many fabulous recipes passed on by Ruby Harris to her granddaughter and Junior Service League member, Mrs. Sealy Harris Ledman. Some of the very best of those recipes grace the pages of this book.

Asparagus Bleu Cheese Rolls

25 fresh thin asparagus spears
8 ounces cream cheese, softened
5 ounces bleu cheese, crumbled
1 egg, lightly beaten
1 teaspoon salt
25 slices sandwich bread
1/4 cup (1/2 stick) butter, melted

Snap off the woody ends of the asparagus spears and discard. Steam or blanch the asparagus until tender-crisp; drain. Let stand until cool and pat dry with paper towels. Combine the cream cheese, bleu cheese, egg and salt in a bowl and mix well.

Roll the bread slices very thin on a hard surface using a rolling pin. Spread 1 side of each slice with some of the cheese mixture. Arrange 1 asparagus spear on each slice and roll to enclose. Brush each roll with some of the butter.

Arrange the rolls on a greased baking sheet. Freeze until firm. Bake at 400 degrees for 15 minutes or until brown on all sides, turning every 5 minutes. Slice as desired and serve warm.

Makes 25 rolls

Green Grapes and Cheese Spread

16 ounces cream cheese, softened
1/3 cup chutney, finely chopped
1/4 cup finely chopped green onions
1/4 cup almonds, toasted and chopped
3 tablespoons brandy
1/4 teaspoon curry powder
1 cup seedless green grapes, cut into halves
green onion tops
grape clusters

Combine the cream cheese, chutney, chopped green onions, almonds, brandy and curry powder in a bowl and mix well. Chill, covered, in the refrigerator until firm. Mound the cream cheese mixture in an oval shape in the middle of a serving tray. Cover the surface of the oval with the grape halves cut side down to resemble the shape of a pineapple. You may chill, covered, at this point for up to 3 days.

Insert the green onion tops at the top of the cheese mound. Surround with the grape clusters and serve with assorted party crackers.

Serves 16

Recipe for this photograph on page 16.

Bleu Cheese and Spiced Pecan Terrine

1/2 teaspoon salt
1/2 teaspoon cumin
1/4 teaspoon cardamom
1/4 teaspoon freshly ground pepper
1 tablespoon olive oil
1 cup pecans
3 tablespoons sugar
16 ounces bleu cheese, crumbled, at
  room temperature
2 1/2 ounces soft fresh goat cheese such
  as Montrachet, at room
  temperature

2 1/2 ounces cream cheese, softened
1/4 cup (1/2 stick) butter, softened
1/2 cup chopped green onions
2 tablespoons brandy
2 tablespoons chopped fresh parsley
1 tablespoon chopped fresh chives
red leaf lettuce leaves
sliced apples
sliced pears

Lightly oil a medium bowl. Line the oiled bowl with plastic wrap, allowing the plastic wrap to extend over the edge. Mix the salt, cumin, cardamom and pepper in a bowl. Heat the olive oil in a heavy skillet over medium heat. Sauté the pecans in the hot olive oil for 5 minutes or until light brown. Sprinkle with the sugar. Sauté for 4 minutes longer or until caramelized. Add the pecans to the salt mixture and toss to coat. Let stand until cool and coarsely chop.

Combine 12 ounces of the bleu cheese, goat cheese, cream cheese and butter in a food processor. Process until smooth. Combine the cheese mixture with the green onions and brandy in a bowl and mix well. Mix the parsley and chives in a small bowl.

Layer 1/3 of the cheese mixture, 1/3 of the remaining bleu cheese, 1/3 of the pecans and 1 tablespoon of the parsley mixture in the prepared bowl. Repeat the layering process using 1/2 of the remaining cheese mixture, 1/2 of the remaining bleu cheese, 1/2 of the remaining pecans and 1 tablespoon of the parsley mixture. Spread with the remaining cheese mixture. Fold the plastic wrap over the top to cover. Chill for 8 to 10 hours. Chill the remaining bleu cheese and parsley mixture separately. Store the remaining pecans, covered, at room temperature.

Line a serving platter with red leaf lettuce. Invert the cheese mold onto the lettuce-lined platter, discarding the plastic wrap. Sprinkle with the remaining bleu cheese, remaining pecans and remaining parsley mixture. Serve with the sliced apples, sliced pears and assorted party crackers.

Serves 12

Champagne Cups

Fill a pitcher or small punch bowl 1/4 full with ice cubes. Add 2 1/2 cups chilled Champagne, 3 1/2 cups brandy, 1/4 cup curaçao, 2 tablespoons maraschino liqueur and 2 tablespoons Grand Marnier and mix gently. Pour into 6 punch cups and garnish each punch cup with an orange slice, a pineapple slice and a mint sprig.

Early Days at the Cove Hotel

Owner J.R. Sealy advertised the Cove Hotel and environs as a paradise for sportsmen. A letter contained the following information:

"A good room with private bath $2.00 per day. Breakfast 50¢; Lunch 75¢ and Dinner 75¢. A good saddle horse for all-day use $5.00 per day. A hunting guide for $4.00 per day. In the event you desire to use your own car and own dogs, you can eliminate the expense of horse and guide. When we furnish the guide, we also furnish dogs for hunting. Our leased hunting land is for quail, deer, turkey, fox, duck and wild geese hunting."

—From a letter signed J.R and C.S. Sealy

Shrimp Cakes with Asparagus

Chive Vinaigrette
1 cup olive oil
²/₃ cup chopped fresh chives or
    green onions
¹/₄ cup fresh lemon juice
3 tablespoons finely chopped shallots

Shrimp Cakes
36 asparagus spears, trimmed to
    6-inch lengths
salt to taste
¹/₄ cup (¹/₂ stick) unsalted butter

²/₃ cup chopped shallots
1¹/₂ pounds medium shrimp, peeled,
    deveined, finely chopped
8 ounces scallops, finely chopped
1¹/₂ cups fresh white bread crumbs
1 cup chopped red bell pepper
2 eggs, beaten
¹/₄ cup chopped fresh chives or
    green onions
pepper to taste
2 tablespoons unsalted butter
3 tablespoons chopped shallots

For the vinaigrette, whisk the olive oil, chives, lemon juice and shallots in a bowl. You may prepare up to 4 hours in advance and store, covered, at room temperature.

For the shrimp cakes, cook the asparagus in boiling salted water in a saucepan for 3 minutes or until tender-crisp; drain. Rinse with cold water and drain. Finely chop 4 of the asparagus spears. Reserve the remaining whole spears.

Heat 2 tablespoons unsalted butter in a heavy skillet over medium heat. Sauté ²/₃ cup shallots in the butter for 2 minutes. Stir in the shrimp, scallops, bread crumbs, bell pepper, eggs and chives. Season generously with salt and pepper. Remove from the heat.

Shape the shrimp mixture into eight 3¹/₂- to 4-inch cakes. You may prepare to this point up to 2 hours in advance and store, covered, in the refrigerator. Heat 2 tablespoons unsalted butter in a nonstick skillet over medium heat. Cook the cakes in batches in the butter for 5 minutes per side or until brown and cooked through.

To serve, arrange 1 shrimp cake in the center of each serving plate. Arrange 4 of the reserved asparagus spears around each cake, overlapping at the corners to form a box. Drizzle with some of the vinaigrette and sprinkle with 3 tablespoons shallots. Serve with the remaining vinaigrette.

Serves 8

Wild Mushroom and Vegetable Soup

1 pound fresh wild mushroom caps, sliced
6 cups chicken broth
1 tablespoon each vegetable oil and water
1 each medium onion and leek bulb, chopped
2 ribs celery, chopped
2 cups chopped carrots
1 garlic clove, chopped
salt and pepper to taste
6 tablespoons unsalted butter
$^1/_2$ cup flour
1 (14-ounce) can diced tomatoes, drained
$^1/_2$ cup each heavy cream and half-and-half
marsala or sherry
thinly sliced fresh wild mushrooms
finely chopped fresh parsley

Bring the mushrooms and broth to a boil in a 2$^1/_2$-quart saucepan. Simmer for 30 minutes, stirring occasionally. Heat the oil and water in a 5-quart saucepan over medium heat. Add the onion, leek, celery, carrots, garlic, salt and pepper. Sauté for 5 to 8 minutes or until the onion is tender. Add the undrained mushrooms and mix well. Bring to a simmer.

Melt the unsalted butter in a saucepan over medium-low heat. Stir in the flour. Cook for 6 to 8 minutes or until bubbly, stirring constantly. Add the vegetable and broth mixture and mix well. Stir in the tomatoes. Simmer for 20 minutes, stirring occasionally. Stir in the heavy cream and half-and-half. Cook for 5 minutes longer or until heated through, stirring frequently. Season with salt and pepper. Process the soup in a food processor until puréed or purée with a hand blender. Ladle into soup bowls. Garnish each serving with a splash of wine, thinly sliced mushrooms and/or parsley.

Serves 8

Sherried She-Crab Soup

$^1/_4$ cup ($^1/_2$ stick) unsalted butter
$^1/_2$ cup minced onion
$^1/_4$ cup minced celery
1 tablespoon minced garlic
2 tablespoons flour
2 cups milk
2 cups heavy cream
1 cup bottled clam juice
1$^1/_2$ teaspoons salt
1 teaspoon grated lemon zest
$^1/_2$ teaspoon mace
$^1/_4$ teaspoon pepper
1 pound lump crab meat, shells and cartilage removed
salt and pepper to taste
$^1/_4$ cup sherry
1 teaspoon paprika
2 tablespoons chopped fresh parsley

Heat the unsalted butter in a Dutch oven over medium-high heat. Sauté the onion, celery and garlic in the butter for 3 to 5 minutes or until the onion and celery are tender. Sprinkle with the flour and stir to mix. Add the milk, heavy cream and clam juice and mix well. Stir in 1$^1/_2$ teaspoons salt, lemon zest, mace and $^1/_4$ teaspoon pepper.

Bring to a low boil; reduce the heat. Stir in $^1/_2$ of the crab meat. Simmer for 10 to 15 minutes, stirring frequently. Season with salt and pepper to taste. Stir in the remaining crab meat and sherry. Bring to a low boil. Cook just until heated through, stirring frequently. Ladle into soup bowls. Sprinkle each serving with the paprika and parsley.

Serves 6

Spinach Salad with Gorgonzola Dressing

2 tablespoons white wine vinegar
2 tablespoons Dijon mustard
1¹/₂ tablespoons honey
salt and pepper to taste
2 (10-ounce) packages fresh spinach, stems removed
3 cups (about 8 ounces) sliced mushrooms
1 cup pitted kalamata olives or other brine-cured olives
1 tablespoon extra-virgin olive oil
1³/₄ cups crumbled Gorgonzola cheese or bleu cheese
¹/₄ cup heavy whipping cream or half-and-half

Whisk the vinegar, Dijon mustard and honey in a bowl until blended. Season with salt and pepper. You may prepare in advance and store, covered, in the refrigerator.

Place the spinach in a large salad bowl or divide evenly among 6 serving plates. Arrange the mushrooms and olives over the spinach. Heat the olive oil in a skillet over high heat. Reduce the heat to medium-low. Add the cheese, whipping cream and vinegar mixture and mix well.

Cook until blended, stirring frequently; do not boil. Drizzle the warm dressing over the salad. Serve immediately. For variety, crumble 10 slices crisp-cooked bacon over the spinach and substitute 1 tablespoon bacon drippings for the olive oil.

Serves 6

Fresh Mozzarella and Tomato Salad

Balsamic Vinaigrette
6 tablespoons balsamic vinegar
3 tablespoons extra-virgin olive oil
3 tablespoons red wine vinegar
2 teaspoons minced garlic
¹/₂ teaspoon English dry mustard
¹/₂ teaspoon salt
¹/₂ teaspoon pepper
1 teaspoon Greek seasoning
¹/₄ teaspoon sugar

Salad
3 large vine-ripe tomatoes, cut into ¹/₄-inch slices
12 ounces mozzarella cheese (preferably fresh),
  cut into ¹/₄-inch slices
12 to 16 fresh basil leaves, thinly sliced

For the vinaigrette, whisk the balsamic vinegar, olive oil, red wine vinegar, garlic, dry mustard, salt, pepper, Greek seasoning and sugar in a bowl.

For the salad, place the tomato slices and cheese slices in a shallow dish and drizzle with the vinaigrette, turning to coat. Marinate at room temperature for 30 minutes, turning occasionally. Arrange the tomato slices and cheese slices alternately on a large platter or on individual salad plates, reserving the vinaigrette. Sprinkle with the basil and drizzle with the reserved vinaigrette.

Serves 6

Grecian-Style Stuffed Tenderloin

1 pound sliced bacon
2 pounds fresh spinach, stems removed
1 tablespoon minced garlic
2 cups feta cheese
1/2 cup cream cheese, softened
1/2 cup sour cream
1/4 cup white wine
1/4 cup grated Parmesan cheese
1 tablespoon Cavender's Greek seasoning
10 (6- to 8-ounce) beef tenderloin steaks, 1 1/2 inches thick
salt and pepper to taste

Fry the bacon in a skillet until crisp. Remove the bacon to paper towels to drain, reserving 3 tablespoons of the bacon drippings. Crumble the bacon.

Heat the reserved bacon drippings over medium-high heat. Stir in the spinach. Sauté for 3 to 5 minutes. Add the garlic. Sauté for 1 minute longer. Stir in the feta cheese, cream cheese, sour cream, wine, Parmesan cheese and Cavender's seasoning. Cook until combined, stirring frequently. Spoon into a bowl. Chill, covered, for 1 to 2 hours.

Make an "X" in the top of each steak with a sharp knife, cutting approximately 3/4 of the way through the steaks. Fill each "X" with 3 tablespoons of the cheese mixture. Sprinkle with salt and pepper.

Arrange the steaks stuffed side down on a grill rack. Grill the steaks over hot coals for 3 minutes or until brown. Turn the steaks carefully with a metal spatula scraping up the cheese crust with the steaks. Grill for 1 minute longer or until brown on the remaining side. Remove the steaks to a large ovenproof sauté pan. Bake at 400 degrees for 12 minutes for rare or to the desired degree of doneness.

Serves 10

Spice-Encrusted Beef Tenderloin

1 1/2 teaspoons onion powder
1 1/2 teaspoons garlic powder
1/2 teaspoon cumin
1/2 teaspoon nutmeg
1 tablespoon salt
1 1/2 teaspoons black pepper
1 teaspoon red pepper
1 (5-pound) beef tenderloin, trimmed
1/4 cup olive oil

Mix the onion powder, garlic powder, cumin, nutmeg, salt, black pepper and red pepper in a small bowl. Rub the tenderloin with the olive oil and coat completely with the spice mixture. Arrange the tenderloin in a roasting pan and cover with plastic wrap. Marinate in the refrigerator for 8 hours or longer.

Roast, uncovered, at 500 degrees for 20 minutes. Reduce the oven temperature to 375 degrees and roast for 20 to 25 minutes longer or to the desired degree of doneness. Let stand for 10 minutes before slicing. Serve with prepared horseradish sauce.

Serves 8

Celebrating with Champagne

Serving Champagne with style—removing the cork quietly, cooling the wine to the proper temperature, keeping it in the glass and not on your guests—is not a natural gift. It requires a little practice. Champagne should be served in long-stemmed flutes or tulip-shaped glasses. These are designed to enhance the flow of bubbles to the crown and to concentrate the aromas of the wine. Never chill or ice the glass, because it takes away from the enjoyment of the wine.

Beef Tenderloin with Sun-Dried Tomato Aïoli

Beef Tenderloin
1 (2-pound) beef tenderloin
1 cup extra-virgin olive oil
³/₄ cup dry red wine
1 tablespoon chopped fresh thyme
1 tablespoon minced fresh parsley
1 garlic clove, minced
¹/₂ teaspoon freshly ground
    pepper

Sun-Dried Tomato Aïoli
¹/₄ cup drained oil-pack sun-dried
    tomatoes
1 egg
1 garlic clove, minced
1¹/₂ teaspoons Dijon mustard
1¹/₂ teaspoons fresh lemon juice
³/₄ cup extra-virgin olive oil
salt and pepper to taste

For the tenderloin, arrange the tenderloin in a shallow dish. Whisk the olive oil, wine, thyme, parsley, garlic and pepper in a bowl. Pour the olive oil mixture over the tenderloin, turning to coat. Marinate, covered, in the refrigerator for 2 hours or longer, turning occasionally.

Drain the tenderloin, discarding the marinade. Grill the tenderloin over indirect heat or medium heat for 45 minutes or to the desired degree of doneness, turning occasionally. Remove the tenderloin to a heated platter. Let stand for 10 minutes before slicing.

For the aïoli, process the sun-dried tomatoes in a food processor until chopped. Add the egg, garlic, Dijon mustard and lemon juice. Process until blended. Add the olive oil gradually, processing constantly until smooth and thick. Season with salt and pepper. Serve with the sliced tenderloin. You may prepare the sauce in advance and store, covered, in the refrigerator for up to 4 days. To avoid uncooked eggs that may carry salmonella, we suggest using an equivalent amount of pasteurized egg substitute.

Serves 6

Scalloped Parmesan New Potatoes

4 to 5 pounds new potatoes or red creamer
    potatoes, sliced
2 cups chicken broth
2 cups water
2 cups heavy cream
2 teaspoons cornstarch
1 teaspoon salt
1 teaspoon pepper
$^1/_2$ teaspoon garlic powder
1 teaspoon MSG (optional)
$1^1/_4$ cups grated Parmesan cheese
chopped fresh parsley (optional)

Combine the potatoes, broth and water in a saucepan. Bring to a boil. Boil for 5 minutes. Drain, reserving 1 cup of the liquid. Combine the reserved liquid with the heavy cream, cornstarch, salt, pepper, garlic powder and MSG in a bowl and mix well.

Layer $^1/_2$ of the potatoes, 1 cup of the cheese and remaining potatoes in a 9×13-inch baking dish. Pour the cream mixture over the top. Bake, covered, at 350 degrees for 45 minutes, stirring gently halfway through the baking process. Turn off the oven. Let the potatoes stand in the oven with the door closed for 15 minutes.

Sprinkle the remaining $^1/_4$ cup cheese and parsley over the top of the potatoes just before ready to serve. Broil until golden brown. You may prepare in advance and store, covered, in the refrigerator. Reheat before serving.

Serves 8 to 10

Spinach Soufflé with Gouda Cheese

1 (10-ounce) package frozen chopped spinach, thawed
    and drained
$2^1/_2$ cups milk
$^1/_4$ cup ($^1/_2$ stick) butter
$^1/_4$ cup flour
4 egg yolks, lightly beaten
1 tablespoon butter
1 cup chopped shallots
$1^1/_3$ cups shredded smoked Gouda cheese
$^3/_4$ teaspoon salt
$^1/_2$ teaspoon each pepper and nutmeg
4 egg whites
$^2/_3$ cup shredded smoked Gouda cheese

Squeeze the excess moisture from the spinach. Bring the milk to a boil in a medium saucepan. Remove from the heat. Melt $^1/_4$ cup butter in a medium heavy saucepan over low heat. Stir in the flour. Cook for 3 to 4 minutes or until bubbly, stirring constantly. Whisk in the warm milk gradually. Increase the heat to medium. Cook for 4 minutes longer or until thickened and of a sauce consistency, whisking constantly. Remove from the heat. Stir a small amount of the hot mixture into the egg yolks. Stir the egg yolk mixture into the hot mixture. Cool slightly.

Heat 1 tablespoon butter in a large skillet over medium heat. Sauté the shallots in the butter for 4 minutes or until tender. Spoon the undrained shallots into a large bowl. Stir in the spinach, warm sauce, $1^1/_3$ cups cheese, salt, pepper and nutmeg. Beat the egg whites in a mixing bowl until stiff but not dry peaks form. Fold the egg whites $^1/_2$ at a time into the spinach mixture. Spoon into a buttered 7×11-inch baking dish. Sprinkle with $^2/_3$ cup cheese. Bake at 350 degrees for 45 minutes or until puffed and set. Serve immediately.

Serves 8

Amaretto Crème Brûlée

2 cups heavy cream
4 ounces white chocolate, chopped (optional)
4 egg yolks, lightly beaten
1/3 cup sugar
2 teaspoons amaretto or Frangelico
1/4 cup each sugar and packed light brown sugar
cinnamon (optional)

Heat the heavy cream in a saucepan until bubbly. Stir in the white chocolate. Cook until blended, stirring constantly. Remove from the heat. Whisk the egg yolks, 1/3 cup sugar and liqueur in a bowl until blended. Whisk in the hot cream mixture gradually.

Pour the cream mixture into 6 ovenproof ramekins. Arrange the ramekins in a large baking pan. Add enough water to the baking pan to reach 3/4 way up the sides of the ramekins. Bake at 325 degrees for 30 to 35 minutes or until set. Cool slightly. Chill for 1 hour or up to 2 days.

Process 1/4 cup sugar, brown sugar and cinnamon in a food processor. Sprinkle over the custards. Caramelize with a blow torch or broil until brown. Increase the egg yolks to 5 if omitting the white chocolate.

Serves 6

White Chocolate Raspberry Cake

2 (2-layer) packages white cake mix
1 (1-ounce) bottle pure almond extract
2 (12-ounce) packages frozen raspberries
2 (1-pound) packages confectioners' sugar
1 cup (2 sticks) butter, softened
3 to 5 tablespoons half-and-half
1 teaspoon almond extract
fresh raspberries
white chocolate curls

Prepare the cake mixes using the package directions; stir in the bottle of almond extract. Spoon into 3 greased and floured 10-inch cake pans. Bake using package directions. Cool in pans for 10 minutes. Remove to a wire rack to cool completely.

Heat the raspberries in a saucepan over medium heat until bubbly, stirring frequently. Press through a fine mesh strainer into a bowl.

Beat the confectioners' sugar and butter in a mixing bowl to the consistency of a light paste. Add the half-and-half and 1 teaspoon almond extract gradually, beating constantly until smooth and of a spreading consistency, scraping the bowl occasionally.

Cut each cake layer horizontally into halves. Arrange 1 layer on a cake plate. Spread with 1/3 of the raspberry sauce. Top with another cake layer and spread with 1/3 of the frosting. Repeat the process with the remaining cake layers, remaining sauce and remaining frosting, ending with the frosting. Garnish with fresh raspberries and white chocolate curls.

Serves 12

White Chocolate and Raspberry Cheesecake

Chocolate Graham Cracker Crust
2 sleeves chocolate graham crackers
6 tablespoons (³/₄ stick) butter, melted

Filling
1 (12-ounce) package frozen raspberries, thawed
32 ounces cream cheese, softened
1¹/₃ cups sugar

2 tablespoons flour
4 eggs
2 tablespoons heavy cream
2 teaspoons vanilla extract
¹/₂ teaspoon almond extract
6 ounces white chocolate, finely chopped
white chocolate curls
fresh raspberries

For the crust, spray a 9-inch springform pan with a 2³/₄-inch side with nonstick cooking spray and double wrap the outside with heavy-duty foil.

Process the graham crackers in a food processor until coarse crumbs form. Add the butter. Process until mixed well. Press the crumb mixture over the bottom and halfway up the side of the prepared springform pan. Bake at 325 degrees for 8 minutes. Cool on a wire rack. Retain oven temperature.

For the filling, process the raspberries in a food processor until puréed. Press the purée through a sieve into a measuring cup until the purée measures ¹/₂ cup, discarding the seeds. Combine the cream cheese and sugar in a mixing bowl and beat until smooth. Add the flour and mix well. Beat in the eggs 1 at a time, beating well after each addition. Stir in the heavy cream and vanilla. Remove 2¹/₄ cups of the batter to a medium bowl and reserve. Stir the raspberry purée and almond extract into the batter remaining in the bowl. Pour into the crust.

Place the springform pan in a roasting pan. Add enough hot water to the roasting pan to reach halfway up the side of the springform pan. Bake for 50 minutes or just until set in the center. Cool on a wire rack for 5 minutes.

Melt the white chocolate in a heavy saucepan or microwave and stir until smooth. Add to the reserved batter and mix well. Spoon the white chocolate batter over the filling, starting at the edge and moving toward the center; smooth the top. Bake for 30 minutes longer. Cool on a wire rack. Chill for at least 4 hours before covering with plastic wrap. You may store in the refrigerator for up to 2 days.

Place the cheesecake on a serving plate. Run a sharp knife around the edge of the pan to loosen. Garnish with white chocolate curls and fresh raspberries.

Serves 12

Chilling Champagne

Champagne should be served cold at about 43 to 48 degrees Fahrenheit. In this range, the smell and taste of the wine can be fully appreciated. This temperature can be achieved by placing the unopened bottle in an ice bucket filled half with ice and half with water for 20 to 30 minutes or in the refrigerator for 3 to 4 hours. Never place Champagne in the freezer.

MENU

A View of Grand Lagoon

Take advantage of Florida's weather by beginning an elegant dinner party on the patio with refreshing cocktails and seafood appetizers. Entice guests into the dining room for an elegant dinner. Dessert is served as everyone enjoys the fabulous view of the lagoon.

Crab Cakes with Lemon Dill Sauce

Lemon Dill Sauce

³/₄ cup mayonnaise

¹/₂ cup buttermilk

2 teaspoons fresh lemon juice

1 tablespoon grated lemon zest

2 small garlic cloves, minced

2 tablespoons chopped fresh dill weed

1 tablespoon minced fresh parsley

Crab Cakes

2 to 3 tablespoons chopped green
    onions

1 tablespoon chopped fresh parsley

2 tablespoons mayonnaise

1 tablespoon Worcestershire sauce

juice of 1 lemon

1 tablespoon baking powder

1 tablespoon dry mustard

1 teaspoon seafood seasoning

¹/₂ teaspoon salt

1 egg

bread crumbs

1 pound crab meat, shells and
    cartilage removed

For the sauce, blend the mayonnaise with the buttermilk in a bowl. Add the lemon juice, lemon zest, garlic, dill weed and parsley and mix well. Chill, covered, until thickened.

    For the crab cakes, combine the green onions, parsley, mayonnaise, Worcestershire sauce, lemon juice, baking powder, dry mustard, seafood seasoning and salt in a bowl and mix well.

    Beat the egg in a small bowl. Add enough bread crumbs to the egg to bind the crab cakes and mix to moisten. Add to the green onion mixture and mix gently. Fold in the crab meat.

    Shape the crab meat mixture into small cakes. Brown on both sides in a lightly oiled nonstick skillet. Serve with the sauce.

    Serves 4

Bay Point Yacht and Country Club

Founded in 1972, the resort village of Bay Point Yacht and Country Club rests on a site along Grand Lagoon that was once known for its towering dunes and bubbling springs. Long ago, couples and families came for quiet picnics amidst these dunes, but now visitors and residents come to Bay Point to experience one of Florida's most popular destinations.

    Few resorts anywhere have attracted more attention and acclaim than Bay Point. It is home to one of Florida's premier marinas, a world-renowned Marriott Resort, one of America's top ten golf courses, a luxurious condominium resort, and an established residential community. There is just no end to the good life at Bay Point!

Spicy Baked Shrimp

¹/₂ cup olive oil
2 tablespoons lemon juice
1 tablespoon honey
1 tablespoon soy sauce
cayenne pepper to taste
2 tablespoons chopped fresh parsley
2 tablespoons Cajun seasoning or Creole seasoning
1 pound shrimp, peeled and deveined

Combine the olive oil, lemon juice, honey, soy sauce, cayenne pepper, parsley and Cajun seasoning in a 9×13-inch baking dish and mix well. Add the shrimp and toss to coat. Marinate, covered, in the refrigerator for 1 hour, turning occasionally.

Bake the shrimp in the marinade at 450 degrees for 10 minutes or until cooked through, stirring occasionally. Garnish with lemon wedges and serve with French bread.

Serves 4

Grilled Whole Red Snapper

1 cup olive oil
¹/₂ cup fresh lemon juice
1 (5- to 8-pound) whole red snapper
¹/₄ cup Cavender's seasoning
¹/₄ cup coarse salt
hot sauce to taste

Blend the olive oil and lemon juice in a small bowl. Pour over the fish in a shallow dish. Sprinkle with the Cavender's seasoning, salt and hot sauce, turning to coat both sides. Marinate, covered, in the refrigerator for 1 hour or longer. Remove the fish from the marinade, reserving the marinade.

Score the skin on both sides of the fish in 3 shallow cuts parallel to the ribs. Place on a piece of heavy-duty foil slightly larger than the fish and fold up the sides to create a rim. Brush with some of the reserved marinade.

Place the fish on a hot grill rack over indirect heat and cover. Grill for 40 minutes or until the fish flakes easily, basting once with the reserved marinade; do not let the juices in the fish cavity dry out completely.

Remove the foil with the fish to a platter and trim or fold down the edges. Garnish with an olive eye if desired. Serve with lemon wedges, chopped or sliced red onion and assorted hot sauces and crackers. Provide a long-pronged fork for guests to use to serve themselves. You may add hickory or other wood chips to the coals for additional flavor if desired.

Serves 6 to 10

Roasted Garlic and Brie Soup

2 garlic bulbs, separated into cloves
2 tablespoons olive oil
1 medium onion, finely chopped
1/4 cup olive oil
2 ribs celery, finely chopped
1 carrot, finely chopped
1/4 cup flour
6 cups chicken stock
1 teaspoon chopped fresh oregano, or 1/2 teaspoon
    dried oregano
1/2 teaspoon chopped fresh thyme, or 1/4 teaspoon
    dried thyme
7 ounces Brie cheese, rind removed and cut
    into cubes
salt and white pepper to taste

Place the unpeeled garlic cloves in a medium baking dish and drizzle with 2 tablespoons olive oil; cover with foil. Roast at 325 degrees for 30 minutes or until very tender. Remove the dish to a wire rack to cool.

Sauté the onion in 1/4 cup olive oil in a large saucepan over medium heat for 10 minutes. Add the celery and carrot and sauté for 10 minutes or until tender. Stir in the flour and cook for 3 minutes, stirring frequently. Add the chicken stock gradually and bring to a boil, stirring constantly; reduce the heat to medium-low. Cook for 15 minutes or until slightly thickened, stirring constantly.

Peel the garlic and combine with 1 cup of the soup in a food processor. Process until smooth. Return the soup to the saucepan and add the oregano and thyme. Bring to a simmer over medium-low heat. Add the cheese gradually, stirring until melted after each addition. Season with salt and white pepper. Ladle into soup bowls.

Serves 6

St. Andrew Bay Scallop Chowder

1 small onion, chopped
3 tablespoons olive oil
3 medium white potatoes, chopped
1 small carrot, chopped
1 rib celery, chopped
2 cups chicken broth
1 teaspoon Old Bay seasoning
1/2 teaspoon herbes de Provence
salt and pepper to taste
8 ounces fresh button mushrooms, sliced
2 tablespoons unsalted butter
1 pound bay scallops
1/2 cup dry white wine
1 cup heavy cream
paprika to taste
crumbled crisp-cooked bacon (optional)
sprigs of fresh parsley

Sauté the onion in the olive oil in a saucepan. Stir in the potatoes, carrot and celery. Sauté for 5 minutes. Add the broth, Old Bay seasoning, herbes de Provence, salt and pepper and mix well. Simmer until the vegetables are tender, stirring occasionally. Let stand until cool. Process the potato mixture in a food processor until puréed.

Sauté the mushrooms in the unsalted butter in a skillet. Add the scallops and wine. Cook for 1 minute, stirring frequently. Stir in the heavy cream. Add the puréed mixture and mix well. Cook just until heated through, stirring frequently. Ladle into soup bowls and sprinkle with paprika and bacon. Top each serving with a sprig of parsley. Serve with crusty French bread.

Serves 4

Romaine Salad with Grapefruit

8 cups torn romaine hearts
Pomegranate and Port Vinaigrette (this page)
salt and pepper to taste
2 1/2 cups Ruby Red grapefruit sections
 (about 2 grapefruits)
3/4 cup crumbled Roquefort cheese
3/4 cup walnuts, lightly toasted and skins removed
seeds from 1 pomegranate

Toss the romaine with the Pomegranate and Port
Vinaigrette in a salad bowl until coated. Season with salt
and pepper. Divide the romaine mixture evenly among
8 chilled salad plates. Top evenly with grapefruit sections.
Sprinkle with the cheese, walnuts and pomegranate seeds.
Serve immediately.

Serves 8

Pomegranate and Port Vinaigrette

1 cup pomegranate juice or cranberry juice
1/3 cup ruby port
1/3 cup orange juice
1 teaspoon minced garlic
1 tablespoon minced shallots
1 egg yolk
2 tablespoons red wine vinegar
1/2 cup peanut oil
2 tablespoons olive oil
salt and pepper to taste

Combine the pomegranate juice, wine, orange juice and
garlic in a nonreactive saucepan. Bring to a boil; reduce
the heat. Simmer until reduced to 1/3 cup, stirring
occasionally. Place the shallots in a stainless steel bowl.
Strain the reduction over the shallots. Let stand until cool.

Whisk the reduction, egg yolk and vinegar in a bowl.
Mix the peanut oil and olive oil in a bowl. Drizzle the olive
oil mixture into the yolk mixture, whisking constantly to
emulsify. Season with salt and pepper. Serve immediately
or chill, covered, in the refrigerator.

Serves 8

Greek Salad with Shrimp and Crab

1 garlic clove, cut into halves
6 cups torn mixed salad greens
1 medium tomato, cut into wedges
1 medium green bell pepper, thinly sliced into rings
1 cucumber, thinly sliced
4 radishes, thinly sliced
3 green onions, thinly sliced
1 cup crumbled feta cheese
1/2 cup large Greek olives
1/2 cup pepperoncini chiles
1 pound medium shrimp, cooked, peeled and deveined
12 ounces lump crab meat, shells and cartilage removed
1/2 cup olive oil
1/4 cup lemon juice
1/2 teaspoon salt
1/4 teaspoon oregano
1/4 teaspoon freshly ground pepper

Rub the bottom and side of a large wooden salad bowl with the cut sides of the garlic; discard the garlic. Add the salad greens, tomato, bell pepper, cucumber, radishes, green onions, feta cheese, olives and pepperoncini chiles to the salad bowl and toss to mix.

Arrange the shrimp and crab meat over the top of the salad. Whisk the olive oil, lemon juice, salt, oregano and pepper in a bowl. Drizzle the olive oil mixture over the salad and toss gently to coat. Serve immediately.

Serves 4 to 6

Floridian Cocktail

Combine 1/2 cup each orange vodka, orange curaçao and orange juice over ice in a shaker. Add 1/4 cup pineapple juice and 1/4 cup cranberry juice. Shake well and pour into 2 chilled balloon glasses. Add ice if desired and garnish each with an orange slice.

Lemon Drop Martini

Squeeze a lemon wedge around the rims of 2 chilled martini glasses and dip the rims in sugar. Fill a cocktail shaker with ice cubes and add 1/2 cup lemon-flavored vodka, 1/2 cup Cointreau, 1/4 cup fresh lemon juice, 2 tablespoons lemon-lime soda and 1 tablespoon sweet-and-sour mix. Shake well and strain into the glasses. Garnish with lemon twists.

To make Lemon Drop Martinis for a crowd, combine 6 cups lemon vodka, 6 cups Cointreau, 3 cups fresh lemon juice, 2 cups lemon-lime soda and 1 cup sweet-and-sour mix in a large pitcher and mix well. Keep chilled and stir before pouring over a shaker of ice. Shake well and pour into glasses.

Grilled Tuna Steaks

8 (8-ounce) tuna steaks, ³/₄ inch thick
¹/₄ cup olive oil
¹/₄ cup soy sauce
2 tablespoons chopped fresh thyme
2 tablespoons fresh lemon juice
2 teaspoons minced fresh gingerroot
¹/₂ teaspoon salt
¹/₄ teaspoon freshly ground pepper
Spicy Tomato and Basil Salsa (this page)

Arrange the steaks in a shallow dish. Whisk the olive oil, soy sauce, thyme, lemon juice, gingerroot, salt and pepper in a bowl. Pour the olive oil mixture over the steaks, turning to coat. Marinate, covered, in the refrigerator for 30 minutes. Drain, discarding the marinade.

Arrange the steaks on an oiled grill rack. Grill over medium heat (300 to 350 degrees) for 2 minutes per side for rare or 5 minutes per side for cooked through. Serve with Spicy Tomato and Basil Salsa.

Serves 8

*Recipe for this photograph
on facing page.*

Spicy Tomato and Basil Salsa

2 cups chopped seeded peeled tomatoes
¹/₂ cup finely chopped green onions
¹/₂ cup chopped fresh basil
4 garlic cloves, minced
2 teaspoons finely chopped seeded jalapeño chile
¹/₂ cup olive oil
¹/₄ cup red wine vinegar
¹/₂ teaspoon salt
¹/₄ teaspoon freshly ground pepper

Combine the tomatoes, green onions, basil, garlic and jalapeño chile in a bowl and mix well. Stir in the olive oil, vinegar, salt and pepper. Let stand, covered, at room temperature for 1 hour or longer.

Serves 8

Lobster Soufflé in the Shell

4 (1¼-pound) lobsters, cooked
6 tablespoons unsalted butter
5 tablespoons flour
2 cups milk, scalded
1 teaspoon salt
½ teaspoon freshly ground pepper
6 egg yolks
8 egg whites
¼ cup grated Parmesan cheese

Split the lobsters into halves with a heavy knife, cutting from the head to the tail. Remove and reserve the tail meat and any bits of meat from the body; reserve the shells. Remove the other bits, such as the tomally and roe, and discard. Separate the claws from the body and remove the meat from each in 1 piece using kitchen shears. Remove the meat from the claw joints; discard the claw shells.

Cut away and discard the sand sac in the head. Scrape out and wash the half shells, leaving the small legs intact if possible; pat the shells dry. Set aside the claw meat and chop the remaining lobster meat.

Melt the butter in a heavy medium saucepan over medium heat and stir in the flour. Cook for 3 minutes, stirring constantly; do not allow to brown. Whisk in the hot milk gradually. Bring to a boil and cook for 2 minutes or until thickened, whisking constantly. Add the chopped lobster, salt and pepper. Process in a food processor until smooth.

Return the mixture to the saucepan. Bring to a boil over medium-high heat. Remove from the heat and cool slightly. Beat in the egg yolks 1 at a time.

Beat the egg whites in a mixing bowl until stiff but not dry. Fold half the egg whites into the egg yolks. Fold in the remaining eggs whites quickly.

Place the lobster shells on a large baking sheet. Spoon the lobster mixture into the shells. Place on a rack in the lower third of the oven and bake at 375 degrees for 15 minutes or until puffed and golden brown but still slightly soft. Sprinkle each shell with the cheese and bake for 5 minutes longer or until the cheese melts.

Steam or microwave the claw meat in a shallow dish just until warmed through. Serve the soufflés immediately, garnishing each lobster half with a whole piece of claw meat.

Serves 8

Alvin's Island Tropical Department Stores

Much has changed since Alvin Walsingham and his family opened their first beach store in 1958. At that time, the store sold the new "two-piece" bathing suit, beach towels, inner tubes now lovingly referred to as "floats," alligator ash trays, and various other Florida souvenirs. In those days, there was no air-conditioning, so the store's doors and windows were thrown wide open to let in the cool Gulf breezes.

Gary Walsingham, Alvin's son, convinced his dad to build the first "Alvin's Island" as a department store with the idea of combining everything under one roof in a tropical motif. The idea took off, and today Alvin's stores are one of America's top retail resort chains. Visitors who have shopped for years can attest that Alvin's Island is a must-stop place on every vacationer's list.

Bay Point Invitational Billfish Tournament

The Bay Point Invitational Billfish Tournament ranks as one of the top billfishing tournaments in the country. Held each July, the tournament draws thousands of spectators who come to the Bay Point Marina to join in what is now a huge summer party with plenty of food, music, and excitement that accompany the weighing-in of the catch as the anglers return from the sea.

Scallops Provençal on Toast

12 ounces thickly sliced lean bacon,
    julienned
2 tablespoons butter, softened
¹/₄ cup olive oil
3 (5-inch-long) pieces French bread,
    cut lengthwise into halves
¹/₂ cup minced shallots
2 garlic cloves, minced
¹/₂ teaspoon fennel seeds, crushed
¹/₂ teaspoon thyme, crushed
¹/₂ teaspoon dill seeds, crushed
1 cup dry white wine

¹/₄ cup Pernod
¹/₂ cup drained canned chopped
    tomatoes
¹/₂ cup tomato juice (from canned
    tomatoes)
2 tablespoons minced fresh parsley
2 pounds bay scallops
1¹/₂ tablespoons fresh lemon juice
1 teaspoon freshly ground pepper
¹/₂ teaspoon salt
¹/₂ cup pitted black olives, sliced
    into rings

Blanch the bacon in boiling water in a saucepan for 10 minutes. Drain on paper towels. Mix the butter and 1 tablespoon of the olive oil in a bowl. Spread the butter mixture evenly over the cut sides of the bread.

Heat the remaining 3 tablespoons olive oil in a nonreactive skillet over low heat. Cook the shallots and garlic in the olive oil for 5 minutes or until tender, stirring frequently. Stir in the bacon, fennel seeds, thyme and dill seeds. Cook for 5 minutes, stirring frequently. Increase the heat to medium-high. Add the wine, liqueur, tomatoes, tomato juice and parsley and mix well.

Cook for 10 minutes or until slightly thickened, stirring occasionally. Stir in the scallops. Cook for 5 minutes or until the scallops turn white, stirring frequently. Remove from the heat. Stir in the lemon juice, pepper and salt. Cover to keep warm.

Arrange the bread slices directly on the oven rack. Toast at 400 degrees for 5 minutes or until golden brown. Arrange 1 piece of the toasted bread on each of 6 dinner plates. Spoon the scallops and sauce over the bread and sprinkle with the olives. Serve immediately.

Serves 6

Broccoli and Olives Vinaigrette

florets of 1 large head broccoli (about 1½ pounds)
salt to taste
¼ cup olive oil
2 teaspoons red pepper flakes
2 tablespoons pine nuts
1 medium red bell pepper, chopped
2 garlic cloves, minced
2 tablespoons red wine vinegar
salt and black pepper to taste
1 cup pitted black olives

Blanch the broccoli in boiling salted water in a saucepan for 3 minutes or until tender-crisp; drain. Plunge the broccoli into a bowl of ice water to stop the cooking process. Drain on paper towels.

Heat the olive oil in a skillet until hot but not smoking. Add the red pepper flakes and stir for 20 to 30 seconds or until the oil begins to turn red. Remove from the heat. Cool slightly. Strain the red pepper oil through a sieve into a bowl.

Return the red pepper oil to the skillet. Stir in the pine nuts. Cook over medium heat for 1 minute, stirring constantly. Add the bell pepper and mix well. Sauté for 2 to 3 minutes or until the bell pepper is tender and the pine nuts begin to turn golden brown. Stir in the garlic, vinegar, salt and black pepper. Add the broccoli and olives and toss gently to coat. Serve warm.

Serves 4 to 6

Fresh Corn and Bacon Casserole

10 ears fresh yellow sweet corn
1 pound thick-slice smoked bacon, julienned
    (about 10 to 12 slices)
1 large green bell pepper, chopped
1 medium sweet onion, chopped
1 teaspoon salt
¾ teaspoon pepper
¾ teaspoon dry mustard
1 (14-ounce) can chopped tomatoes, drained and
    finely chopped

Cut the corn kernels from the cobs into a bowl with a sharp knife. Fry the bacon in a skillet until brown and crisp. Drain, reserving 2 tablespoons of the bacon drippings. Sauté the bell pepper and onion in the reserved bacon drippings for 2 minutes. Stir in the corn. Sauté for 3 minutes longer.

Combine the bacon, salt, pepper and dry mustard in a bowl and toss to coat. Layer the corn mixture, bacon mixture and tomatoes ½ at a time in a 9×13-inch baking dish sprayed with nonstick cooking spray. Bake at 350 degrees for 30 to 40 minutes or until bubbly.

Serves 8 to 10

Florida Orange Rice

2 tablespoons chopped onion
2 tablespoons butter or margarine
2 cups water
$1/2$ cup fresh orange juice
1 teaspoon salt
$1/2$ teaspoon grated orange zest
$1/8$ teaspoon whole marjoram
$1/8$ teaspoon whole thyme
1 cup long grain rice

Sauté the onion in the butter in a large saucepan until tender. Stir in the water, orange juice, salt, orange zest, marjoram and thyme. Bring to a boil. Stir in the rice. Return to a boil; reduce the heat. Simmer, covered, for 20 minutes or until the rice is tender and the liquid has been absorbed.

Serves 4 to 6

Piña Colada Mousse

1 cup cream of coconut
1 cup crushed pineapple in unsweetened syrup
1 cup whipping cream
6 tablespoons dark rum
2 teaspoons unflavored gelatin
2 tablespoons water
grated nutmeg to taste

Combine the cream of coconut, crushed pineapple, whipping cream and dark rum in a blender and process until smooth. Remove to a bowl. Sprinkle the unflavored gelatin over the water in a small heavy saucepan and let stand for 10 minutes. Cook over low heat until the gelatin is completely dissolved, stirring constantly. Stir into the coconut cream mixture and spoon into 6 wine glasses or dessert ramekins. Chill, covered, for 8 hours or longer. Sprinkle with nutmeg to serve.

Serves 6

Chocolate and Almond Soufflé Torte

1 cup (about 5 ounces) whole
    almonds, toasted and cooled
2 tablespoons sugar
2 tablespoons vegetable oil
³/₄ cup (1¹/₂ sticks) unsalted butter
¹/₂ cup whipping cream
1 pound bittersweet or semisweet
    chocolate, finely chopped

6 egg whites, at room temperature
¹/₃ cup sugar
6 egg yolks, at room temperature
1 cup chilled whipping cream
2 tablespoons amaretto
2 tablespoons sugar
¹/₂ cup sliced almonds, toasted
fresh raspberries

Position the oven rack in the center of the oven. Butter and flour a 9-inch springform pan with a 2³/₄-inch side; shake out excess flour. Line the bottom of the pan with baking parchment and coat with butter.

Combine ¹/₂ cup of the almonds and 2 tablespoons sugar in a food processor. Pulse until the almonds are finely ground. Remove the almond mixture to a large bowl. Process the remaining ¹/₂ cup almonds and oil in the food processor for 3 minutes or until the mixture is thick and pasty and similar to the consistency of peanut butter, scraping the bowl frequently.

Combine the unsalted butter and ¹/₂ cup whipping cream in a large heavy saucepan. Cook over medium heat until the mixture comes to a simmer and the butter melts, stirring occasionally. Remove from the heat. Whisk in the chocolate until smooth. Stir in both almond mixtures. Cool slightly.

Beat the egg whites in a large mixing bowl until soft peaks form. Add ¹/₃ cup sugar gradually, beating constantly until stiff peaks form. Beat the egg yolks in a mixing bowl for 5 minutes or until pale and thick. Add the chocolate mixture to the egg yolks gradually, beating constantly until blended. Fold the egg whites in 3 additions to the chocolate mixture. Spoon the batter into the prepared pan. Bake at 350 degrees for 35 to 45 minutes or until the side cracks and puffs and a wooden pick inserted in the center comes out with moist batter attached. Begin checking at 3 minute intervals after 35 minutes baking time has elapsed. Cool in the pan on a wire rack for 2 hours or until room temperature; the center will fall slightly. You may prepare up to this point 4 days in advance and store, covered, in the refrigerator. Bring to room temperature before serving.

Beat 1 cup whipping cream, liqueur and 2 tablespoons sugar in a mixing bowl until soft peaks form. Serve the torte with dollops of the whipped cream and sprinkle with the sliced almonds. Add raspberries on the side.

Serves 12

Dill Muffins

Combine 2 cups baking mix, 1 cup sour cream, ¹/₂ cup (1 stick) butter and 2 tablespoons finely chopped fresh dill weed in a bowl and mix well. Drop the batter by tablespoons into greased miniature muffin cups. Bake at 425 degrees for 10 to 15 minutes or just until golden brown. Serve immediately.

MENU

Puttin' on the Ritz

In the midst of the tropical atmosphere of Florida, uptown style may also be found. In this chic setting, cocktails and hors d'oeuvre are offered as guests enjoy the view of St. Andrew Bay. The table is set with Royal Crown Derby Black Aves china, Tiffany flatware, mouth-blown crystal, and a brilliant floral centerpiece. The sophisticated food is the highlight.

Cosmopolitan

1¹/₂ ounces vodka
1 ounce Cointreau
¹/₂ ounce lime juice

1 teaspoon superfine sugar
1 ounce cranberry juice
lemon twist or lime twist

Fill a cocktail shaker with ice. Add the vodka, liqueur, lime juice, sugar and cranberry juice to the cocktail shaker and shake to mix. Strain into a cocktail glass. Garnish with a lemon or lime twist.

Serves 1

Pecan and Stilton Napoleons

96 pecan halves
3 ounces cream cheese, softened
2 ounces Stilton cheese, at room
    temperature

2 teaspoons port
¹/₂ teaspoon honey
¹/₈ teaspoon cracked pepper
2 tablespoons chopped fresh chives

Arrange the pecans flat side down on a baking sheet. Toast at 350 degrees for 8 to 10 minutes or until fragrant. Remove the pecans to a wire rack to cool. You may prepare in advance and store, covered, in an airtight container at room temperature. Combine the cream cheese, Stilton cheese, wine, honey and pepper in a food processor. Process for 30 seconds and scrape the side of the bowl. Process until smooth. You may prepare the cheese mixture up to 3 days in advance and store, covered, in the refrigerator.

Spoon the cheese mixture into a pastry bag fitted with a medium star tip. Arrange 24 of the pecan halves flat side down on a hard surface, reserving the best pecans for the tops. Pipe ¹/₄ teaspoon of the cheese mixture down the middle of each pecan. Top each with 1 pecan half round side up and press lightly. Pipe another ¹/₄ teaspoon of the cheese mixture on top. Sprinkle with the chives. Repeat the process with the remaining pecan halves, remaining cheese mixture and remaining chives.

Makes 4 dozen napoleons

The Dixie-Sherman Legacy

John Henry Sherman, whose home provides the setting for "Puttin' on the Ritz," is one of the most artful interior decorators of the Gulf Coast. His eye for stylish décor must have been passed down from his father, W.C. Sherman, because his is truly a vision of good taste in the area.

W.C. Sherman built the famed Dixie-Sherman Hotel in 1926 on Jenks Avenue in downtown Panama City. Each of the 101 rooms in the eight-story hotel offered a private bath and telephone and were described as being "furnished in the elegance of the era." The hotel also boasted a rooftop garden from which guests could take in a panoramic view of the town and bay.

The Dixie-Sherman is said to have attracted movie stars and celebrities such as Clark Gable and Hank Greenberg, who visited the hotel while stationed at Tyndall Field in 1942. Beatrice Houdini, wife of the Great Houdini, is also said to have stayed there in 1937. A landmark in its day, the Dixie-Sherman was torn down in 1970, to great sadness.

Bargain Rates at the Dixie-Sherman

An early advertisement for the Dixie-Sherman Hotel listed 100 outside rooms, each with bath. Single rooms were offered on the European plan for $2.00 to $3.50. Rooms on the American plan went for $4.50 to $6.00. For a double room, rates on the European plan increased to $3.50 and $5.00 and on the American plan to $8.50 and $10.00. Rates for parties and weekly rates were offered on request, with special rates for summer or winter season.

Bleu Cheese Shortbread with Walnuts and Chutney

1/2 cup flour

1/4 cup cornstarch

1/4 teaspoon pepper

1/4 teaspoon salt

1/2 cup sharp bleu cheese, at room temperature

3 tablespoons butter, softened

1/3 cup walnuts, chopped

3 tablespoons (about) cream cheese, softened

1/2 cup walnut halves, toasted

3 tablespoons (about) Major Grey's chutney

36 fresh parsley leaves

Mix the flour, cornstarch, pepper and salt together. Process the bleu cheese and butter in a food processor until smooth and creamy. Add the flour mixture. Pulse until blended. Add the chopped walnuts. Process just until mixed; do not overprocess. Shape the bleu cheese mixture into a disk and wrap with plastic wrap. Chill for 1 hour or until firm.

Let the chilled dough stand at room temperature for 10 to 15 minutes or just until softened. Place the dough on a hard surface and cover with a sheet of plastic wrap. Roll 1/8 inch thick and discard the plastic wrap. Cut the dough into 1-inch rounds with a fluted cookie cutter.

Arrange the rounds on a baking sheet lined with baking parchment. Bake at 325 degrees for 25 minutes or until light brown. Cool on the baking sheet for 2 minutes. Remove to a wire rack to cool completely. You may prepare the rounds up to 3 days in advance and store, covered, at room temperature.

To serve, top each shortbread round with a dollop of cream cheese. Layer each with 1 walnut half, chutney and 1 parsley leaf.

Makes 3 dozen

Roasted Red Pepper Soup

2 tablespoons olive oil
1¹/₂ medium onions, finely chopped
3 red bell peppers, chopped
2 tablespoons minced garlic
1 (16-ounce) can Italian tomatoes
6 jalapeño chile slices (jar or can)
¹/₈ teaspoon oregano
¹/₈ teaspoon basil
¹/₈ teaspoon thyme
¹/₄ cup water
1 tablespoon cornstarch
2 cups heavy whipping cream
salt to taste

Heat the olive oil in a skillet. Stir in the onions, bell peppers and garlic. Cook over low heat until the onions and bell peppers are very tender, stirring frequently. Stir in the undrained tomatoes, jalapeño chile slices, oregano, basil and thyme. Simmer for 20 minutes, stirring occasionally.

Mix the water and cornstarch in a bowl. Set aside. Process the tomato mixture in a food processor or blender until puréed. Stir a small amount of the tomato purée into the cornstarch mixture. Return the tomato mixture to the saucepan. Add the remaining cornstarch mixture to the tomato mixture gradually, stirring constantly. Cook for 15 to 20 minutes or until slightly thickened, stirring frequently. Stir in the whipping cream. Simmer just until heated through, stirring occasionally. Season with salt. Ladle into soup bowls.

Makes 1 quart

Tomato Soup with Rosemary

1 onion, finely chopped
1 tablespoon minced garlic
2 tablespoons butter
2 (15-ounce) cans stewed tomatoes
3 beef bouillon cubes
1 sprig of fresh rosemary, tied in cheesecloth
2 tablespoons butter
2¹/₂ tablespoons flour
2 cups half-and-half
chopped fresh parsley

Sauté the onion and garlic in 2 tablespoons butter in a saucepan until the onion is tender. Stir in the undrained tomatoes, bouillon cubes and rosemary. Simmer for 15 to 20 minutes, stirring occasionally.

Heat 2 tablespoons butter in a saucepan. Add the flour and mix well. Cook until bubbly, stirring constantly. Stir in the half-and-half. Cook until thickened, stirring frequently. Add the sauce to the tomato mixture and mix well. Cook for 15 minutes, stirring frequently. Discard the rosemary. Ladle into soup bowls and sprinkle with parsley. Serve immediately.

Makes 4 appetizer servings

Rouille Garlic Toasts

Process ¹/₂ cup chopped pimentos, ¹/₃ cup bread crumbs, 6 garlic cloves, 12 large fresh basil leaves, 1 egg yolk and ¹/₂ teaspoon salt in a food processor untl puréed. Add ¹/₄ cup olive oil gradually, processing constantly until blended. Season with hot pepper sauce to taste. Cut a baguette into ¹/₂-inch slices and toast the slices lightly. Spread with the pimento mixture.

To avoid uncooked eggs that may carry salmonella, we suggest using an equivalent amount of pasteurized egg substitute.

Florida-Style Bouillabaisse

1 medium red bell pepper
1 medium yellow bell pepper
¹/₃ cup olive oil
1 bunch leeks (white and pale green parts only), thinly sliced
1 fennel bulb with top, trimmed and finely sliced
1 medium onion, chopped
3 garlic cloves, minced
1 tablespoon chopped fresh thyme, or 2 teaspoons dried thyme
1 teaspoon turmeric
¹/₂ teaspoon crushed red pepper
1¹/₂ cups dry white wine
4 (8-ounce) bottles clam juice
2 cups drained canned Italian tomatoes, chopped
2 pounds littleneck clams
1 pound medium shrimp, peeled and deveined
1 pound fresh fish, cut into 1-inch cubes
1 pound bay scallops
¹/₂ cup chopped fresh basil
salt and freshly ground black pepper to taste
Rouille Garlic Toasts (this page)

Roast the bell peppers over the flame of a gas burner or under a broiler until the skin is blackened and charred on all sides, turning frequently. Remove the blackened skin under running water. Cut the bell peppers into ¹/₈-inch slices, discarding the seeds and membranes.

Heat the olive oil in a large saucepan. Add the leeks, fennel, onion and garlic and mix well. Cook, covered, over medium heat for 10 minutes, stirring occasionally. Stir in the thyme, turmeric and red pepper. Cook for 5 minutes or until fragrant, stirring frequently. Stir in the wine. Bring to a boil over high heat.

Boil for 5 to 7 minutes or until most of the liquid evaporates, stirring frequently. Stir in the clam juice. Bring to a boil. Boil for 12 minutes or until the liquid is reduced by ¹/₂, stirring occasionally. Stir in ¹/₂ of the tomatoes, clams and shrimp. Cook, covered, for 3 minutes. Add the fish and scallops and mix gently.

Cook, covered, for 3 to 4 minutes or just until the seafood is cooked through, stirring occasionally. Stir in the remaining tomatoes, bell peppers and basil. Cook just until heated through, stirring occasionally. Season with salt and black pepper. Ladle into soup bowls. Serve with Rouille Garlic Toasts.

Serves 6 to 8

Goat Cheese Salad

1 head favorite lettuce, separated into leaves
2 or 3 tomatoes, cut into wedges
1 egg
1 cup (about) finely ground fresh bread crumbs
1 (4- to 6-ounce) log goat cheese
freshly ground pepper to taste
olive oil
French Vinaigrette (this page)

Arrange the lettuce and tomato wedges on 4 salad plates. Whisk the egg in a shallow dish. Spread the bread crumbs in a shallow dish. Cut the goat cheese into 8 equal rounds and sprinkle with pepper. Coat the rounds with the egg and then with the bread crumbs.

Sauté the goat cheese rounds in olive oil in a sauté pan until golden brown on both sides. Arrange 2 of the rounds on each salad. Drizzle with French Vinaigrette.

Serves 4

French Vinaigrette

1/4 cup red wine vinegar
1 tablespoon Dijon mustard
1 to 2 tablespoons minced fresh herbs, such as chives or
    parsley (optional)
1 teaspoon sugar
1/2 teaspoon salt
1/2 teaspoon freshly ground pepper
1/2 cup olive oil

Whisk the vinegar, Dijon mustard, herbs, sugar, salt and pepper in a bowl until combined. Add the olive oil gradually, whisking constantly until thickened. Taste and adjust the seasonings. Whisk before serving.

Makes 1 cup

Caesar Salad with Bleu Cheese

Parmesan Croutons

1 tablespoon butter
1 cup small bread cubes
1 tablespoon grated Parmesan cheese

Salad

1 head romaine, torn into bite-size pieces
2 cups seedless grapes
1 cup crumbled bleu cheese
Caesar Salad Dressing (this page)

For the croutons, melt the butter in a skillet over medium heat. Add the bread cubes and cheese and mix well. Cook until the bread cubes are golden brown, stirring frequently. Remove from the heat. Let stand until cool.

   For the salad, mix the lettuce, grapes, bleu cheese and croutons in a bowl. Add the Caesar Salad Dressing and toss gently to coat. Serve immediately.

   Serves 6

Caesar Salad Dressing

¹/₄ cup lemon juice
1 garlic clove, crushed
1 teaspoon Worcestershire sauce
³/₄ teaspoon salt
¹/₄ teaspoon freshly ground pepper
¹/₃ cup extra-virgin olive oil

Whisk the lemon juice, garlic, Worcestershire sauce, salt and pepper in a bowl. Add the olive oil gradually, whisking constantly until mixed.

   Serves 6

Roast Pork Tenderloin with Port and Bleu Cheese Sauce

8 ounces sliced bacon
3 quarts water
3 pounds pork tenderloins
salt and pepper to taste
2 cups port
2 cups heavy cream
1¹/₂ cups crumbled bleu cheese
¹/₂ cup beef broth
2 tablespoons drained green peppercorns

Parboil the bacon in the water in a saucepan for 10 minutes; drain. Arrange the tenderloins in a roasting pan and tuck the ends under. Sprinkle with salt and pepper. Arrange the bacon over the tops. Bake at 375 degrees for 45 minutes or until a meat thermometer registers 140 degrees. Remove the tenderloins to a platter and tent with foil to keep warm, reserving the pan drippings.

Deglaze the roasting pan with the wine. Pour the wine mixture into a saucepan. Cook until reduced by ¹/₂, stirring occasionally. Add the heavy cream, bleu cheese, broth and peppercorns and mix well. Cook until the cheese melts, stirring constantly. Simmer until the mixture is reduced by ¹/₂, stirring occasionally.

Slice the tenderloins as desired. Spoon or ladle some of the sauce on each serving plate. Arrange the sliced tenderloins in a fan shape over the sauce. Pass the remaining sauce.

Serves 6 to 8

Manhattan

Combine 2 ounces whiskey, ¹/₄ ounce dry vermouth and ¹/₄ ounce sweet vermouth in a bar glass filled with ice and mix for 30 seconds. Strain into a cocktail glass and serve straight up or on the rocks. Garnish with a stemmed maraschino cherry and a strip of fresh lemon peel tied in the middle to release the oils.

Panama City Music Association

PCMA's concert season literally circles the globe and offers the finest classical and popular programs the world has to offer, as it has done for the past 61 years. All performances are at the Marina Civic Center in Panama City.

PCMA is a volunteer organization operating as a not-for-profit corporation. Its purpose is to bring culture and an appreciation of various types of music to citizens of Panama City and surrounding areas and visitors to the area. Its goal is to keep the performances at an affordable rate for all citizens.

— From a publication, circa 1941

Veal Scaloppine with Shrimp and Brandy Cream Sauce

1 red onion, thinly sliced
$^{1}/_{2}$ cup (1 stick) unsalted butter
8 ounces shiitake mushrooms, stems removed and caps thinly sliced
6 tablespoons brandy
1 cup each beef broth and chicken broth
1 cup whipping cream
6 (4-ounce) veal cutlets
salt and pepper to taste
flour
24 medium shrimp, peeled and deveined

Sauté the onion in 2 tablespoons of the unsalted butter in a large heavy skillet over medium-high heat for 3 to 4 minutes or until tender. Add the mushrooms and mix well. Sauté for 4 minutes or until the mushrooms begin to brown. Remove from the heat. Stir in the brandy and ignite carefully. Return the skillet to the heat when the flames subside.

Simmer for 1 minute or until the brandy almost evaporates, stirring frequently. Add the beef broth and chicken broth and mix well. Bring to a boil. Boil for 5 minutes, stirring occasionally. Stir in the whipping cream. Bring to a boil. Boil for 15 minutes longer or until the sauce coats the back of a spoon, stirring occasionally. Pour the sauce into a bowl and cover to keep warm. Wipe the skillet with paper towels to clean.

Pound the cutlets $^{1}/_{4}$ inch thick between sheets of waxed paper. Sprinkle with salt and pepper and coat with flour. Heat 2 tablespoons of the remaining unsalted butter in the same skillet over high heat. Sauté 3 of the cutlets in the butter for 2 minutes per side or until brown and cooked through. Remove to a platter and cover to keep warm. Repeat the process with the remaining cutlets and 2 tablespoons of the remaining unsalted butter, reserving the pan drippings.

Heat the remaining 2 tablespoons unsalted butter with the reserved pan drippings. Sauté the shrimp in the butter mixture for 3 minutes or just until the shrimp are opaque in the center. Add the sauce and mix well. Cook until heated through, scraping up any browned bits from the bottom of the skillet. To serve, arrange 1 cutlet on each of 6 serving plates. Drizzle with the shrimp sauce.

Serves 6

Rack of Lamb Dijon

1/4 cup olive oil
2 tablespoons Dijon mustard
2 tablespoons soy sauce
1 tablespoon chopped fresh parsley
freshly ground pepper to taste
1 garlic clove, minced
1 (8-rib) rack of lamb

Whisk the olive oil, Dijon mustard, soy sauce, parsley, pepper and garlic in a bowl until the mixture is of a mayonnaise consistency. Spread the mixture over the surface of the lamb. Arrange the lamb on a broiler rack in a broiler pan.

Broil for 5 minutes per side. Bake at 400 degrees for 10 minutes for rare or to the desired degree of doneness. Let stand for 5 minutes before carving. Serve with minted peas and garlic mashed potatoes.

Serves 2 to 4

Lamb Chops in Red Wine Sauce

6 lamb chops, 2 inches thick
salt and freshly ground pepper to taste
1/3 cup plus 1/4 cup olive oil
2 1/2 cups chopped onions
3 tablespoons minced garlic
2 cups beef broth or beef stock
2 cups dry red wine
1 cup barbecue sauce
3 (6-inch) sprigs of fresh rosemary
1 (2-inch) cinnamon stick
sprigs of fresh rosemary

Sprinkle the lamb with salt and pepper. Heat 1/3 cup olive oil in a large heavy skillet over medium-high heat and brown the lamb chops on both sides in batches in the oil. Remove the lamb to a roasting pan; drain the skillet and wipe with a paper towel.

Heat the remaining 1/4 cup olive oil in the same skillet over medium-high heat. Add the onions and sprinkle with salt and pepper. Sauté for 8 minutes or until tender. Add the garlic and sauté for 1 minute. Pour in the beef broth and wine and bring to a boil. Add the barbecue sauce, 3 sprigs of rosemary and cinnamon stick. Pour over the lamb and cover tightly with foil.

Roast at 350 degrees for 1 hour. Turn the lamb and roast for 1 hour longer or until the chops are tender and the meat pulls easily from the bones. Remove from the oven and tent with foil to keep warm.

Skim the cooking juices and then strain into a small saucepan. Bring to a boil over medium-high heat. Boil until the liquid is reduced by 1/2; keep warm.

Serve the lamb chops on a bed of grits or mashed potatoes and top with the warm sauce. Garnish with additional sprigs of fresh rosemary.

Serves 6

Garlic Gruyère Mashed Potatoes

6 medium potatoes, peeled and cut into 1-inch pieces
³/₄ cup milk, heated
¹/₂ cup sour cream
¹/₄ cup (¹/₂ stick) butter or margarine, softened
¹/₂ teaspoon salt
¹/₈ teaspoon red pepper
1 garlic clove, minced
¹/₄ cup shredded Gruyère cheese
2 green onions, thinly sliced
¹/₃ cup chopped baked ham (optional)
sliced green onions (optional)

Combine the potatoes with enough water to cover in a saucepan. Bring to a boil. Boil for 15 minutes or until tender; drain. Mash the potatoes in a bowl with a potato masher. Stir in the hot milk, sour cream, butter, salt, red pepper and garlic.

Add the cheese, 2 thinly sliced green onions and ham to the potato mixture and mix well. Spoon into a serving bowl and sprinkle with sliced green onions if desired.

Serves 6 to 8

Potato Gratin with Goat Cheese

1 cup milk
1 cup heavy cream
6 ounces fresh goat cheese, crumbled
3 garlic cloves, minced
¹/₈ teaspoon ground nutmeg
1¹/₂ teaspoons salt
³/₄ teaspoon pepper
2 pounds Yukon gold potatoes, peeled and thinly sliced

Combine the milk, cream, goat cheese, garlic, nutmeg, salt and pepper in a medium bowl and whisk to mix well. Arrange ¹/₃ of the potatoes in an overlapping layer in a greased 7×11-inch baking dish. Pour ¹/₃ of the goat cheese mixture over the potatoes. Repeat the process 2 more times.

Bake at 400 degrees for 1¹/₄ hours or until the potatoes are tender and the top is golden brown. Serve hot. You may prepare the dish in advance and chill for 6 to 8 hours before baking. You may also double the recipe and bake in a larger dish.

Serves 6

Balsamic-Glazed Carrots

3 pounds carrots, julienned
1/2 cup beef broth
1/4 cup maple syrup
2 tablespoons butter
1/4 teaspoon salt
1/4 teaspoon balsamic vinegar

Combine the carrots, broth, maple syrup, butter and salt in a skillet and cover. Bring to a boil over medium-high heat. Cook for 5 minutes, stirring occasionally. Remove the cover and increase the heat to high.

Cook until the liquid is reduced to 2 tablespoons, stirring occasionally. Stir in the vinegar. Cook for 1 to 2 minutes longer or until the carrots are glazed, stirring occasionally.

Serves 6 to 8

Carrots with Black Olives Provençal

2 pounds carrots
2 tablespoons extra-virgin olive oil
cloves of 2 garlic bulbs, cut lengthwise into halves
sea salt to taste
1/2 cup (about) brine-cured black olives, pitted and cut
    lengthwise into halves

Peel the carrots and slice diagonally 1/4 inch thick. Heat the olive oil in a large skillet over medium-high heat and add the carrots, stirring to coat well. Reduce the heat to medium and cook, covered, for 20 minutes or until the carrots are almost tender. Add the garlic and season with sea salt.

Reduce the heat to low and cook for 15 minutes longer or until the carrots begin to caramelize and are tender, stirring constantly. Stir in the olives and correct the seasonings. Serve hot or at room temperature.

Serves 8 to 10

Seven-Minute Frosting

Combine ¹/₄ cup sugar, 2 tablespoons water and 1 tablespoon light corn syrup in a medium saucepan. Cook over medium heat until the sugar dissolves, stirring constantly. Bring to a boil. Boil for 5 minutes; do not stir. Remove from the heat.

Beat 5 egg whites in a mixing bowl at medium speed for 2 to 3 minutes or until soft peaks form. Add ¹/₂ cup sugar gradually, beating constantly until blended. Add the syrup mixture gradually, beating constantly at medium-low speed until blended. Beat at medium speed for 5 to 10 minutes longer or until thickened and shiny. Prepare just before assembling the cake to be frosted.

Coconut Layer Cake

Coconut Cream Filling
³/₄ cup sugar
¹/₄ cup cornstarch
¹/₈ teaspoon salt
3 cups milk
6 egg yolks, beaten
1¹/₂ cups flaked coconut
1¹/₂ teaspoons vanilla extract

Cake
2 cups flour
¹/₂ teaspoon baking powder
¹/₂ teaspoon baking soda
¹/₄ teaspoon salt
³/₄ cup (1¹/₂ sticks) butter, softened
1 cup sugar
1 teaspoon vanilla extract
4 egg yolks, beaten
²/₃ cup sour cream
1 (11-ounce) package sweetened
    coconut (about 3³/₄ cups)
12 tablespoons flaked coconut
Seven-Minute Frosting (this page)
Raspberry Coulis (page 49)

For the filling, mix the sugar, cornstarch and salt in a medium saucepan. Whisk in the milk gradually. Cook over medium heat for 10 to 12 minutes or until thickened, stirring frequently. Remove from the heat. Whisk 1 cup of the hot milk mixture into the egg yolks ¹/₂ cup at a time. Add the egg yolk mixture to the remaining hot milk mixture and mix well. Cook over medium heat for 2 minutes or until bubbly, stirring constantly. Remove from the heat. Stir in the coconut and vanilla. Pour into a medium bowl. Press buttered plastic wrap directly on the filling. Chill for 1 to 10 hours.

For the cake, grease and flour three 8-inch cake pans. Line the bottoms with baking parchment and grease and flour the parchment. Sift the flour, baking powder, baking soda and salt together. Cream the butter in a mixing bowl at low speed. Beat at medium speed for 1 to 2 minutes longer or until light. Beat in the sugar and vanilla gradually. Beat in the egg yolks 1 at a time. Beat for 3 to 4 minutes longer or until fluffy. Add the flour mixture to the creamed mixture alternately with the sour cream, beating at low speed and beginning and ending with the flour mixture. Stir in 1 package coconut. Spoon into the prepared pans. Bake at 350 degrees for 30 minutes or until a wooden pick comes out clean. Cool in the pans for 10 to 15 minutes. Remove to a wire rack to cool.

To assemble, cut each cake layer horizontally into halves; save the best dome for the top layer. Arrange 1 cake layer on a cake plate. Sprinkle with 2 to 3 tablespoons of the flaked coconut and spread with ¹/₂ cup of the filling. Repeat this process with the remaining layers, coconut and filling, ending with a layer. Frost with Seven-Minute Frosting. Serve with Raspberry Coulis.

Serves 12

Vanilla Ice Cream

1 vanilla bean
3 cups half-and-half
³/₄ cup sugar
6 egg yolks

Cut the vanilla bean lengthwise into halves. Combine the vanilla bean and half-and-half in a medium heavy saucepan. Bring to a simmer over medium-high heat. Remove from the heat. Let stand, covered, for 30 minutes. Scrape the seeds from the vanilla bean with the tip of a small knife and return the seeds to the saucepan.

Bring the half-and-half mixture to a simmer over medium-high heat. Whisk the sugar and egg yolks in a metal bowl until blended. Add the hot half-and-half mixture to the egg yolk mixture gradually, whisking constantly. Return the egg yolk mixture to the saucepan.

Cook over medium-low heat for 5 minutes or until the mixture is thickened and coats the back of a spoon, stirring constantly; do not boil. Strain the custard through a sieve into a bowl. Chill, covered, for 1 hour. Pour the chilled custard into an ice cream freezer container. Freeze using manufacturer's directions. Cover and freeze in a freezer until firm. You may substitute 2 teaspoons vanilla extract for the vanilla bean, but the minimal effort of using a fresh vanilla bean is definitely worthwhile!

Makes (about) 5 cups

Recipe for this photograph on facing page.

Raspberry Coulis

1 pint fresh raspberries
¹/₂ cup sugar
¹/₂ cup water
2 tablespoons Grand Marnier

Combine the raspberries, sugar, water and liqueur in a medium saucepan. Bring to a boil. Boil for 1 minute, stirring occasionally. Purée the raspberry mixture in a blender or food processor. Be sure to remove the lid of the food processor carefully to allow the steam to escape.

Strain the raspberry purée into a bowl through a fine sieve, discarding the seeds. Repeat the process until all of the seeds have been removed. Chill, covered, for 4 to 10 hours. You may prepare up to 2 days in advance and store, covered, in the refrigerator.

Makes (about) 1 cup

The Night before Christmas

AWAITED CHRISTMAS MORNING

GINGERBREAD COTTAGES

NUTCRACKER SWEETS

MENU

Awaited Christmas Morning

Christmas mornings in Florida are often warm outside, but we still take the opportunity to open presents in front of the fireplace. Breakfast is made the night before, so even Mother doesn't miss all of the excitement.

Artichoke and Smoked Ham Strata

2 cups milk
1/4 cup olive oil
8 cups cubed sourdough bread, crusts removed
1 1/2 cups whipping cream
5 eggs
1 tablespoon minced garlic
1/2 teaspoon nutmeg
salt and freshly ground pepper to taste
12 ounces soft goat cheese such as Montrachet or chèvre, crumbled
1 tablespoon chopped fresh thyme
1 1/2 teaspoons herbes de Provence
1 teaspoon finely chopped fresh sage
12 ounces smoked ham, coarsely chopped
2 1/2 cups marinated artichoke hearts, drained and cut lengthwise into halves
1 cup (heaping) shredded fontina cheese or Gruyère cheese
1 1/2 cups (heaping) grated Parmesan cheese

Whisk the milk and olive oil in a large bowl. Add the bread cubes and stir gently until completely coated. Let stand at room temperature for 10 minutes or until the liquid is absorbed, stirring occasionally. Whisk the whipping cream, eggs, garlic, nutmeg, salt and pepper in a bowl. Stir in the goat cheese. Mix the thyme, herbes de Provence and sage in a bowl.

Layer the bread cube mixture, ham, artichoke hearts, herb mixture, fontina cheese, Parmesan cheese and whipping cream mixture 1/2 at a time in the order listed in a buttered 9×13-inch baking dish. Bake at 350 degrees for 1 hour or until the center is set and the edges are brown. You may prepare up to 1 day in advance and store, covered, in the refrigerator, extending the baking time up to 1 1/2 hours if needed. Substitute a mixture of dried basil and dried rosemary for the herbes de Provence if desired.

Serves 10

Christmas in Florida, Circa 1900

In the early 1900s, Christmas was quite different in Panama City, and the actual holiday wasn't recognized in Florida until 1881. Times were much simpler, and shopping wasn't the main focus of the season as it is today. Most people did their shopping on Christmas Eve, and sent cards only a day or two before Christmas. The most popular items were fruits, nuts, and candies, and fireworks were the main entertainment on Christmas Eve.

Southern pines or cedars were used for Christmas trees, and they were cut and set up on Christmas Eve. Decorations included apples, oranges, nuts, palm leaves, and seashells; magnolia boughs and holly were dipped in pine rosin and placed throughout the home. Christmas dinner included wild turkey, cured ham, collard greens, sweet potatoes, Lane cakes, pecan pies, and eggnog. After the big dinner, most people went hunting or boating, while some visited friends and family, or fished off the city dock.

Breakfast Omelet

3 tablespoons butter
1/4 cup flour
2 ounces cream cheese, softened
1/2 teaspoon salt
1/2 teaspoon pepper
1/4 teaspoon dry mustard
1 cup milk
4 eggs, separated
Crab Sauce (this page)

Heat the butter in a saucepan. Stir in the flour, cream cheese, salt, pepper and dry mustard. Cook until blended, stirring constantly. Stir in the milk gradually. Cook until thickened, stirring constantly. Cool slightly.

Whisk the egg yolks in a bowl until thickened. Add the warm sauce and mix well. Beat the egg whites in a mixing bowl until stiff peaks form. Fold the egg whites into the sauce. Pour the egg mixture into a greased 7×12-inch baking dish. Bake at 325 degrees for 20 minutes.

Serves 6

Crab Sauce

1/4 cup (1/2 stick) butter
1 1/2 cups sliced mushrooms
2 tablespoons chopped onion
1/4 cup flour
1/2 teaspoon salt
pepper to taste
1/2 teaspoon paprika
1 1/2 cups milk
2 egg yolks, lightly beaten
12 ounces lump crab meat, shells removed and flaked
2 tablespoons white wine
1 teaspoon Worcestershire sauce

Heat the butter in a skillet. Cook the mushrooms and onion in the butter until tender, stirring frequently. Stir in the flour, salt, pepper and paprika. Cook until bubbly, stirring frequently. Add the milk and mix well.

Cook over medium heat until thickened, stirring frequently. Cool slightly. Stir in the egg yolks. Add the crab meat, wine and Worcestershire sauce and mix well. Serve with the Breakfast Omelet. You may prepare the crab sauce in advance and keep warm in a double boiler.

Serves 6

Recipe for this photograph on facing page.

Christmas Torta

1 pound puff pastry

1 pound fresh spinach, blanched and
   chopped

1 tablespoon olive oil

3 tablespoons butter

3 garlic cloves, finely chopped

$^1/_2$ teaspoon nutmeg

salt and pepper to taste

2 large red bell peppers, thinly sliced

5 eggs

2 teaspoons chopped fresh chives

2 teaspoons chopped fresh flat-leaf
   parsley

1 teaspoon chopped fresh thyme

$^1/_8$ teaspoon salt

8 ounces Gruyère cheese or Swiss
   cheese, shredded

8 ounces smoked ham, thinly sliced

1 egg, beaten

Roll 1 of the puff pastry sheets $^1/_4$ inch thick on a hard surface. Store the remaining pastry, covered, in the refrigerator. Line the bottom and side of a greased 8-inch springform pan with the pastry and trim the edge. Press the excess moisture from the spinach. Heat the olive oil and 1 tablespoon of the butter in a large sauté pan over medium heat. Sauté the spinach and garlic in the olive oil mixture for 3 minutes. Stir in the nutmeg and salt and pepper to taste. Spoon into a bowl. Sauté the bell peppers in the same sauté pan for 4 minutes or until tender-crisp. Remove the bell peppers to a small bowl.

Whisk 5 eggs, chives, parsley, thyme and $^1/_8$ teaspoon salt lightly in a bowl. Heat 1 tablespoon of the remaining butter in an 8-inch skillet over medium heat until melted and swirl to evenly coat the skillet. Add $^1/_2$ of the egg mixture to the hot skillet, tilting the skillet to ensure even coverage. Cook until set, lifting the edge of the omelet gently with a spatula as the eggs set to allow the uncooked eggs to flow underneath; do not stir. Slide the omelet onto a heated plate. Repeat the process with remaining 1 tablespoon butter and egg mixture.

Layer 1 omelet, $^1/_2$ of the spinach, $^1/_2$ of the cheese, $^1/_2$ of the ham and sautéed bell peppers in the prepared springform pan. Top with the remaining ham, cheese, spinach and omelet. Roll the remaining pastry $^1/_4$ inch thick on a work surface. Cut an 8-inch round and place over the layers, sealing the edge. Make several slits in the top of the pastry. Cut the remaining pastry scraps into decorative shapes with cookie cutters and arrange over the top. Brush with 1 beaten egg. Place on a baking sheet. Bake in the lower third of the oven at 350 degrees for $1^1/_4$ to $1^1/_2$ hours or until golden brown.

Serves 8

Bloody Mary

Combine 3 tablespoons vodka or chile-flavored vodka with $1^1/_2$ teaspoons sherry and 5 ounces tomato juice in a large bar glass half filled with ice and mix well. Add 1 tablespoon fresh lemon or lime juice, 1 tablespoon Worcestershire sauce, 2 or 3 dashes of Tabasco sauce and $^1/_2$ teaspoon creamy horseradish. Add 1 teaspoon celery salt and pepper to taste and mix well. Strain into a tall glass half filled with ice and add a celery stick stirrer. Thread an olive, a cherry tomato and another olive on a cocktail pick to lay across the rim of the glass.

Mimosa

Pour 3 ounces chilled fresh orange juice into a Champagne flute. Add 3 ounces chilled Champagne and mix gently. Garnish with an orange twist.

Shrimp and Grits

1 cup grits
2 tablespoons butter or margarine
milk to taste
salt and pepper to taste
6 ounces sharp Cheddar cheese, shredded
8 ounces sliced bacon
1 garlic clove, minced
2 cups sliced fresh mushrooms
1 cup finely sliced green onions
1 pound fresh shrimp, peeled and deveined
4 teaspoons lemon juice
hot sauce to taste
2 teaspoons chopped fresh parsley

Cook the grits using the package directions, adding the butter and milk to the cooked grits for a creamier consistency. Season with salt and pepper. Stir in the cheese, adding additional milk if needed for the desired consistency.

Fry the bacon in a skillet until crisp. Remove the bacon to paper towels to drain, reserving the bacon drippings. Sauté the garlic in the reserved bacon drippings for 1 minute. Stir in the mushrooms. Sauté until the mushrooms are slightly softened. Add the green onions and mix well. Sauté for 1 minute longer. Stir in the shrimp.

Cook until the shrimp turn pink, stirring frequently. Stir in the lemon juice and hot sauce. Spoon the shrimp mixture over the grits on a serving platter. Sprinkle with the parsley. Crumble the bacon over the top.

Serves 4

Hash Brown Potato Casserole

1 (2-pound) package frozen hash brown potatoes
10 ounces Cheddar cheese, shredded
1 (10-ounce) can cream of chicken soup
1 cup sour cream
1/2 cup chopped onion
1/4 cup (1/2 stick) margarine, melted
1 teaspoon salt
1/2 teaspoon pepper
1 1/2 to 2 cups bread crumbs or croutons (optional)
1/4 cup (1/2 stick) margarine, melted

Combine the potatoes, cheese, soup, sour cream, onion, 1/4 cup margarine, salt and pepper in a bowl and mix well. Spoon the potato mixture into a greased 9×13-inch baking dish. Bake at 350 degrees for 50 to 55 minutes. Remove from the oven.

Sprinkle with a mixture of the bread crumbs and 1/4 cup margarine. Bake for 15 to 20 minutes longer or until brown and crisp on top. Serve immediately.

Serves 10 to 12

Miniature Orange Muffins

1 teaspoon baking soda
1 cup buttermilk
1 cup sugar
1/2 cup dried cherries
1/2 cup (1 stick) unsalted butter, softened
2 eggs
2 cups flour
grated zest and juice of 1 orange
1/2 cup packed dark brown sugar

Dissolve the baking soda in the buttermilk in a small bowl. Process the sugar and cherries in a food processor until the cherries are finely chopped. Add the unsalted butter and eggs. Process until mixed.

Combine the flour and orange zest in a bowl and mix well. Fold in the cherry mixture and buttermilk mixture just until moistened; do not overmix. Spoon the batter into greased miniature muffin cups. Bake at 350 degrees for 10 to 12 minutes or until the muffins test done.

Remove the muffins to a wire rack immediately. Dip the warm muffins in a mixture of the orange juice and brown sugar. Let stand until cool. Serve as an appetizer or for breakfast. You may prepare in advance and freeze for future use.

Makes 4 to 5 dozen muffins

Stuffed French Toast

1 (16-ounce) loaf French bread, cut into 18 slices
1 pound cooked ham, thinly sliced and chopped
9 slices Swiss cheese
1 1/2 cups milk
6 eggs
2 tablespoons orange juice
1 teaspoon vanilla extract
1/4 cup (1/2 stick) butter
1/4 cup confectioners' sugar

Arrange 9 slices of the bread in a single layer in a lightly greased 9×13-inch baking dish. Layer each bread slice with some of the ham and 1 slice of the cheese. Top with the remaining bread slices. Whisk the milk, eggs, orange juice and vanilla in a bowl until blended. Pour over the prepared layers. Let stand for 10 minutes, turning once.

Heat 2 tablespoons of the butter in a large skillet over medium-high heat. Add 1/2 of the French toast to the skillet. Cook for 1 to 2 minutes per side, turning once. Remove to a lightly greased baking sheet. Repeat the process with the remaining butter and remaining French toast. Bake at 375 degrees for 20 to 25 minutes or until golden brown. Sprinkle with the confectioners' sugar. Serve immediately. You may prepare 1 day in advance and store, covered, in the refrigerator. Cook just before serving.

Serves 9

Snowdrift

Combine one 12-ounce thawed frozen piña colada mix with 3 cups lemonade and 1 cup crushed ice in a blender and process until slushy. Pour into glasses and garnish with grated coconut and maraschino cherries. You may add rum if desired.

Christmas Stollen

1 envelope dry yeast
1/4 cup warm water
1/2 cup (1 stick) butter
1 cup milk, scalded and hot
1/3 cup sugar
1 egg
1 teaspoon salt
1/2 teaspoon cardamom
1 cup raisins
1/2 cup dried currants
1/4 cup chopped candied fruit
1/4 cup almonds, chopped
2 tablespoons grated orange zest
1 tablespoon grated lemon zest
4 1/2 to 5 cups flour
3 tablespoons butter, melted
confectioners' sugar

Soften the yeast in the warm water in a small bowl. Combine 1/2 cup butter and the hot milk in a bowl and stir until the butter melts. Add the sugar, egg, salt and cardamom and mix well. Cool to lukewarm. Stir in the yeast mixture, raisins, currants, candied fruit, almonds, orange zest and lemon zest.

Add the flour to the yeast mixture gradually and stir until a stiff dough forms. Knead the dough on a floured surface for 5 minutes or until smooth and satiny. Place the dough in a greased bowl, turning to coat. Let rise, covered, in a warm place for 1 1/2 hours or until doubled in bulk.

Divide the dough into 3 equal portions. Roll each portion into a 7×12-inch rectangle on a lightly floured surface. Lift the 12-inch side and fold over to within 1 inch of the opposite side. Arrange on a greased baking sheet. Let rise, covered, in a warm place for 1 hour or until doubled in bulk. Bake at 350 degrees for 20 to 25 minutes or until golden brown. Brush the warm loaves with 3 tablespoons melted butter and sprinkle with confectioners' sugar.

Makes 3 stollen

Lemon Cranberry Loaf

chopped pecans (optional)
2¼ cups all-purpose flour or bread flour
2 teaspoons baking powder
½ teaspoon baking soda
1½ cups fresh or frozen cranberries, coarsely chopped
8 ounces cream cheese, softened
1¼ cups sugar
⅓ cup margarine
1 teaspoon vanilla extract
3 eggs
2 tablespoons lemon juice
1 teaspoon grated lemon zest

Spread the pecans in a single layer on a baking sheet. Toast at 300 degrees for 10 to 13 minutes or until light brown, stirring frequently. Let stand until cool. Increase the oven temperature to 350 degrees. Mix the flour, baking powder and baking soda in a large bowl. Add the cranberries and toss to coat.

Beat the cream cheese, sugar, margarine and vanilla in a mixing bowl at medium speed until blended, scraping the bowl occasionally. Add the eggs 1 at a time, beating well after each addition. Stir in the lemon juice and lemon zest. Add the pecans and mix well. Add the cream cheese mixture to the cranberry mixture and mix well.

Pour the batter into a greased and floured 5×9-inch loaf pan. Bake for 1¼ hours. Cool in the pan for 5 minutes. Remove to a wire rack to cool completely. You may freeze for future use.

Makes 1 loaf

Glazed Orange Bread

Bread
16 ounces cream cheese
2 (8-count) cans Grands buttermilk biscuits
¾ cup sugar
½ cup chopped pecans
1 tablespoon grated orange zest
½ cup (1 stick) butter, melted

Orange Glaze
1½ cups confectioners' sugar
3 tablespoons orange juice
¼ teaspoon vanilla extract
½ teaspoon orange extract

For the bread, cut the cream cheese into 16 equal portions and flatten slightly. Make a slit down the middle in the top of each biscuit. Insert 1 portion of the cream cheese in each slit and pinch the edges to seal.

Combine the sugar, pecans and orange zest in a shallow dish and mix well. Dip each biscuit in the butter and coat with the sugar mixture. Arrange the biscuits upright in a circle in a bundt pan sprayed with nonstick cooking spray. Drizzle with any remaining butter and sprinkle with any remaining sugar mixture. Bake at 350 degrees for 35 to 45 minutes or until brown. Invert onto a rimmed serving platter.

For the glaze, combine the confectioners' sugar, orange juice and flavorings in a bowl and mix until of a glaze consistency. Drizzle over the warm bread.

Serves 16

Menu

Gingerbread Cottages

What better time of year than Christmas to host an open house that allows you to display your holiday best. Greet guests with a steaming cup of hot chocolate and treat them to holiday goodies. Gingerbread cottages set amongst the platters of food add to the magical spirit of Christmas. Perhaps St. Nicholas will appear to hear last-minute wishes.

Cranberry Mulled Cider

1 orange
24 whole cloves
8 cups apple cider
4 cups cranberry juice
½ cup sugar

2 cinnamon sticks
1 teaspoon angostura bitters
24 whole allspice
1 cup dark rum (optional)

Stud the orange with the cloves and place the orange in a heavy saucepan. Add the cider, cranberry juice, sugar, cinnamon sticks, bitters and allspice to the saucepan and mix well. Bring to a simmer over medium heat.

Simmer until the sugar dissolves, stirring occasionally. Cover and reduce the heat to low. Simmer for 1½ hours, stirring occasionally. Strain the mulled cider into a heatproof punch bowl or slow cooker. Stir in the rum. Ladle into punch cups or mugs.

Serves 12

Festive Punch

¼ cup packed light brown sugar
2 cinnamon sticks, broken into halves
8 cups boiling water
4 orange pekoe tea bags

2 cups pineapple juice, chilled
2 cups white grape juice, chilled
2 cups strained orange juice, chilled
sliced star fruit (optional)

Combine the brown sugar and cinnamon in a large heatproof container. Add the boiling water and stir until the brown sugar dissolves. Add the tea bags. Steep, covered, for 5 minutes. Discard the tea bags and cinnamon sticks.

Pour the tea mixture into a heatproof punch bowl. Stir in the pineapple juice, grape juice and orange juice. Top with sliced star fruit. Ladle into punch cups.

Serves 16

Christmas Lights

The month of December marks the time for many popular Christmas traditions in Panama City. One in particular is piling into the car and driving throughout Bay County's many neighborhoods looking at Christmas lights and decorations. While everyone has his favorite holiday tour, we recommend a good starting place at the Downtown Marina, where Jolly Old St. Nicholas stands guard over angels, reindeer, toy soldiers, and lights of every color imaginable. Once you hit the bay, wind back around and travel north along Harrison Avenue, where lampposts and store-front windows are vaguely reminiscent of seasons past.

You may wish to meander through the Cove, where carolers gather to sing Christmas songs and enjoy hot chocolate at the homes of their neighbors and friends. A cruise along historic Beach Drive will give you a glimpse of graceful old antebellum homes decked out in their holiday best. No matter where your tour begins and ends, take the time to see Panama City in its wintertime glory, and you'll find we are home to more than just the world's most beautiful beaches.

Low Country Cheese Straws

16 ounces extra-sharp Cheddar cheese, shredded
1¾ cups flour
½ cup (1 stick) butter, softened
½ teaspoon red pepper
¼ teaspoon salt

Combine the cheese, flour, butter, red pepper and salt in a food processor. Pulse until the mixture forms a ball, scraping the side as needed. Spoon the dough into a cookie press fitted with the desired shape. Press ½ inch apart onto an ungreased baking sheet.

    Bake at 400 degrees for 20 minutes; watch carefully to prevent overbrowning. Cool on paper towels. Serve standing up, like flower stems, in decorative glasses, small vases or mint julep cups. Store leftovers in an airtight container.

Makes (about) 6 dozen straws

Holiday Fruit Ball

1 (20-ounce) can juice-pack crushed pineapple, drained
16 ounces cream cheese, softened
1 cup confectioners' sugar
¾ cup chopped pecans
1 cup golden raisins
1 cup chopped dates
1 (3-ounce) can shredded coconut
1 teaspoon vanilla extract
¼ cup chopped pecans

Press the excess juice from the pineapple. Beat the cream cheese and confectioners' sugar in a mixing bowl until blended. Stir in the pineapple, ¾ cup pecans, raisins, dates, coconut and vanilla. Shape the cream cheese mixture into a ball and coat with ¼ cup pecans. Chill, wrapped in plastic wrap, until firm. Serve with crackers.

Serves 12 to 15

Roquefort Fondue

8 ounces cream cheese, softened
4 ounces Roquefort cheese
¾ cup sour cream
2 tablespoons lemon juice
1 teaspoon Worcestershire sauce
1 splash of Tabasco sauce
3 garlic cloves, crushed
3 or 4 green onions, chopped
1 teaspoon sugar
¼ teaspoon pepper
¼ teaspoon salt
French bread, cubed

Beat the cream cheese, Roquefort cheese, sour cream, lemon juice, Worcestershire sauce and Tabasco sauce in a mixing bowl until blended. Stir in the garlic, green onions, sugar, pepper and salt.

Spoon the cream cheese mixture into an ovenproof serving dish and carefully wipe the edges of the dish. Bake at 300 degrees for 20 minutes. Serve with cubed French bread and skewers.

Serves 10 to 12

Hot Goat Cheese Appetizer

2 tablespoons extra-virgin olive oil
8 ounces soft goat cheese, such as Montrachet or chèvre
20 imported black or green olives, pitted and coarsely chopped
¼ cup fresh basil, coarsely chopped
1 cup canned chopped peeled seeded tomatoes
salt and freshly ground pepper to taste

Coat the bottom of a medium baking dish with the olive oil. Crumble the cheese over the bottom of the dish. Sprinkle the olives and basil over the cheese. Top with the tomatoes and sprinkle with salt and pepper, taking into account the saltiness of the goat cheese and olives.

Broil for 5 minutes or until the cheese melts and the tomatoes are sizzling. Serve warm with crusty French bread. Fresh tomatoes may be substituted for the canned tomatoes. You may add chopped prosciutto or additional herbs such as rosemary, thyme and/or oregano and roasted garlic.

Serves 10

Peppermint Hot Chocolate

Prepare a single-serving package of instant hot chocolate mix in a mug, using the package directions. Add a shot of peppermint schnapps. Top with whipped topping and garnish with a candy cane.

Hot Cocoa for a Crowd

Combine 1½ cups sugar with 1¼ cups baking cocoa and 1¼ teaspoons salt in a large saucepan. Add ¾ cup hot water gradually, mixing well. Cook over medium heat until the mixture boils, stirring constantly. Boil for 2 minutes, stirring constantly. Add 1 gallon milk and heat just to serving temperature, stirring occasionally; do not boil. Remove from the heat and add 1 teaspoon vanilla extract and ¼ teaspoon cinnamon if desired; whisk until smooth. Serve hot with whipped cream or marshmallows. This will serve a crowd and can be kept warm in a slow cooker.

Holiday Ham

1 (8- to 10-pound) fully cooked bone-in ham
48 whole cloves
1 (1-pound) package dark brown sugar
1 cup spicy mustard
1 cup apple cider
½ cup bourbon or chicken broth
1 cup hot strong coffee

Remove the skin from the ham and trim the fat to ¼ inch thickness. Score the ham in a diamond pattern and stud with the cloves in a decorative pattern. Arrange the ham in a lightly greased 9×13-inch baking pan.

Combine the brown sugar, mustard, cider and bourbon in a bowl and mix well. Drizzle the brown sugar mixture over the ham. Place the baking pan on the lower oven rack. Bake at 350 degrees for 2½ hours or until a meat thermometer inserted in the thickest portion of the ham registers 140 degrees, basting with pan drippings every 15 to 20 minutes. Remove the ham to a platter, reserving the pan drippings.

Add the coffee to the reserved pan drippings and stir to loosen any browned bits from the bottom of the pan. Pour the coffee mixture into a small saucepan. Cook over medium heat for 5 to 7 minutes or until heated through, stirring frequently. Serve with the ham.

Serves 12

Quick Yeast Rolls

1¹/₂ cups milk
2 tablespoons vegetable oil
3¹/₂ cups flour
2 envelopes fast-rising yeast
2 tablespoons sugar
1 teaspoon salt
1 egg, lightly beaten

Heat the milk and oil in a saucepan to 130 degrees. Remove from the heat. Combine the flour, yeast, sugar and salt in a bowl and mix well. Add the hot milk mixture and mix well. Stir in the egg. Knead for 5 to 6 minutes or until smooth and elastic, adding additional flour as needed to make an easily handled dough. Let rest, covered, for 10 minutes.

Divide the dough into 24 equal portions. Roll each portion into a ball and arrange in muffin cups or in 2 round baking pans. Let rise for 30 minutes. Bake at 400 degrees for 10 to 15 minutes or until golden brown.

Makes 2 dozen rolls

Mustard Butter

1¹/₂ cups (3 sticks) butter
1 cup pecans, toasted and finely chopped
¹/₂ cup spicy brown mustard

Combine the butter, pecans and brown mustard in a mixing bowl. Beat until mixed, scraping the bowl occasionally. Store, covered, in the refrigerator.

Makes (about) 2 cups

Bacon and Onion Spiral Bread

enough white bread dough for 1 (1-pound) loaf
3/4 cup chopped onion
2 tablespoons butter
1 cup (4 ounces) shredded Swiss cheese
1/4 cup crumbled crisp-cooked bacon (about 6 slices)
1 egg white, lightly beaten
poppy seeds or dill seeds

Let the bread dough rise until doubled in bulk; punch the dough down. Roll the dough into a 7×17-inch rectangle on a lightly floured surface. Sauté the onion in the butter in a skillet until tender. Sprinkle the sautéed onion over the rectangle. Sprinkle with the cheese and bacon. Roll as for a jelly roll, sealing the edge and ends.

Arrange the roll seam side down in a circle on a greased baking sheet. Make 1/4-inch slits crosswise in the top of the dough at equal intervals. Let rise, covered, in a warm place for 30 to 45 minutes or until almost doubled in bulk. Brush with the egg white and sprinkle with poppy seeds. Bake at 350 degrees for 25 to 30 minutes or until light brown. Slice and serve warm. You may substitute one 1-pound frozen bread loaf for the homemade bread dough.

Makes 1 round loaf

Cranberry Yam Bread

1 cup flour
1 teaspoon baking soda
1 teaspoon cinnamon
1/4 teaspoon allspice
1 1/3 cups sugar
1 cup mashed cooked yams
1/3 cup vegetable oil
2 eggs, lightly beaten
1 teaspoon vanilla extract
1 cup chopped fresh cranberries

Coat a 5×9-inch loaf pan with nonstick cooking spray and dust lightly with flour. Mix 1 cup flour, baking soda, cinnamon and allspice in a bowl. Make a well in the center of the flour mixture. Combine the sugar, yams, oil, eggs and vanilla in a bowl and mix well. Add the yam mixture to the well and stir just until moistened. Stir in the cranberries.

Spoon the batter into the prepared loaf pan. Bake at 350 degrees for 1 hour or until a wooden pick inserted in the center comes out clean. Cool in the pan for 10 minutes. Remove to a wire rack to cool completely.

Makes 1 loaf

Old-Fashioned Divinity

1 (1-pound) package light brown sugar
3 cups sugar
1½ cups water
1 cup light corn syrup
2 egg whites
1 tablespoon vanilla extract
2 cups chopped pecans

Combine the brown sugar, sugar, water and corn syrup in a 3-quart saucepan and mix well. Cook over low heat until the sugar dissolves and the syrup registers 240 degrees on a candy thermometer, soft-ball stage.

Beat the egg whites in a mixing bowl until stiff peaks form. Pour ½ of the hot syrup over the egg whites gradually, beating constantly at high speed for 10 minutes. Cook the remaining syrup over medium heat to 272 degrees on a candy thermometer, soft-crack stage; the syrup separates into hard threads that are not brittle.

Pour the hot syrup mixture and vanilla over the egg white mixture gradually, beating constantly for 10 minutes or until the mixture thickens and holds its shape. Stir in the pecans.

Drop the candy by teaspoonfuls onto lightly greased waxed paper. Let stand until firm; the divinity will have a dull luster. Store in an airtight container.

Makes 5 dozen

Molasses Spice Cookies

4 cups flour
4 teaspoons baking soda
2 teaspoons cinnamon
2 teaspoons allspice
1 teaspoon salt
1½ cups (3 sticks) butter, softened
2 cups sugar
½ cup molasses
2 eggs
sugar

Sift the flour, baking soda, cinnamon, allspice and salt together. Combine the butter, 2 cups sugar, molasses and eggs in a mixing bowl and mix well. Add the sifted dry ingredients gradually, beating constantly.

Shape the dough into 1-inch balls and roll in additional sugar. Place on a cookie sheet and bake at 350 degrees for 8 minutes or until light golden brown. Cool on the cookie sheet for 5 minutes and remove to a wire rack to cool completely.

Makes 7 dozen cookies

Decorations for Gingerbread Houses

- *Red and black licorice bites, ropes, and twists*
- *Pretzel sticks for fences and logs*
- *Candy pebbles for chimneys and accents*
- *Chocolate bars for shutters and walkways*
- *Chocolate chips*
- *Frosted ice cream cones for trees and turrets*
- *Sliced almonds for roof material*
- *Silver dragees*
- *Shredded wheat for thatched roofs*
- *Gumdrops*
- *Peppermints*

Sugar Cookies with Royal Icing

Cookies

$^3/_4$ cup ($1^1/_2$ sticks) unsalted butter, softened

$^1/_2$ cup sugar

3 egg yolks

$^1/_2$ teaspoon vanilla extract

$1^1/_4$ cups flour

$^1/_4$ teaspoon salt

Royal Icing

$^1/_4$ cup plus 2 tablespoons warm water

3 tablespoons meringue powder

1 (1-pound) package confectioners' sugar, sifted

paste food coloring

For the cookies, beat the unsalted butter and sugar in a mixing bowl until light and fluffy, scraping the bowl occasionally. Add the egg yolks 1 at a time, beating well after each addition; scrape the bowl. Beat for 1 minute longer. Add the vanilla and mix well.

Add the flour and salt to the creamed mixture. Beat at low speed until blended. Increase the speed to medium. Beat for 2 minutes longer or until the dough is thick and creamy. Remove the dough to a large sheet of waxed paper or plastic wrap and top with another sheet of waxed paper or plastic wrap. Pat the dough into a disk. Chill, wrapped in waxed paper or plastic wrap, for 4 hours. Roll the dough $^1/_2$ inch thick on a generously floured work surface. Cut with cookie cutters. Arrange the cookies 2 inches apart on a cookie sheet lined with baking parchment. Bake at 350 degrees for 15 minutes or until light brown. Cool on the cookie sheet.

For the icing, combine the warm water and meringue powder in a large mixing bowl and mix well. Add $^1/_2$ of the confectioners' sugar and beat until blended. Add the remaining confectioners' sugar. Beat at high speed for 5 to 7 minutes or to the desired consistency, scraping the bowl occasionally. Add the desired amount of color paste and mix well. Decorate the cooled cookies with the icing, keeping the bowl covered with a damp towel, as the icing dries quickly. Let the cookies stand for 8 to 10 hours or until set.

Makes about $1^1/_4$ dozen cookies

Gingerbread Cookies

3¼ cups flour
1¾ cups sugar
⅔ cup shortening
1 cup sour cream
2 eggs
1 tablespoon cinnamon
1 tablespoon ginger
2 teaspoons double-acting baking powder
1¼ teaspoons salt
1 teaspoon baking soda
1 teaspoon vanilla extract
2¾ cups flour

Combine 3¼ cups flour, sugar, shortening, sour cream, eggs, cinnamon, ginger, baking powder, salt, baking soda and vanilla in a mixing bowl. Beat at low speed until blended, scraping bowl constantly with a rubber spatula. Knead in 2¾ cups flour with hands until a soft dough forms. Chill, wrapped in plastic wrap, for 2 hours or until the dough is not sticky and easily kneaded.

Divide the dough into 2 equal portions. Place 1 portion on a lightly floured work surface, keeping the remaining portion in the refrigerator. Knead the dough with lightly floured hands until smooth. Roll ⅛ inch thick on a greased and floured 14×17-inch cookie sheet with a lightly floured rolling pin. Cut into cookies or pieces for a gingerbread house. Bake at 350 degrees until golden brown and very firm to the touch. Cool on the cookie sheet on a wire rack for 5 minutes. Remove to a wire rack to cool completely. Repeat the process with the remaining portion of dough.

Makes 4 dozen cookies

Holiday Gingerbread House

1 recipe Gingerbread Cookie dough (this page)
3 egg whites
½ teaspoon cream of tartar
1 (1-pound) package confectioners' sugar
decorations (see page 68)

Make the pattern pieces for the gingerbread house of heavy cardboard. Arrange the patterns on the dough, allowing ½ inch between the each pattern. Cut around the patterns with a sharp knife, removing the scraps and reserving for the re-rolling process. Bake at 350 degrees until golden brown and very firm when lightly touched with your finger. Cool on the cookie sheet on a wire rack for 5 minutes. Remove to a wire rack to cool completely. Repeat the process with the reserved scraps and remaining dough portion. Trim the pattern pieces if needed while warm. You may need to make several batches of the dough to complete your project, but do not double or triple the recipe. Make 1 batch at a time.

Combine the egg whites with the cream of tartar and confectioners' sugar in a mixing bowl. Beat for 7 minutes or until smooth and thick and a knife blade drawn through the icing leaves a clean cut. Spoon into a pastry bag fitted with a medium tip.

To assemble, shave the edges of the cookie pieces with a sharp knife to ensure a close fit. Pipe the icing along 1 edge of 1 house piece and fit it against the adjoining piece. Let stand until firm and dry, propping if necessary. Smooth the seams with a damp cloth and pipe along the inside seam. Continue until all the pieces are assembled and decorate as desired. You may need to make several batches of icing for your house.

Makes 1 gingerbread house

MENU

Nutcracker Sweets

After the ballet, an elegant dessert party provides a sinfully delicious opportunity to show off your hosting talents. You can invite a multitude of guests for sweets, cheeses, and drinks, and showcase your favorite serving pieces. What a perfect ending to an enchanting evening.

Hot Scandinavian Christmas Punch

1 (750-milliliter) bottle dry red wine
1/2 cup sugar
grated zest of 1 lemon
grated zest of 1 navel orange
3 whole cloves
1 cinnamon stick
1/4 teaspoon whole allspice

1 green cardamom pod
1 thin slice fresh gingerroot
1/2 cup tawny port
1/2 cup aquavit
1/4 cup each kirsch and vodka
1/2 cup raisins
1/3 cup blanched sliced almonds

Combine 1/2 of the red wine, sugar, lemon zest, orange zest, cloves, cinnamon stick, allspice, cardamom pod and gingerroot in a heavy nonreactive saucepan. Cook over medium heat until the sugar dissolves, stirring occasionally.

Simmer for 10 minutes, stirring occasionally. Let stand until cool. Strain the wine mixture through a fine sieve into a bowl. Stir in the remaining red wine, tawny port, liqueurs and vodka. Pour into a clean saucepan. Heat just until warm.

Divide the raisins and almonds evenly among 6 small coffee mugs or heatproof glasses. Ladle the warm punch over the raisin mixture. Serve with small spoons for eating the raisins and almonds.

Serves 6

Strawberry Champagne Punch

4 cups fresh strawberry juice
10 cups fresh orange juice
1 cup fresh lemon juice
1 1/2 cups Campari

16 cups Champagne
16 cups ice cubes
fresh strawberries or strawberry
    ice ring

Combine the strawberry juice, orange juice and lemon juice in a 2-gallon container and chill in the refrigerator. Pour into a punch bowl and add the Campari, Champagne and ice cubes; mix gently. Garnish with fresh strawberries or a strawberry ice ring.

Serves 44

The Martin Theatre

The Martin Theatre, which opened its doors in 1937 as the Ritz, is a perfect example of the movie palace era. During its heyday, the theatre hosted movies, vaudeville shows, beauty pageants, and talent shows, and was billed as the "Showplace of Northwest Florida." The state-of-the-art theatre featured leather seats, climate control, dressing rooms with showers, and a silk gauze rainbow curtain that opened right before each movie began.

In the late 1950s, the Ritz became the Martin Theatre, and was extensively redecorated, receiving its trademark marquee. By the time the early 1970s rolled around, the theatre closed and stood vacant for more than a decade. Luckily, with the aid of the Downtown Improvement Board, the historic Martin Theatre was returned to its original art deco glory, and the doors reopened in 1990. It now serves as a center for cultural activity in Bay County.

Classic Eggnog

1 gallon vanilla ice cream
2 cups whipping cream, chilled
12 egg yolks
1 cup confectioners' sugar
1½ cups each brandy or whiskey and rum
12 egg whites
1 cup confectioners' sugar
1 pint vanilla ice cream
nutmeg to taste

Soften 1 gallon ice cream in a chilled punch bowl. Beat the whipping cream in a mixing bowl until stiff peaks form. Beat the egg yolks and 1 cup confectioners' sugar in a mixing bowl. Add the brandy and rum gradually to the yolk mixture, beating constantly.

Beat the egg whites in a mixing bowl until stiff peaks form. Add 1 cup confectioner's sugar gradually, beating constantly. Fold into the yolk mixture. Fold in the whipped cream. Pour over the ice cream in the punch bowl. Chill, covered, for 8 to 10 hours. To serve, scoop 1 pint ice cream into the eggnog. Top each serving with nutmeg.

Serves 12

Baked Brie with Caramelized Onions

3 large onions, thinly sliced
2 tablespoons butter
1 tablespoon minced fresh thyme
4 garlic cloves, minced
½ cup dry white wine
1 teaspoon sugar
salt and freshly ground pepper to taste
1 (32-ounce) round Brie cheese packed in wooden box

Sauté the onions in the butter in a large skillet over medium-high heat for 5 minutes or just until tender. Stir in the thyme. Reduce the heat to medium-low. Cook for 25 minutes or until the onions are very tender and golden in color, stirring frequently.

Add the garlic and sauté for 2 minutes. Stir in ¼ cup of the wine. Cook for 2 minutes. Sprinkle with the sugar. Cook for 10 minutes. Add the remaining ¼ cup wine and mix well. Cook for 2 minutes or just until the liquid evaporates. Season with salt and pepper. Cool slightly. You may prepare up to this point 2 days in advance and store, covered, in the refrigerator.

Remove the Brie from the wooden box, reserving the bottom. Wrap the bottom of the box with foil and secure with kitchen twine. Place on a baking sheet.

Cut the rind from the top of the Brie and place the Brie rind side down in the box. Spoon the onion mixture evenly over the top. Bake at 350 degrees for 30 minutes or just until the Brie begins to melt. Serve in the box on a platter with sliced apples, bread and/or Belgian endive.

The Brie becomes almost like fondue after being baked so be careful moving the wooden box to a platter. This method is also suitable with Brie alone if it is a very high quality cheese. For variety, use other toppings such as fruit sauces.

Serves 10

Peppermint and Pecan Chocolate Bark

20 ounces mint chocolate such as Ghirardelli, chopped
1 (7-ounce) package hard peppermint candies, chopped
1 cup pecans, toasted and chopped

Line an 11×17-inch baking sheet with sides with baking parchment. Sprinkle the chocolate evenly over the baking parchment. Heat at 250 degrees for 5 minutes or until the chocolate is soft. Remove from the oven. Spread the chocolate evenly on the parchment paper with a rubber spatula or the back of a spoon. Sprinkle with the peppermint candies and pecans. Chill for 2 hours or until firm. Break into bite-size pieces.

> *Makes (about) 2 pounds*

Perfect Peppermint Patties

1 (1-pound) package confectioners' sugar
3 tablespoons butter, softened
2 to 3 teaspoons peppermint extract
$1/2$ teaspoon vanilla extract
$1/4$ cup evaporated milk
2 cups (12 ounces) chocolate chips
2 tablespoons shortening

Combine the confectioners' sugar, butter and flavorings in a bowl and mix well. Stir in the evaporated milk. Shape the candy mixture into $1^1/2$-inch balls and arrange on a baking sheet lined with waxed paper. Chill for 20 minutes. Flatten each ball with the bottom of a glass. Freeze for 30 minutes.

Heat the chocolate chips and shortening in a double boiler or microwave until blended, stirring frequently. Dip the patties in the chocolate until coated on all sides. Arrange the patties on the baking sheet lined with waxed paper. Chill until set.

> *Makes 3 to 5 dozen patties*

Toasted Pecans

Melt 3 tablespoons butter in a heavy skillet. Stir in 3 tablespoons Worcestershire sauce, 1 teaspoon cinnamon, $1/4$ teaspoon garlic powder, 1 teaspoon salt, $1/4$ teaspoon cayenne pepper and a dash of hot sauce. Add 1 pound pecan halves and toss to coat well. Spread in a single layer on a baking sheet and bake at 300 degrees for 20 to 25 minutes or until the pecans are golden brown and crisp, stirring frequently.

Orange Syrup

Bring ¹/₂ cup water and ¹/₂ cup sugar to a boil in a saucepan; reduce the heat. Simmer for 5 minutes, stirring occasionally. Cool for 10 minutes. Stir in ¹/₄ cup Grand Marnier.

Semisweet Chocolate Glaze

Heat 1 cup chopped Swiss semisweet chocolate and 2 tablespoons unsalted butter in a double boiler or microwave until blended, stirring frequently. Cool just to room temperature.

Milk Chocolate Glaze

Heat ¹/₂ cup chopped Swiss milk chocolate in a double boiler or microwave until melted, stirring frequently. Cool just to room temperature.

Fudge Yule Log

Cake
¹/₄ cup cornstarch
¹/₄ cup flour
¹/₄ cup baking cocoa
¹/₃ cup egg yolks (about 5)
1 teaspoon very strong coffee
1 teaspoon orange liqueur, such as
    Grand Marnier
³/₄ cup egg whites (about 5)
¹/₃ cup sugar
Orange Syrup (this page)

apricot jam, heated
Semisweet Chocolate Glaze (this page)
Milk Chocolate Glaze (this page)
Meringue Mushrooms (page 75)

Truffle Mousse Filling
1¹/₄ cups heavy cream
1¹/₂ cups coarsely chopped Swiss
    semisweet chocolate
¹/₄ cup (¹/₂ stick) unsalted butter,
    softened

For the cake, grease a jelly roll pan and line with baking parchment or waxed paper. Grease the baking parchment and dust lightly with flour. Sift the cornstarch, flour and baking cocoa twice. Whisk the egg yolks, coffee and liqueur in a bowl. Beat the egg whites in a mixing bowl until foamy. Add the sugar gradually, beating constantly until stiff but not dry peaks form. Fold ¹/₄ of the egg whites into the egg yolk mixture. Fold the egg yolk mixture into the egg whites. Sift the cornstarch mixture over the egg white mixture and fold just to incorporate. Spread the batter in the prepared pan. Bake at 400 degrees for 10 to 12 minutes or until the cake tests done. Invert the cake immediately onto a tea towel dusted with confectioners' sugar. Discard the baking parchment. Roll the warm cake in the tea towel from the short side. Let rest for 1 minute. Unroll and let stand until cool.

For the mousse, bring the heavy cream to a boil in a saucepan. Stir in the chocolate. Cook for 1 minute or until the chocolate melts, stirring constantly. Turn off the heat and continue stirring for 1 minute longer or until smooth, without removing from the burner. Pour into a bowl and chill, covered, for 1 hour or until set. Beat in a mixing bowl until the mixture lightens in color and increases in volume. Add the butter gradually, beating constantly until light and fluffy.

To assemble, brush the cake with the Orange Syrup and spread with the mousse; reroll. Brush with warm apricot jam. Chill, covered, in the refrigerator. Place on a wire rack over a baking sheet. Pour the Semisweet Chocolate Glaze over the cake roll until completely covered. Let stand until set. Pour the Milk Chocolate Glaze into a small decorator's paper cone and drizzle over the roll. Garnish with Meringue Mushrooms and/or sprigs of holly.

Serves 8 to 10

Meringue Mushrooms

4 large egg whites, at room temperature
1/4 teaspoon cream of tartar
1 cup sugar
1/2 teaspoon vanilla extract
baking cocoa (optional)
3 ounces semisweet chocolate, melted

Beat the egg whites and cream of tartar in a mixing bowl at medium speed until frothy. Add 1/2 cup of the sugar and vanilla gradually, beating constantly at high speed. Add the remaining 1/2 cup sugar gradually, beating until stiff and shiny peaks form.

Spoon the meringue into a pastry bag fitted with a #6 tip or a similar plain tip using a rubber spatula; do not overfill. Pipe about 30 mushroom stems onto a baking sheet lined with baking parchment, lifting and twisting the bag to separate the stems from the tip. Dust with baking cocoa. Pipe the mushroom caps by holding the tip a short distance over the prepared baking sheet and gently squeezing the bag to make the cap billow out. Lift and twist to separate the tip from the cap. Smooth the caps as needed by gently patting with a moist fingertip. Dust with baking cocoa.

Bake caps and stems at 200 degrees for 2 hours or until dry and crisp, watching carefully. Trim the mushroom stems so they have flat tops. Brush the bottom of each mushroom cap with melted chocolate and attach a stem. Surround your Yule Log with the mushrooms or attach to the roll.

Makes 30 mushrooms

Frosted Red Velvet Cake

Cake
2 1/2 cups flour, sifted
1 teaspoon baking soda
1 teaspoon baking cocoa
1 1/2 cups sugar
2 eggs
1 teaspoon vanilla extract
1 1/2 cups vegetable oil
1 cup buttermilk
1 teaspoon vinegar
2 tablespoons red food coloring

Cream Cheese Frosting
1/2 cup (1 stick) butter or margarine, softened
8 ounces cream cheese, softened
1 (1-pound) package confectioners' sugar
1 cup pecans, chopped
1 teaspoon vanilla extract

For the cake, sift the flour, baking soda and baking cocoa together. Beat the sugar and eggs in a mixing bowl until blended. Add the oil, buttermilk and vinegar and beat until smooth. Add the flour mixture and beat until blended. Stir in the food coloring.

Spoon the batter into 3 nonstick cake pans. Bake at 350 degrees for 30 minutes. Cool in the pans for 10 minutes. Remove to a wire rack to cool completely.

For the frosting, beat the butter and cream cheese in a mixing bowl until creamy. Add the confectioners' sugar and beat until of a spreading consistency. Stir in the pecans and vanilla. Spread the frosting between the layers and over the top and side of the cake.

Serves 12

Toffee

Combine 1 cup sugar, ³/₄ cup (1¹/₂ sticks) butter and 1 tablespoon corn syrup in a saucepan and mix well. Bring to a boil and boil until the mixture registers 290 degrees on a candy thermometer, stirring constantly. Stir in 1¹/₄ cups pecans quickly. Spread evenly in a pan and let stand until set. Melt 3 bars chocolate bark in a double boiler, stirring until smooth. Spread over the toffee layer and let cool until set. Break into pieces and store in an airtight container.

Chocolate Fondue

6 ounces semisweet chocolate, chopped
2 ounces unsweetened chocolate, chopped
1¹/₂ cups sugar
1 cup half-and-half
¹/₂ cup (1 stick) butter, sliced
¹/₈ teaspoon salt
2 teaspoons vanilla extract

Combine the chocolate, sugar, half-and-half, butter and salt in a fondue pot. Heat over medium heat until blended, stirring occasionally. Reduce the heat to low. Heat for 5 minutes longer or until thickened, stirring occasionally. Stir in the vanilla. Maintain the temperature to serve. Serve with whole strawberries, cubed pound cake and sliced bananas dipped in lemon juice.

Makes 3 cups

Key Lime Fudge

3 cups (18 ounces) white chocolate chips
1 (14-ounce) can sweetened condensed milk
2 tablespoons Key lime juice or lime juice
2 teaspoons finely grated lime zest
1 cup chopped macadamia nuts, toasted
coarsely chopped macadamia nuts to taste

Line an 8x8-inch or 9x9-inch dish with foil, allowing a 4- to 5-inch overhang. Coat the foil with butter. Combine the white chocolate chips and condensed milk in a heavy saucepan. Cook over low heat just until the chocolate melts and the mixture is smooth, stirring frequently. Remove from the heat. Stir in the lime juice and lime zest. Add 1 cup macadamia nuts and mix well. Spread the chocolate mixture in the prepared dish and sprinkle with coarsely chopped macadamia nuts. Chill, covered, for 2 hours or until firm. Lift the fudge out of the dish using the edges of the foil. Cut the fudge into squares and store in an airtight container at room temperature for 1 week or freeze for up to 2 months.

Makes 64 squares

Raspberry Pecan Fluff Pie

4 egg whites, at room temperature
1½ teaspoons cream of tartar
2 cups sugar
1 teaspoon vanilla extract
1 cup butter cracker crumbs
½ cup chopped pecans
1 cup whipping cream
1 cup whipped topping
1 cup fresh raspberries or sliced fresh strawberries

Beat the egg whites and cream of tartar in a mixing bowl at medium speed until frothy. Add ½ cup of the sugar gradually, beating constantly at high speed. Beat in the vanilla. Add another ½ cup of the sugar gradually, beating constantly until stiff. Fold in the cracker crumbs and pecans. Spoon into a lightly greased pie plate and pat lightly to form a crust. Bake at 325 degrees for 1 hour or until dry and crisp. Cool on a wire rack.

Beat the whipping cream in a mixing bowl until soft peaks form. Add the remaining 1 cup sugar gradually, beating constantly until blended. Fold in the whipped topping and raspberries. Spoon the raspberry filling into the prepared pie plate. Chill, covered, until serving time.

Serves 6 to 8

Hot Chocolate Pie

4 eggs
1⅓ cups sugar
½ cup flour
⅓ cup baking cocoa
2 cups milk
¼ cup (½ stick) butter or margarine
1 teaspoon vanilla extract
1 (9-inch) pie shell
⅓ cup sugar

Separate the eggs and place the egg whites in the refrigerator, reserving the yolks. Sift 1⅓ cups sugar, flour and baking cocoa into a bowl and mix well. Heat 1½ cups of the milk in a double boiler.

Beat the reserved egg yolks in a mixing bowl until blended. Add the sugar mixture and remaining ½ cup milk and beat until smooth. Beat in the warm milk. Return the milk mixture to the double boiler. Stir in the butter and vanilla. Cook until thickened, stirring frequently.

Spoon the chocolate filling into a buttered baking dish. Bake the pie shell and heat the chocolate filling at 350 degrees for 15 minutes. Heating the filling makes for a thicker consistency.

Beat the chilled egg whites in a mixing bowl until frothy. Add ⅓ cup sugar gradually, beating constantly until stiff peaks form. Spoon the hot filling into the pie shell. Spread with the meringue, sealing to the edge. Bake at 350 degrees until the meringue is light brown. Serve hot.

Serves 6 to 8

Recipes for this photograph on pages 74 and 75.

Warm Winters

WINNER OF THE GAME

PALMS OF ST. ANDREWS

ARTE ITALICA

MENU

Winner of the Game

When the heat of the summer subsides and the leaves turn to shades of gold, a trip to the country is a natural reprieve. Fall's bounty provides the perfect ingredients for a lakeside feast with fellow hunters. A rustic porch adorned with gourds and pumpkins completes the scene.

Absent Husband Cocktail

Sugar Syrup
¹/₂ cup water
1 cup sugar

Cocktail
1¹/₂ cups cracked ice
6 ounces amaretto
3 ounces bourbon
2 ounces fresh lemon juice
lemon zest

For the syrup, bring the water to a boil in a saucepan. Remove from the heat. Add the sugar gradually, stirring constantly until the sugar dissolves. Let stand until cool. Pour into a glass jar with a tight-fitting lid. Store in the refrigerator for up to 1 month. You may purchase sugar syrup at the liquor store.

   For the cocktail, combine the cracked ice, amaretto, bourbon, lemon juice and 2 tablespoons of the sugar syrup in a cocktail shaker and cover. Shake until blended and chilled. Pour into 2 glasses. Garnish with lemon zest.

   Serves 2

Buttered Bourbon and Cider

2 cups apple cider
¹/₂ cup water
3 tablespoons brown sugar
4 whole cloves
1 cinnamon stick
3 tablespoons unsalted butter, chilled

³/₄ cup bourbon
2¹/₂ tablespoons fresh lemon juice
grated nutmeg
4 cinnamon sticks
4 lemon slices

Combine the apple cider, water, brown sugar, cloves and 1 cinnamon stick in a saucepan and bring to a simmer. Remove from the heat and steep, covered, for 15 minutes. Return to the stove and add 2 tablespoons of the unsalted butter. Bring to a simmer, stirring to melt the butter. Remove from the heat and stir in the bourbon and lemon juice. Strain into a large glass measuring cup with a pouring spout. Pour into 4 mugs. Cut the remaining tablespoon of butter into 4 pats and place 1 pat in each mug. Sprinkle with nutmeg and garnish with a fresh cinnamon stick and a lemon slice placed on the rim. Serve hot.

   Serves 4

Life in North Bay County

While the original settlers of this area were fishermen, it didn't take long for the word to spread that the area was also rich in yellow pines. Once the word got out, capitalists came quickly to take advantage of the natural resources of the forest and the perfect proximity to the coastal waters. Sawmills were built, and lumber was harvested, processed, and loaded onto ships for transport.

   Most of the rural areas of Bay County are made up of land dedicated to tree farming today. However, one of the great side effects of owning such property is the opportunity to take advantage of the terrific hunting in those areas. The farms furnish a bounty of wild game, and hunting boar, turkey, dove, wood ducks, quail, squirrel, rabbit, and deer is a favorite pastime and tradition among the residents.

Nutty Pinecones

1 cup sliced almonds
8 ounces cream cheese, softened
1/2 cup reduced-fat mayonnaise
1 cup (4 ounces) shredded Vermont Cheddar cheese
5 slices bacon, crisp-cooked and crumbled
1 tablespoon chopped green onions
1 tablespoon chopped bell pepper
1/2 teaspoon lemon dill seasoning
salt and pepper to taste

Spread the sliced almonds in a single layer on a baking sheet. Toast at 300 degrees for 15 minutes, stirring frequently. Remove to a platter. Let stand until cool.

Combine the cream cheese and mayonnaise in a mixing bowl and beat until smooth. Mix in the Cheddar cheese, bacon, green onions, bell pepper, lemon dill seasoning, salt and pepper until thoroughly combined. Chill, covered, for 8 to 10 hours.

Divide the cheese mixture into 2 equal portions. Shape each portion to resemble a pinecone. Beginning at the narrow end of each portion, press the almonds at a slight angle into the pinecones forming rows. Continue overlapping the rows until completely covered. Arrange the pinecones on a serving platter and garnish with sprigs of fresh pine. Serve with assorted party crackers.

Serves 12

Venison Meatballs

Meatballs
1 pound ground venison or ground beef
1 medium onion, minced
1 cup flour
1/2 cup soft bread crumbs
1/4 cup milk
3/4 teaspoon salt
1/2 teaspoon pepper
Worcestershire sauce to taste
3 tablespoons butter

Mustard Sauce
1/4 cup ketchup
3 tablespoons molasses or honey
3 tablespoons cider vinegar
3 tablespoons prepared mustard
1/4 teaspoon thyme

For the meatballs, combine the ground venison, onion, flour, bread crumbs, milk, salt, pepper and Worcestershire sauce in a bowl and mix well. Shape the venison mixture into bite-size balls. Heat the butter in a large skillet. Brown the meatballs on all sides in the butter; drain.

For the sauce, combine the ketchup, molasses, vinegar, prepared mustard and thyme in a large saucepan and mix well. Bring to a boil, stirring frequently. Add the meatballs and stir gently.

Simmer for 10 minutes or until heated through, stirring occasionally. Double or triple the recipe for a large crowd and serve in a chafing dish.

Serves 8 to 10

Curried Butternut Squash Soup

3 tablespoons butter or margarine
2 large onions, sliced
1 tablespoon curry powder, or to taste
3½ pounds butternut squash, peeled, seeded and
    cut into ½-inch pieces
2 (14-ounce) cans chicken broth
2¼ cups water
½ teaspoon salt
¼ cup sour cream (optional)
1½ teaspoons nutmeg (optional)

Melt 2 tablespoons of the butter in a 5-quart Dutch oven or saucepan over medium heat. Stir in the onions. Cook for 18 to 20 minutes or until very tender, stirring frequently. Add the curry powder and remaining 1 tablespoon butter. Cook for 1 minute, stirring constantly. Add the squash, broth, water and salt and mix well. Bring to a boil; reduce the heat to low.

Simmer, covered, for 20 minutes or until the squash is tender, stirring occasionally. Process the soup in batches in a blender until smooth, removing the center portion of the cover to allow the steam to escape. Return the soup to the Dutch oven. Simmer just until heated through, stirring occasionally. Ladle into soup bowls. Top each serving with 1 teaspoon of the sour cream and sprinkle with ⅛ teaspoon of the nutmeg.

Makes 12 cups

Collard Greens Soup

2 (32-ounce) cans chicken broth
1 (8-ounce) ham hock
2 bacon slices, chopped
2 teaspoons olive oil
⅓ onion, chopped
2 ribs celery, chopped
½ cup water
3 tablespoons flour
2 (16-ounce) packages fresh collard greens, trimmed
⅓ cup whipping cream
2 tablespoons cider vinegar
1 tablespoon hot sauce
1 teaspoon pepper

Bring the broth and ham hock to a boil in a Dutch oven over high heat; reduce the heat. Simmer, partially covered, for 30 minutes. Fry the bacon in the olive oil in a medium skillet until crisp. Remove the bacon to a paper towel to drain, reserving the pan drippings.

Sauté the onion and celery in the reserved pan drippings until tender. Mix the water and flour in a bowl until smooth. Add the flour mixture to the onion mixture and mix well. Add the onion mixture and collard greens to the broth mixture and mix well.

Simmer, covered, for 1 hour or until the collard greens are tender, stirring occasionally. Remove the ham hock to a platter. Cool slightly. Remove the ham from the bone and chop, discarding the bone. Return the ham to the Dutch oven. Stir in the whipping cream, vinegar, hot sauce, pepper and bacon. Simmer just until heated through, stirring occasionally. Ladle into soup bowls.

Makes 15 cups

Stuffed Pepper Soup

1½ pounds ground sirloin
3 large green bell peppers, chopped
1 large onion, chopped
1 (28-ounce) can chopped tomatoes
2 (14-ounce) cans beef broth
2 (10-ounce) cans tomato soup
1 teaspoon salt
½ teaspoon pepper
1½ cups cooked white or brown rice

Brown the ground sirloin in a Dutch oven, stirring until crumbly; drain. Add the bell peppers and onion and mix well. Sauté until the onion is tender.

Stir in the undrained tomatoes, broth, tomato soup, salt and pepper. Simmer for 45 to 60 minutes or to the desired consistency, stirring occasionally. Stir in the rice. Simmer just until heated through, stirring occasionally. Ladle into soup bowls. Add a yellow bell pepper or red bell pepper for variety.

Serves 6

Corn Bread Salad

1 recipe Jalapeño Corn Bread (page 93)
1½ cups mayonnaise
½ cup sweet pickle juice
¼ cup sweet pickle relish
4 tomatoes, chopped
1 green bell pepper, chopped
1 sweet onion, chopped
12 slices bacon, crisp-cooked and crumbled

Prepare the corn bread. Let stand until cool and crumble. Combine the mayonnaise, pickle juice and pickle relish in a bowl and mix well. Toss the tomatoes, bell pepper and onion in a bowl.

Layer the corn bread, tomato mixture and mayonnaise mixture ½ at a time in the order listed in a clear salad bowl or trifle dish with straight sides. Sprinkle with the bacon. Chill, covered, until serving time.

Serves 4 to 6

Stuffed Pork Tenderloin

2 (10-ounce) packages frozen chopped spinach, thawed and drained
1 onion, chopped
1 red bell pepper, chopped
2 garlic cloves, minced
1/4 cup olive oil
1/2 cup crumbled feta cheese
1/4 cup shredded mozzarella cheese
3 tablespoons pine nuts
1 egg, lightly beaten
2 pork tenderloins, trimmed and butterflied
8 slices prosciutto
8 slices provolone cheese
Apple Glaze (this page)

Press the excess moisture from the spinach. Sauté the onion, bell pepper and garlic in the olive oil in a skillet until the onion and bell pepper are tender. Combine the onion mixture, spinach, feta cheese, mozzarella cheese, pine nuts and egg in a bowl and mix well.

Flatten the tenderloins slightly. Arrange 4 slices of the prosciutto and 4 slices of the provolone cheese on each tenderloin. Spoon 1/2 of the spinach mixture down the center of each tenderloin. Roll and secure with kitchen twine.

Arrange the tenderloins in a roasting pan. Roast at 400 degrees for 40 minutes or to the desired degree of doneness. Cool for 10 minutes before slicing into medallions. Drizzle with the Apple Glaze.

Serves 8 to 10

Apple Glaze

Combine 1 peeled and chopped large apple, 1/2 cup sugar, 1/2 cup water, 1/2 cup white wine and 1/8 teaspoon nutmeg in a saucepan. Bring to a boil and boil until thickened, stirring frequently. Stir in a mixture of 2 tablespoons water and 1 tablespoon cornstarch if needed to thicken.

Venison Backstrap Medallions

8 venison backstrap pieces, cut into 1-inch medallions
½ cup bourbon
6 tablespoons dark brown sugar
¼ cup balsamic vinegar
2 teaspoons salt
2 teaspoons pepper
2 teaspoons finely chopped garlic
2 tablespoons Worcestershire sauce
2 bay leaves
1 red bell pepper, julienned
Béarnaise Sauce (this page)
sprigs of fresh parsley
2 tablespoons pine nuts, toasted
freshly grated nutmeg

Place the venison in a large sealable plastic bag. Combine
the bourbon, brown sugar, vinegar, salt, pepper, garlic,
Worcestershire sauce and bay leaves in a bowl and mix
well. Pour the bourbon mixture over the venison and seal
tightly. Marinate in the refrigerator for 8 to 10 hours,
turning occasionally. Combine the bell pepper strips
with enough cold water to cover in a bowl. Chill in
the refrigerator.

   Grill the venison over hot coals until medium-rare.
Spoon some of the Béarnaise Sauce on each serving plate.
Top with the venison. Garnish with the drained bell pepper
strips and sprigs of fresh parsley. Sprinkle with the pine
nuts and freshly grated nutmeg.

   Serves 4

Recipe for this photograph on facing page.

Béarnaise Sauce

4 egg yolks
juice of 1 lemon
2 cups (4 sticks) butter, melted
salt and white pepper to taste
2 tablespoons rinsed drained capers
¼ cup fresh parsley, chopped
1 tablespoon tarragon vinegar

Whisk the egg yolks and lemon juice in a double boiler
until blended. Cook over low heat, stirring constantly;
do not allow the water to boil. Add the butter gradually,
stirring constantly. Cook to the desired consistency,
stirring constantly. Stir in the salt, white pepper, capers,
parsley and vinegar. Cover to keep warm.

   Makes 3 cups

Grilled Quail with Mushroom Sauce

Quail

1/4 cup olive oil

1 tablespoon chopped garlic

1 tablespoon chopped fresh rosemary

1 (3-pound) quail, cut into quarters

salt and pepper to taste

Creamy Grits (this page)

Mushroom Sauce

1 cup beef stock or beef broth

1 cup chicken stock or chicken broth

1/2 cup dry white wine

3 ounces pancetta, thinly sliced and
   julienned (about 3/4 cup)

8 ounces fresh mushrooms, such as
   cremini or shiitake, sliced
   (about 3 cups)

3/4 cup whipping cream

1 tablespoon thinly sliced
   fresh sage

salt and pepper to taste

For the quail, combine the olive oil, garlic and rosemary in a 9×13-inch dish
and mix well. Season the quail with salt and pepper. Add the quail to the olive
oil mixture and turn to coat. Marinate, covered, in the refrigerator for 4 to
10 hours, turning occasionally; drain. Grill over medium-high heat for 30 minutes
or until cooked through.

For the sauce, bring the beef stock, chicken stock and wine to a boil in
a heavy saucepan. Boil for 15 minutes or until the liquid is reduced to 1 cup.
Remove from the heat. Fry the pancetta in a large heavy skillet over medium-high
heat for 3 minutes or until brown and crisp, stirring constantly. Remove the
pancetta to a bowl using a slotted spoon and reserving the pan drippings.

Sauté the mushrooms in the reserved pan drippings for 4 to 5 minutes or
until golden brown. Add the stock mixture and whipping cream and mix well.
Simmer for 5 minutes or until slightly thickened and of a sauce consistency,
stirring frequently. Stir in the pancetta and sage. Season with salt and pepper.
Remove from the heat. Cover to keep warm.

To serve, mound half of the Creamy Grits in the center of each of 2 serving
plates. Top with the quail and drizzle with the sauce. Serve immediately. You may
substitute an equivalent amount of chicken for the quail.

Serves 2

Creamy Grits

Bring 1 1/2 cups chicken stock or chicken broth,
1/2 cup whipping cream and 2 tablespoons
butter to a simmer in a heavy saucepan over
medium heat, stirring occasionally. Whisk in
1/2 cup quick-cooking grits gradually. Reduce
the heat to low. Simmer, covered, for 6 minutes
or until the grits are creamy and tender,
stirring occasionally. Season with salt
and pepper.

Native Americans in Bay County

Native Americans lived in Bay County long before the white settlers came, and the area was home to several groups, including the Choctaw and Creeks. There is still a section of land in North Bay County that is occupied by the North Bay Clan of Lower Muscogee Creeks, and traditional celebrations are still held.

Dove Breast Kabobs

¹/₂ cup vegetable oil
¹/₄ cup Worcestershire sauce
¹/₄ cup soy sauce
1 teaspoon each garlic powder and ginger
¹/₂ teaspoon each salt and pepper
12 dove breasts
8 ounces sliced bacon
1 large onion, cut into 1-inch pieces
1 green bell pepper, cut into 1-inch pieces
cherry tomatoes

Mix the oil, Worcestershire sauce, soy sauce, garlic powder, ginger, salt and pepper in a shallow dish. Fillet the meat from each side of the dove breast bones and add to the oil mixture, turning to coat. Marinate, covered, in the refrigerator for several hours, turning occasionally. Drain, reserving the marinade.

Thread the dove, bacon, onion, bell pepper and cherry tomatoes alternately on skewers. Grill the kabobs over hot coals until the dove is cooked through and the vegetables are the desired degree of crispness, basting frequently with the reserved marinade. Watch carefully as the dove may cook quickly. The vegetables may be placed directly on the grill rack for greater color and for grill markings.

Serves 6

Creamed Collard Greens

1 cup water
2 ounces bacon, cut into 1/4-inch strips
4 pounds fresh collard greens, stems and tough inner ribs
    removed
1 large onion, chopped
1 cup heavy cream
salt and freshly ground pepper to taste
2 eggs, lightly beaten
Parmesan Herb Crumbs (this page)

Bring the water and bacon to a boil in a large stockpot.
Add the collard greens by handfuls, stirring after each
addition until the greens are wilted before adding the next
handful. Bring to a boil; reduce the heat. Stir in the onion.

Simmer, covered, over medium heat for 30 to
40 minutes or until the greens are tender. Remove from
the heat. Let stand until cool. Drain the greens in a
colander and press until almost dry; coarsely chop.

Combine the greens and heavy cream in a bowl and
mix well. Season with salt and pepper. Stir in the eggs.
Spoon the greens mixture into a buttered shallow 2-quart
baking dish. Bake, covered with foil, for 40 minutes. You
may prepare up to this point 1 day in advance and store,
covered, in the refrigerator. Bring to room temperature
before proceeding with the recipe.

Sprinkle the Parmesan Herb Crumbs over the baked
layer. Bake for 20 minutes longer or until golden brown.
Broil 10 inches from the heat source until crisp. Serve
immediately. You may substitute 3 packages frozen collard
greens for the fresh collard greens.

Serves 6

Parmesan Herb Crumbs

3/4 cup coarse dry bread crumbs
1/4 cup plus 2 tablespoons freshly grated Parmesan cheese
1 tablespoon olive oil
1 1/2 teaspoons minced fresh parsley
1/2 teaspoon minced fresh sage
1 garlic clove, minced

Combine the bread crumbs, cheese, olive oil, parsley, sage
and garlic in a food processor. Pulse just until blended.

Makes 1 cup

Accompaniments for Game

Good side dishes to serve with game include wild rice, pasta, rosemary potatoes, and seasonal vegetables. Seasoned butters are good to flavor the game and vegetables, as well as natural seasonings that are compatible with the animal's diet. Nuts, fresh and dried berries, and herbs such as sage, rosemary, and thyme are particularly good with game.

Corn Pudding

1 (15-ounce) can whole kernel corn, drained
1 (15-ounce) can creamed corn
1 (9-ounce) package corn bread mix
1 cup sour cream
1 cup (2 sticks) butter, melted
2 eggs, beaten

Combine the corn, corn bread mix, sour cream, butter and eggs in a bowl and mix well. Spoon the corn mixture into a greased 2-quart baking dish. Bake at 350 degrees for 1 hour. Double the ingredients for a large crowd and bake in a 9×13-inch baking dish.

Serves 4 to 6

Glazed Julienne of Root Vegetables

1 pound carrots, peeled and cut into 1^1/$_2$-inch julienne strips
1 pound turnips, peeled and cut into 1^1/$_2$-inch julienne strips
12 ounces rutabagas, peeled and cut into 1^1/$_2$-inch julienne strips
^{1}/$_4$ cup (^{1}/$_2$ stick) butter
2^1/$_2$ tablespoons sugar
2^1/$_2$ tablespoons water
^{1}/$_2$ teaspoon salt
^{1}/$_4$ teaspoon pepper

Combine the carrots, turnips, rutabagas, butter, sugar, water, salt and pepper in a large skillet. Bring to a boil, stirring occasionally; reduce the heat to low. Cook, covered, for 10 to 12 minutes or until the vegetables are tender-crisp, stirring occasionally. Serve immediately.

Serves 8

Crowder Peas with Spinach

2 cups fresh or frozen crowder peas
1 cup chicken broth, ham broth or vegetable broth
1/2 teaspoon salt
1 slice bacon, chopped
1 small sweet onion, chopped
1 bunch green onions, chopped
2 garlic cloves, minced
10 ounces fresh spinach, trimmed
1/2 teaspoon salt
1/2 teaspoon crushed red pepper

Bring the peas, broth and 1/2 teaspoon salt to a boil in a saucepan. Reduce the heat to low. Simmer, covered, for 30 minutes or until the peas are tender, stirring occasionally.

Sauté the bacon in a large skillet over medium heat. Stir in the onion, green onions and garlic. Sauté for 3 minutes. Add the spinach, 1/2 teaspoon salt and red pepper. Sauté for 2 minutes or until the spinach wilts. Stir in the undrained peas. Serve immediately.

Serves 4

Whipped Sweet Potatoes with Pears

8 medium sweet potatoes or yams
1 cup evaporated milk
1/2 cup packed brown sugar
1/4 cup (1/2 stick) butter
2 teaspoons vanilla extract
4 fresh pears, peeled, cored, poached and puréed
2 tablespoons orange juice
1/2 teaspoon freshly ground cinnamon
1/8 teaspoon freshly grated nutmeg
1 cup chopped pecans

Bake the sweet potatoes at 375 degrees until tender. Cool slightly and peel. Place the sweet potato pulp in a mixing bowl and beat until smooth. Heat the evaporated milk, brown sugar, butter and vanilla in a saucepan until bubbles form around the edge of the pan. Add the hot milk mixture to the sweet potatoes and mix until blended.

Stir the puréed pears, orange juice, cinnamon, nutmeg and pecans into the sweet potato mixture. Spoon the sweet potato mixture into a baking dish. Bake at 350 degrees for 15 minutes or until heated through. Serve immediately.

Serves 10 to 12

Savory Wild Rice

Prepare 4 cups uncooked wild rice using the package directions and set aside. Melt 2 tablespoons butter in a saucepan and add 1 chopped red onion, 1 chopped garlic clove, 1/2 cup chopped mushrooms, 1/2 cup raisins and 1/2 cup chopped pecans or walnuts. Sauté until the onion is tender. Add 3 tablespoons canola or other vegetable oil and the rice and cook until heated through. Season with salt and pepper.

Cranberry Bake

2 cups fresh cranberries
3 cups sliced peeled apples
1 (8-ounce) can crushed pineapple
1 cup packed brown sugar
1 cup chopped pecans
3/4 cup sugar
1/3 cup rolled oats
1/3 cup flour
1/2 cup (1 stick) margarine, melted

Layer the cranberries, apples and undrained pineapple in the order listed in a 9×13-inch baking dish. Combine the brown sugar, pecans, sugar, oats and flour in a bowl and mix well. Spread the pecan mixture over the prepared layers and drizzle with the margarine. Bake at 350 degrees for 30 minutes or until brown and bubbly.

Serves 10 to 12

Fluffy Angel Biscuits

1/2 envelope dry yeast
1/4 cup warm water
2 1/2 cups sifted flour
1 1/2 tablespoons sugar
1 1/2 teaspoons baking powder
1/2 teaspoon baking soda
1/4 teaspoon salt
6 tablespoons shortening
1 cup buttermilk

Sprinkle the yeast over the warm water in a cup and stir to dissolve. Sift together the flour, sugar, baking powder, baking soda and salt 3 times. Cut the shortening into the flour mixture in a bowl until crumbly. Add the yeast mixture and buttermilk and mix just until the mixture adheres.

Knead the dough on a lightly floured surface for 30 seconds or until smooth. Place the dough in a greased bowl, turning to coat the surface. Chill, covered, for 1 hour or up to 3 days in advance.

Pat the dough into a rectangle on a floured surface and cut with a floured biscuit cutter. Arrange on a greased baking sheet and let stand until risen. Bake at 350 degrees for 15 minutes or until light brown.

Makes 1 dozen biscuits

Jalapeño Corn Bread

3 cups corn bread mix
2 cups milk
1/2 cup vegetable oil
3 tablespoons sugar
3 eggs, beaten
1/2 teaspoon garlic powder
1 1/2 cups (6 ounces) shredded Cheddar cheese
1 large onion, chopped
1 cup canned creamed corn
4 slices bacon, crisp-cooked and crumbled
1/2 cup chopped jalapeño chiles
1 (2-ounce) jar pimento, drained and chopped

Combine the corn bread mix, milk, oil, sugar, eggs and garlic powder in a bowl and mix well. Stir in the cheese, onion, creamed corn, bacon, jalapeño chiles and pimento. Spoon the corn bread mixture into a greased 9×13-inch baking pan. Bake at 350 degrees for 30 to 40 minutes or until brown. Slice and serve warm. You may freeze for future use.

Serves 15

Gingersnap Crust

Process 1½ cups gingersnap crumbs and 3 tablespoons sugar in a food processor until finely ground. Add 3 tablespoons melted butter gradually to the crumb mixture, processing constantly until mixed. Pat the crumb mixture over the bottom of a 9-inch springform pan sprayed with nonstick cooking spray. Freeze for 15 minutes.

Pumpkin Frangelico Cheesecake

Cheesecake
16 ounces cream cheese, softened
1 (16-ounce) can pumpkin purée
12 eggs
¾ cup packed brown sugar
½ cup Frangelico or hazelnut
    liqueur
1 teaspoon cinnamon
1 teaspoon vanilla extract
1 teaspoon ginger
¼ teaspoon nutmeg
¼ teaspoon ground cloves
Gingersnap Crust (this page)

Sour Cream Topping
2 cups sour cream
¼ cup sugar
¼ cup Frangelico
½ to 1 cup chopped or whole
    hazelnuts, toasted

For the cheesecake, combine the cream cheese, pumpkin purée, eggs, brown sugar, liqueur, cinnamon, vanilla, ginger, nutmeg and cloves in a food processor. Process until smooth, scraping the side of the bowl once during the process. Spoon the filling into the Gingersnap Crust. Bake at 350 degrees for 50 to 60 minutes or until the side pulls from the edge of the pan; the center will be almost set.

For the topping, whisk the sour cream, sugar and liqueur in a bowl until blended. Spread over the baked layer. Bake for 15 to 25 minutes longer or until the edge begins to bubble. Let stand until cool. Chill, covered, for 12 hours or for up to 2 days.

To serve, let the cheesecake stand at room temperature for 15 to 20 minutes. Sprinkle the hazelnuts around the outer edge of the cheesecake. Drizzle additional Frangelico on each serving plate and top with a slice of the cheesecake if desired.

Serves 10 to 12

Pumpkin Pound Cake

2 cups flour
2 teaspoons baking soda
2 teaspoons baking powder
1 teaspoon salt
2 cups sugar
$1^1/_2$ cups vegetable oil
4 eggs
2 cups pumpkin
2 teaspoons cinnamon
Cream Cheese Frosting (this page)
1 cup chopped pecans

Sift the flour, baking soda, baking powder and salt
together. Combine the sugar and oil in a mixing bowl and
beat until blended. Add the eggs 1 at a time, beating well
after each addition. Beat in the pumpkin and cinnamon.
Add the flour mixture and beat until blended. Spoon
the batter into a greased and floured tube pan. Bake at
350 degrees for 1 hour. Cool in the pan for 10 minutes.
Invert onto a wire rack to cool completely.

Spread the Cream Cheese Frosting over the top and
side of the cake. Pat some of the pecans over the side of
the cake and sprinkle the remaining pecans over the top
of the cake. Store, covered, in the refrigerator.

Serves 16

Cream Cheese Frosting

3 ounces cream cheese, softened
$^1/_4$ cup ($^1/_2$ stick) margarine, softened
$^1/_2$ (1-pound) package confectioners' sugar
$^1/_2$ teaspoon vanilla extract

Beat the cream cheese and margarine in a mixing bowl
until smooth. Add the confectioners' sugar gradually,
beating constantly until smooth and of a spreading
consistency and adding additional confectioners' sugar
if needed for the desired consistency. Stir in the vanilla.

Makes enough to frost 1 cake

Wine with Dessert

Although coffee is most often served with dessert in this country—or Champagne for special occasions—there are several wines that go well with dessert and are gaining popularity. An interesting way to introduce guests to the idea is to serve a sweet wine, such as port, Madeira, or sherry, over ice cream as an accompaniment to cake. The apple, pumpkin, or spice cake would be especially good served in this manner.

Fresh Apple Cake

Cake
2¹/₂ cups flour
2 teaspoons baking powder
1 teaspoon baking soda
1 teaspoon salt
1¹/₂ cups vegetable oil
2 cups sugar
2 eggs
1 teaspoon vanilla extract
3 cups finely chopped apples
1 cup chopped pecans

Brown Sugar Icing
¹/₂ cup (1 stick) butter, softened
1 cup packed brown sugar
¹/₄ cup evaporated milk

For the cake, combine the flour, baking powder, baking soda and salt in a bowl. Combine the oil, sugar, eggs and vanilla in a mixing bowl and mix until smooth. Add the flour mixture gradually, beating constantly. Fold in the apples and pecans.

Spoon the batter into a greased and floured tube pan. Bake at 350 degrees for 35 minutes. Cool in the pan for 5 minutes and remove to a wire rack to cool completely.

For the icing, combine the butter, brown sugar and evaporated milk in a mixing bowl and beat until smooth and of a spreading consistency. Spread the frosting over the top and side of the cake.

Serves 12

Spice Cake

3¼ cups cake flour
2 teaspoons baking powder
1½ teaspoons baking cocoa
1 teaspoon baking soda
1 teaspoon cinnamon
1 teaspoon cardamom
½ teaspoon Chinese five-spice powder
½ teaspoon nutmeg
½ teaspoon ground cloves
½ teaspoon salt
1 cup (2 sticks) butter, softened
1 cup packed brown sugar
1 cup sugar
4 eggs
2 teaspoons brandy or vanilla extract
1½ cups buttermilk
Caramel Frosting (this page)

Sift the cake flour, baking powder, baking cocoa, baking soda, cinnamon, cardamom, five-spice powder, nutmeg, cloves and salt into a bowl and mix well. Beat the butter, brown sugar and sugar in a mixing bowl until creamy, scraping the bowl occasionally. Add the eggs 1 at a time, beating well after each addition. Beat in the brandy until blended. Add the cake flour mixture alternately with the buttermilk, mixing well after each addition.

Spoon the batter into 3 greased and floured 9-inch cake pans. Bake at 350 degrees for 35 to 40 minutes or until the layers test done. Cool in the pans for 10 minutes. Invert onto a wire rack to cool completely. Spread the Caramel Frosting between the layers and over the top and side of the cake.

Serves 12

Caramel Frosting

¾ cup (1½ sticks) butter
1½ cups packed brown sugar
¼ teaspoon salt
⅓ cup milk
3 cups confectioners' sugar

Melt the butter in a large saucepan. Stir in the brown sugar and salt and bring to a boil. Boil for 2 minutes, stirring constantly. Remove from the heat. Stir in the milk. Let stand until lukewarm. Add the confectioners' sugar and beat to a spreading consistency. The frosting will thicken as it cools. If the frosting becomes too thick, warm slightly to thin.

Makes enough to frost 1 cake

Menu

Palms of St. Andrews

Although Mardi Gras celebrations encompass many styles, the food screams New Orleans. To make the most of the festivities, invite the revelers for an all-day fête. The deck holds oysters and beer, while the tables indoors overflow with Creole and Cajun specialties fit for a king.

American Beauty Cocktail

2 ounces vodka
1 ounce cranberry juice
2 teaspoons rose-flavor syrup
2 teaspoons fresh lime juice
cracked ice
2 or 3 rose petals (optional)

Combine the vodka, cranberry juice, syrup, lime juice and cracked ice in a cocktail shaker and shake vigorously. Strain the cocktail mixture into a cocktail glass. Float the rose petals in the glass.

Serves 1

Hurricane Cocktail

2 ounces red passion fruit cocktail mix
2 ounces fresh lemon juice
2 ounces light rum
2 ounces dark rum
1 orange slice
1 maraschino cherry

Shake the cocktail mix, lemon juice, light rum and dark rum in a cocktail shaker until blended. Pour over crushed ice in a glass. Garnish with the orange slice and cherry.

Serves 1

Mardi Gras St. Andrews Style

The historic waterfront neighborhood of St. Andrews is home to a very popular Mardi Gras parade and celebration that continues to grow larger every year. Each February, local Krewes outdo each other by hosting parties and creating floats for the now famous parade and weekend-long celebration. Locals and visitors line the streets to enjoy the festivities and watch the parade, but mostly to catch the strings of beads and other trinkets that are tossed from the extravagant floats passing by.

Thanks to a major revitalization, the streets of St. Andrews are now lined with antique shops, art galleries, basket shops, and other unique stores that offer great shopping and browsing. A variety of charming local restaurants, such as Hunt's Oyster Bar and Pappy's, offer something for everyone, from the freshest seafood to authentic German food.

Tomato Coulis

Heat 2 teaspoons olive oil in a small skillet. Stir in 2 tablespoons minced shallots and 4 teaspoons minced garlic. Cook for 1 minute, stirring constantly. Remove from the heat. Stir in 1 cup chopped peeled tomatoes, 2 tablespoons Creole mustard, 2 tablespoons olive oil, 1 teaspoon salt and freshly ground pepper to taste.

Chicken and Andouille Cheesecake

1 cup freshly grated Parmesan cheese
1 cup dry bread crumbs
1/2 cup (1 stick) unsalted butter, melted
1 pound andouille, finely chopped or crumbled
1 teaspoon olive oil
8 ounces boneless skinless chicken breasts, finely chopped
1 cup chopped onion
1/2 cup chopped green bell pepper or any color bell pepper

1/2 cup chopped red bell pepper or any color bell pepper
2 teaspoons salt
1/4 teaspoon freshly ground pepper
28 ounces cream cheese, softened
4 eggs
1 cup (4 ounces) shredded smoked Gouda cheese
1/2 cup heavy cream
Tomato Coulis (this page)

Combine the Parmesan cheese, bread crumbs and unsalted butter in a bowl and mix well. Press the crumb mixture over of the bottom of a 9-inch springform pan. Cook the sausage in a skillet until brown, stirring frequently. Drain, pat dry with paper towels and place in a bowl. Wipe the skillet with a paper towel. Heat the olive oil in the same skillet over high heat. Sauté the chicken in the olive oil for 2 minutes. Stir in the onion, bell pepper, salt and pepper. Sauté for 3 minutes; drain. Add the chicken mixture to the sausage and mix well. Let stand until cool.

Beat the cream cheese and eggs in a mixing bowl for 4 minutes, scraping the bowl occasionally. Fold in the Gouda cheese, heavy cream and sausage mixture. Spoon the cream cheese mixture into the prepared springform pan. Place the springform pan in a roasting pan. Add enough hot water to the roasting pan to reach halfway up the side of the springform pan. Bake at 350 degrees for 1 hour or until golden brown and set. Remove the springform pan from the roasting pan. Cool on a wire rack to room temperature.

Choose one of the following presentations. Serve whole at room temperature with the coulis spread over the top, allowing the guests to slice as desired. Or, cut the cheesecake into wedges and place the wedges on the stem end of endive spears, on party bread or on assorted party crackers, drizzling each with some of the coulis. Store leftovers in the refrigerator.

Serves 48

Cheddar Ring

16 ounces Cheddar cheese, shredded
1 cup mayonnaise
1 small onion, finely chopped
1 cup pecans or walnuts, chopped
cayenne pepper to taste
strawberry preserves

Combine the cheese, mayonnaise, onion, pecans and cayenne pepper in a bowl and mix well. Shape the cheese mixture into a ring. Chill, covered, until firm. To serve, arrange the cheese ring on a serving platter. Place a small bowl filled with strawberry preserves in the center of the ring. Serve with butter crackers and/or assorted party crackers.

Serves 16

Oysters Rockefeller

4 sprigs of flat-leaf parsley, minced
4 green onions with tops, minced
celery leaves to taste, minced
6 fresh tarragon leaves, minced
6 fresh chervil leaves, minced
¾ cup (1½ sticks) unsalted butter, softened
½ cup dry French bread crumbs
2 tablespoons Herbsaint or Pernod
salt and freshly ground pepper to taste
Tabasco sauce or other hot sauce to taste
rock salt or kosher salt
2 dozen fresh oysters in shells, scrubbed

Combine the parsley, green onions, celery leaves, tarragon and chervil in a bowl and mix well. Add the unsalted butter and bread crumbs and mix until the consistency of a smooth paste with some texture. Stir in the liqueur, salt, pepper and Tabasco sauce.

Spread rock salt over the bottom of a large baking sheet with sides. Open the oysters with the top shells facing up and leave the oyster in its bottom shell, reserving the liquor and discarding the top shell. Arrange the oysters on half shells in the bed of rock salt; the rock salt will prevent the oysters from tipping. Spoon some of the reserved liquor and some of the herb butter over each of the oysters.

Place the baking sheet on the middle oven rack. Broil for 5 to 7 minutes or until the edges of the oysters curl and the herb butter is bubbly; do not overcook. Serve immediately.

Makes 2 dozen

Spicy Shrimp Rémoulade

1¹/₂ pounds medium shrimp
¹/₂ cup finely chopped fresh parsley
3 tablespoons Creole mustard
3 tablespoons white vinegar
1 tablespoon paprika
2 teaspoons minced garlic
2 teaspoons white horseradish
¹/₃ cup olive oil
¹/₈ teaspoon hot pepper sauce
salt and freshly ground pepper to taste
¹/₄ cup finely chopped celery
3 scallions, minced
1 head leaf lettuce, separated
Fried Green Tomatoes (this page)
3 tablespoons chopped fresh chives

Boil the shrimp in boiling water in a stockpot until the shrimp turn pink; drain. Peel and devein the shrimp. Whisk the parsley, Creole mustard, vinegar, paprika, garlic and horseradish in a bowl until mixed. Add the olive oil gradually, whisking constantly until incorporated. Stir in the hot pepper sauce, salt and pepper. Fold in the shrimp, celery and scallions. Chill, covered, for 4 to 10 hours. Taste and adjust the seasonings.

To serve, arrange 1 lettuce leaf on each of 8 plates. Arrange about 3 Fried Green Tomato slices on each plate and top with the shrimp mixture. Sprinkle with the chives. Serve immediately.

Serves 8

Fried Green Tomatoes

4 green tomatoes
1 cup flour
salt and freshly ground pepper to taste
1 cup bread crumbs
¹/₄ cup grated Parmesan cheese
1 tablespoon basil
1 teaspoon oregano
1 cup milk
1 cup water
1 egg, beaten
hot sauce to taste
1¹/₂ cups vegetable oil

Cut the tomatoes into ³/₈-inch slices and pat dry with paper towels. Mix the flour, salt and pepper in a shallow dish. Combine the bread crumbs, cheese, basil and oregano in a shallow dish and mix well. Whisk the milk, water and egg in a bowl until blended. Season with salt, pepper and hot sauce. Coat the tomato slices with the seasoned flour, tapping off the excess. Dip in the egg wash and coat with the bread crumb mixture.

Heat the oil in a large cast-iron skillet until hot but not smoking. Panfry the tomatoes in batches in the hot oil until golden brown on both sides; drain on paper towels.

Serves 8

St. Andrews Salad

2 ounces dried cranberries
1/4 cup ruby port
1/4 cup raspberry vinegar
2 tablespoons vegetable oil
2 tablespoons water
1 teaspoon cinnamon
1 teaspoon sugar

5 dashes hot pepper sauce
24 ounces mesclun
salt and freshly ground pepper
   to taste
2 ounces bleu cheese, crumbled
2 ounces sliced almonds, toasted

Soak the cranberries in the wine in a bowl for 8 to 10 hours. Whisk the vinegar, oil, water, cinnamon, sugar and hot pepper sauce in a large bowl until emulsified. Add the salad mix and toss to coat. Season with salt and pepper.

    Divide the salad mixture evenly among 4 plates. Sprinkle with the cheese, cranberries and almonds. Serve immediately.

    Serves 4

Green and Black Olive Salad

3/4 cup chopped pimento-stuffed green
   olives
3/4 cup chopped pitted kalamata
   olives
1/2 cup plus 2 tablespoons olive oil
1/2 cup thinly sliced celery
1/3 cup minced fresh parsley

2 tablespoons red wine vinegar
2 medium garlic cloves, minced
2 teaspoons oregano
1 teaspoon thyme
1/2 teaspoon sugar
freshly ground pepper to taste

Combine the olives, olive oil, celery, parsley, vinegar, garlic, oregano, thyme, sugar and pepper in a bowl and mix well. Chill, covered, for 24 hours, stirring occasionally. A necessity for muffuletta sandwiches, but good on any sandwich.

    Makes (about) 2 1/2 cups

Sazerac Cocktail

Pour 1/4 teaspoon Herbsaint or Pernod into an elegant cocktail glass and swirl to coat the side and bottom of the glass. Discard the excess liqueur if desired. Combine 5 small ice cubes, 1 teaspoon simple syrup, 2 ounces rye whiskey and 3 or 4 dashes bitters in a cocktail shaker and cover. Shake gently for 5 to 8 seconds. Strain into the cocktail glass. Rub a strip of lemon zest around the edge of the glass and add as a garnish. You can prepare a simple syrup by boiling 2 parts sugar and 1 part water until of a syrupy consistency.

St. Charles Cocktail

Fill a highball glass almost to the top with cracked ice. Add the juice of 1 lime, 2 ounces Bombay Sapphire gin, 5 ounces tonic water and 4 dashes bitters in the order listed. Rub a lime wedge around the rim of the glass and add as a garnish. Stir and serve with the swizzle stick.

Muffuletta Bread

3 to 3¹/₂ cups flour
1 envelope dry yeast
1 tablespoon sugar
1 teaspoon salt
¹/₂ teaspoon each thyme, oregano and basil
¹/₂ teaspoon each onion powder and garlic powder
¹/₂ teaspoon freshly ground black pepper
¹/₄ to ¹/₂ teaspoon cayenne pepper, or to taste
1 cup warm water
1 tablespoon olive oil
1 egg
1 to 2 tablespoons water
sesame seeds to taste

Combine 1¹/₂ cups of the flour, yeast, sugar, salt, thyme, oregano, basil, onion powder, garlic powder, black pepper and cayenne pepper in a large mixing bowl and mix well. Add the warm water and olive oil gradually, beating constantly at medium speed for 2 minutes and scraping the bowl occasionally. Beat for 2 minutes at high speed, scraping the bowl occasionally. Stir in enough of the remaining flour to make a soft dough.

Knead the dough on a lightly floured surface for 5 minutes or until smooth and elastic. Place the dough in an oiled bowl, turning to coat the surface. Let rise, covered, in a warm draft-free environment for 30 to 45 minutes or until doubled in bulk. Punch the dough down. Shape into a loaf and place on a baking sheet. Let rise, covered, in a warm draft-free environment for 30 to 45 minutes or until doubled in bulk. Whisk the egg and water in a bowl. Brush the egg wash over the top of the loaf and sprinkle with sesame seeds. Bake at 400 degrees for 40 to 45 minutes or until golden brown. You may also use the dough for a Filled Muffuletta Twist (this page).

Serves 8 to 10

Muffuletta Twist

1 recipe Muffuletta Bread dough (this page)
3 or 4 thin slices deli ham
3 or 4 slices genoa salami
4 slices provolone cheese
³/₄ cup shredded Monterey Jack cheese
³/₄ cup Green and Black Olive Salad (page 103)
1 egg
1 to 2 tablespoons water
sesame seeds to taste

Roll the dough into a 10×14-inch rectangle on a lightly floured surface. Layer the ham, salami and provolone cheese down the center of the rectangle. Sprinkle with the Monterey Jack cheese and spread with the Green and Black Olive Salad.

Make cuts at 1-inch intervals from the outer edge of the dough to the filling. Fold the strips alternately across the filling for a braided effect. Arrange the loaf on a greased baking sheet. Let rise, covered, in a warm draft-free environment for 30 to 45 minutes or until doubled in bulk.

Whisk the egg and water in a bowl. Brush the egg wash over the top of the loaf and sprinkle with sesame seeds. Bake at 400 degrees for 40 to 45 minutes or until golden brown. Slice as desired.

Serves 8 to 10

Chicken and Smoked Andouille Gumbo

2¹/₂ pounds boneless skinless chicken breasts, cut into 1-inch pieces

2 teaspoons each salt and garlic powder

¹/₂ teaspoon (or more) cayenne pepper

1 large onion, chopped

1 large green bell pepper, chopped

3 ribs celery, chopped

1¹/₄ cups flour

¹/₂ teaspoon each salt, garlic powder and cayenne pepper

3 to 4 cups vegetable oil

8 cups chicken broth or chicken stock

1 pound andouille or other high-quality smoked sausage, chopped

1 teaspoon minced garlic

2 cups cooked white rice

Sprinkle the chicken with 2 teaspoons salt, 2 teaspoons garlic powder and ¹/₂ teaspoon cayenne pepper. Toss the onion, bell pepper and celery in a bowl. Combine the flour, ¹/₂ teaspoon salt, ¹/₂ teaspoon garlic powder and ¹/₂ teaspoon cayenne pepper in a bowl and mix well. Reserve a generous ¹/₂ cup of the flour mixture. Pour the remaining flour mixture into a sealable plastic bag. Add the chicken and seal tightly. Toss to coat. Heat the oil in a cast-iron skillet. Fry the chicken in batches in the hot oil until golden brown on all sides. Remove the chicken to paper towels to drain. Drain the skillet, reserving ¹/₂ cup of the pan drippings and any browned bits in the skillet. Add the reserved flour mixture to the oil gradually, whisking constantly. Cook over high heat for 3 to 5 minutes or until the roux turns a dark reddish-brown color, whisking constantly. Reduce the heat to low. Stir in the onion mixture.

Cook for 5 to 8 minutes or until the vegetables are tender, stirring constantly and scraping any browned bits from the bottom of the skillet. Remove from the heat. Bring the broth to a rolling boil in a stockpot. Add the vegetable mixture by large spoonfuls, stirring well after each addition. Reduce the heat to low. Stir in the sausage and garlic. Simmer for 45 minutes, stirring frequently. Stir in the chicken just before serving. Mound ¹/₄ to ¹/₃ cup of the rice in each bowl. Ladle the gumbo over the rice. Serve immediately.

Serves 6 to 8

St. Andrews, Florida

The tiny coastal village of St. Andrews has been a place of splendor since the Native Americans inhabited the land thousands of years ago. In the 1800s, white settlers came to the area, and it quickly became known for its beauty and bewitching climate. Several years later, the summer population grew, and the first visitors came to enjoy the excellent fishing and bathing in the "healthy sea baths" of its coastal waters.

Roux

The nutty flavor of a rich roux is essential for a good gumbo. A roux is not difficult to make, but it does require the time to let it cook slowly to a warm brown color. If your roux begins to have the least hint of a burned or scorched smell, it should be discarded and begun again, as the flavor of the gumbo will be ruined.

Seafood and Sausage Gumbo with Chicken

1 cup vegetable oil
1 cup flour
2 large onions, chopped
1 large green bell pepper, chopped
6 ribs celery, chopped
1/2 cup fresh parsley, chopped
4 garlic cloves, minced
4 quarts chicken stock
1 pound spicy smoked sausage, cut into 1/2-inch slices and sautéed
1 (16-ounce) can chopped tomatoes, drained
1/2 cup Worcestershire sauce
1/2 cup tomato sauce
4 slices bacon, crisp-cooked and crumbled

2 tablespoons salt
2 bay leaves
1/4 teaspoon rosemary
1/4 teaspoon thyme
1/8 teaspoon cayenne pepper
Tabasco sauce to taste
4 pounds medium shrimp, peeled and deveined
2 pounds crab meat, shells and cartilage removed
2 cups chopped cooked chicken
2 tablespoons fresh lemon juice
1 teaspoon light brown sugar
hot cooked white rice

Heat the oil in a heavy stockpot over medium heat. Add the flour gradually, stirring constantly with a wooden spoon. Cook for 30 to 40 minutes or until the roux is golden brown, stirring constantly. Add the onions, bell pepper, celery, parsley and garlic and mix well.

Cook for 45 minutes or until the vegetables are tender, stirring frequently. Add the stock, sausage, tomatoes, Worcestershire sauce, tomato sauce, bacon, salt, bay leaves, rosemary, thyme, cayenne pepper and Tabasco sauce and mix well.

Simmer for 2 to 3 hours, stirring occasionally. Add the shrimp, crab meat, chicken, lemon juice and brown sugar 30 minutes before serving and mix well. Discard the bay leaves. Ladle the gumbo over rice in soup bowls. Serve with New Orleans French bread.

Serves 20

Chicken and Sausage Jambalaya

2 tablespoons unsalted butter
8 ounces chopped smoked sausage or smoked ham
12 ounces boneless skinless chicken breasts,
    cut into bite-size pieces
3 tablespoons Jambalaya Seasoning Mix (this page)
1¹/₂ tablespoons minced garlic
1 cup each chopped onion and chopped celery
1 cup each chopped red and green bell pepper
¹/₂ cup canned tomato sauce
1 cup chopped peeled fresh tomatoes
2¹/₂ cups canned chicken stock
1¹/₂ cups rice

Melt the unsalted butter in a 2-quart saucepan over high heat. Stir in the sausage. Cook for 3 minutes or until the sausage begins to brown, stirring frequently. Add the chicken and continue cooking for 3 to 5 minutes or until the chicken begins to brown, scraping the bottom of the saucepan frequently. Stir in the Jambalaya Seasoning Mix, garlic and ¹/₂ cup each of the onion, celery, red bell pepper and green bell pepper. Cook for 5 to 8 minutes or until the vegetables begin to soften, stirring constantly and scraping the bottom of the saucepan as needed. Stir in the tomato sauce. Cook for 1 minute, stirring frequently. Stir in the remaining onion, celery, red and green bell peppers and tomatoes. Remove from the heat. Add the stock and rice and mix well.

Spoon the sausage mixture into an ungreased casserole dish. Bake at 350 degrees for 1 hour or until the rice is tender but slightly crunchy. Remove from the oven and stir. Discard the bay leaves. Let stand for 5 minutes.

Makes 8 entrée servings or 16 appetizer servings

Jambalaya Seasoning Mix

2 whole bay leaves
1¹/₂ teaspoons salt
1 teaspoon white pepper
1 teaspoon dried thyme
1 teaspoon cayenne pepper
¹/₂ teaspoon black pepper
¹/₄ teaspoon rubbed sage

Combine the bay leaves, salt, white pepper, thyme, cayenne pepper, black pepper and sage in a bowl and mix well. Use to season jambalaya or gumbo.

Makes 3 tablespoons

Grilled Creole-Seasoned Salmon

Creole Seasoning

4 teaspoons paprika

4 teaspoons chopped fresh thyme

4 teaspoons chopped fresh oregano

4 teaspoons chopped fresh basil

$2^1/_2$ teaspoons garlic powder

$2^1/_2$ teaspoons black pepper

$1^1/_2$ teaspoons white pepper

$1^1/_2$ teaspoons cayenne pepper

$1^1/_2$ teaspoons onion powder

Salmon

8 (6-ounce) salmon fillets

$^1/_2$ to $^3/_4$ cup olive oil

Tomato Parmesan Linguini (this page)

1 cup very finely chopped green bell pepper

For the seasoning, combine the paprika, thyme, oregano, basil, garlic powder, black pepper, white pepper, cayenne pepper and onion powder in a bowl and mix well.

For the salmon, brush both sides of the fillets with the olive oil and sprinkle about 1 tablespoon of the seasoning over the surface of each fillet. Grill the fillets over hot coals just until cooked through, leaving the center a little more rare; do not overcook. The fillets will continue to cook after being taken off the grill.

To serve, spoon about 4 ounces of the Tomato Parmesan Linguini on each serving plate. Top each serving with 1 fillet and about 2 tablespoons of the finely chopped bell pepper.

Serves 8

Tomato Parmesan Linguini

$^1/_2$ cup minced shallots

2 garlic cloves, minced

$^1/_2$ cup (1 stick) butter

4 cups heavy cream

4 large tomatoes, peeled, seeded and chopped into $^1/_4$-inch pieces

1 bunch green onions, chopped

salt and pepper to taste

2 pounds fresh linguini, cooked al dente and drained

1 cup finely grated Parmesan cheese

Sauté the shallots and garlic in the butter in a large sauté pan for 2 minutes or until the shallots are tender. Stir in the heavy cream, tomatoes and green onions. Bring to a boil; reduce the heat.

Simmer for 5 minutes or until thickened, stirring frequently. Season with salt and pepper. Add the pasta and toss to coat. Heat for 1 minute, stirring frequently. Add the cheese and toss to coat. Heat for 1 minute, stirring frequently.

Serves 8

Crawfish Pie

1 large onion, chopped
1 cup chopped green onions
1 bell pepper, chopped
3 ribs celery, chopped
4 garlic cloves, minced
1/2 cup (1 stick) butter
1 pound crawfish tail meat, chopped
1 (10-ounce) can cream of celery soup
1/4 cup tomato sauce
1/4 cup fresh parsley, chopped
1/2 cup bread crumbs
2 teaspoons liquid crab boil
1 egg, beaten
1 cup milk
Cajun seasoning to taste
1 unbaked (9-inch) pie shell

Sauté the onion, green onions, bell pepper, celery, garlic and butter in a skillet over medium-high heat until the vegetables are tender. Stir in the crawfish, soup, tomato sauce and parsley.

Cook for 10 minutes, stirring frequently. Remove from the heat. Stir in the bread crumbs, crab boil and egg. Add the milk and Cajun seasoning and mix well. Spoon the crawfish mixture into the pie shell. Bake at 350 degrees for 40 minutes. Let stand for 30 minutes before serving. Substitute miniature tart shells for the pie shell for a buffet or cocktail party.

Serves 8

King Cakes

King cakes are circular pastries usually decorated in the Mardi Gras colors of purple, green, and gold. They are associated with Carnival because Carnival begins with the feast of Epiphany on January 6, also known as Twelfth Night. The feast commemorates the day that the three kings arrived from the east to honor the Christ child.

Traditionally, a king cake containing a bean or a small baby figurine was cut and served to the unmarried women attending a Mardi Gras banquet. The person who received the slice containing the hidden object was crowned queen of the festival. Today king cakes are served throughout the Carnival season.

Shrimp Étouffée

1/2 cup (1 stick) butter
5 tablespoons flour
1 cup chopped onion
6 green onions with tops, chopped
1/2 cup each chopped green bell pepper and celery
3 pounds shrimp, peeled and deveined
2 cups water
1/2 cup white wine
1/4 cup fresh parsley, chopped
1 bay leaf
Tabasco sauce, salt and pepper to taste
hot cooked rice

Melt the butter in a large heavy saucepan. Stir in the flour. Cook until the mixture is dark brown in color, stirring constantly. Add the onion, green onions, bell pepper and celery and mix well. Cook until the vegetables are tender, stirring constantly. Add the shrimp, water, wine, parsley, bay leaf, Tabasco sauce, salt and pepper and mix well. Simmer for 20 minutes, stirring occasionally. Discard the bay leaf. Ladle the étouffée over rice in bowls.

Serves 4

Buttermilk Cheddar Biscuits

2 cups flour
1/2 cup shredded Cheddar cheese
2 teaspoons baking powder
1/2 teaspoon baking soda
7 tablespoons butter, chilled and cut into pieces
2/3 to 3/4 cup buttermilk
1/2 teaspoon sugar
1/2 teaspoon salt
1 egg yolk
1 cup (4 ounces) shredded Cheddar cheese

Preheat the oven to 425 degrees. Combine the flour, 1/2 cup cheese, baking powder and baking soda in a bowl and mix well. Cut in the butter until crumbly. Whisk 2/3 cup buttermilk, sugar and salt in a bowl until the sugar and salt dissolve. Whisk in the egg yolk. Add the buttermilk mixture to the flour mixture and stir until the mixture forms a ball, adding the remaining buttermilk 1 teaspoon at a time if needed to bind the mixture.

Knead the dough on a lightly floured surface for 30 seconds or just until smooth. Pat the dough 1/2 inch thick on the floured surface and cut into rounds with a 2-inch biscuit cutter. Do not twist the cutter while cutting as this will cause the biscuits to rise unevenly.

Arrange the rounds on a lightly greased baking sheet. Reduce the oven temperature to 400 degrees. Bake for 10 minutes. Sprinkle the biscuits with 1 cup cheese. Bake for 20 minutes longer or until the cheese melts and the biscuits are golden brown. Serve warm.

Makes (about) 1 1/2 dozen biscuits

Chocolate Doberge Cake

Cake

2 cups flour

1 teaspoon baking soda

1 teaspoon salt

1¹/₂ cups sugar

3 tablespoons plus 1 teaspoon butter

3 egg yolks

1 cup buttermilk

2 ounces unsweetened chocolate, melted

3 egg whites, stiffly beaten

2 teaspoons vanilla extract

¹/₂ teaspoon almond extract

Chocolate Filling and Assembly

2¹/₂ cups evaporated milk

2 ounces semisweet chocolate, chopped

1¹/₄ cups sugar

5 tablespoons flour

4 egg yolks

2 tablespoons butter

1 teaspoon vanilla extract

¹/₂ teaspoon almond extract

Chocolate Doberge Frosting (this page)

For the cake, sift the flour, baking soda and salt together. Beat the sugar and butter in a mixing bowl until creamy. Add the egg yolks and beat until blended. Add the flour mixture alternately with the buttermilk, beating well after each addition. Add the chocolate. Beat for 3 minutes, scraping the bowl occasionally. Fold in the egg whites and flavorings.

Spoon the batter into 2 greased and floured 9-inch cake pans. Bake at 300 degrees for 45 minutes or until the layers test done. Cool in the pans for 10 minutes. Remove to a wire rack to cool completely.

For the filling, heat the evaporated milk and chocolate in a double boiler until blended, stirring occasionally. Add the sugar and flour and mix well. Cook over medium heat until thickened, stirring frequently.

Stir a small amount of the hot chocolate mixture into the egg yolks in a bowl; stir the egg yolks into the hot chocolate mixture. Cook for 2 to 3 minutes longer, stirring frequently. Remove from the heat. Stir in the butter and flavorings. Let stand until cool.

To serve, slice each cake layer horizontally into halves. Spread the filling between the layers; do not spread over the top layer. Spread the Chocolate Doberge Frosting over the top and side of the cake.

Serves 12

Chocolate Doberge Frosting

Bring 1¹/₄ cups sugar and 1 cup evaporated milk to a boil in a saucepan over medium-high heat, stirring constantly; reduce the heat. Simmer for 6 minutes; do not stir. Remove from the heat. Stir in 2 ounces chopped unsweetened chocolate. Add ¹/₄ cup (¹/₂ stick) butter and 1 teaspoon vanilla extract and mix well. Cook over medium-low heat for 1 to 2 minutes, stirring frequently. Chill until cooled. Spoon the frosting into a mixing bowl and beat until of spreading consistency.

Praline Sauce

Melt 1 cup (2 sticks) unsalted butter in a heavy saucepan over medium-high heat. Stir in 1 cup packed dark brown sugar, 1 cup heavy cream and ¹/₂ cup toasted chopped pecans. Bring to a boil over high heat; reduce the heat to low. Simmer for 10 minutes, stirring frequently. Cover to keep warm.

Sweet Potato Cheesecake

Gingersnap Crust
*1¹/₂ cups finely ground gingersnap
    cookie crumbs, about 3 dozen
    (1³/₄-inch) cookies
³/₄ cup pecans, toasted and
    finely ground
6 tablespoons butter, melted*

Filling and Assembly
*8 ounces cream cheese or mascarpone
    cheese, softened
¹/₂ cup sugar*

*¹/₂ cup packed dark brown sugar
1 teaspoon cinnamon
³/₄ teaspoon ginger
¹/₂ teaspoon nutmeg
¹/₄ teaspoon ground cloves
1 cup puréed cooked sweet
    potatoes
5 eggs
¹/₂ cup heavy cream
Praline Sauce (this page)
whipped cream
fresh mint sprigs*

For the crust, process the cookie crumbs and pecans in a food processor until combined. Add the butter. Process until mixed. Press the crumb mixture over the bottom of a 9-inch springform pan. Wrap the bottom and side of the pan with foil. Chill in the refrigerator.

For the filling, beat the cream cheese in a mixing bowl until smooth. Add the sugar, brown sugar, cinnamon, ginger, nutmeg and cloves. Beat for 3 to 4 minutes or until light and fluffy. Add the sweet potato purée and beat just until blended. Add the eggs 1 at a time, scraping the bowl after each addition. Add the heavy cream and beat at low speed until blended.

Spoon the filling into the prepared springform pan. Place the springform pan in a large roasting pan. Add enough warm water to the roasting pan to reach halfway up the side of the springform pan. Bake at 350 degrees for 1¹/₄ hours or until the center is set. Remove the springform pan from the roasting pan. Cool on a wire rack at room temperature for 45 minutes. Chill, covered, for 4 to 10 hours.

To serve, arrange 1 slice of the cheesecake on each dessert plate. Drizzle the Praline Sauce over and around each slice. Top each with a dollop of whipped cream and a sprig of fresh mint.

Serves 12 to 16

Banana Bread Pudding

Bread Pudding

4 cups (1-inch) dry French or sourdough bread cubes
1/4 cup (1/2 stick) butter, melted
2 cups milk
1/2 cup sugar
4 eggs
2 teaspoons vanilla extract
1/2 teaspoon each cinnamon, nutmeg and salt
1 cup (1-inch) banana slices, cut into quarters

Whiskey Sauce

3 tablespoons butter
2 tablespoons sugar
1 tablespoon cornstarch
2/3 cup milk
1/4 cup light corn syrup
2 tablespoons whiskey
1 teaspoon vanilla extract

For the pudding, toss the bread cubes with the butter in a large bowl. Beat the milk, sugar, eggs, vanilla, cinnamon, nutmeg and salt in a mixing bowl until blended. Stir in the bananas. Add the banana mixture to the bread cube mixture and mix gently. Pour into a buttered 2- or 3-quart baking dish. Bake at 375 degrees for 40 minutes.

For the sauce, melt the butter in a small saucepan. Mix the sugar and cornstarch in a small bowl. Add the sugar mixture to the butter and mix well. Stir in the milk and corn syrup. Bring the mixture to a boil over medium heat. Stir in the whiskey. Boil for 1 minute. Remove from the heat. Stir in the vanilla. Drizzle over the servings.

Serves 6

Easy Pecan Pralines

2 cups sugar
1 teaspoon baking soda
1 cup buttermilk
3/4 cup (1 1/2 sticks) butter, cut into pieces
1 1/2 cups chopped pecans or pecan halves
1 1/2 teaspoons vanilla extract

Combine the sugar and baking soda in a heavy saucepan and mix well. Stir in the buttermilk and butter. Cook over medium heat to 234 to 240 degrees on a candy thermometer, soft-ball stage, stirring constantly. Remove from the heat.

Beat for 3 to 5 minutes or until the mixture lightens in color and slightly thickens. Stir in the pecans and vanilla. Drop by tablespoonfuls onto waxed paper. Let stand until firm. Store in an airtight container.

Makes 3 dozen small pralines

MENU

Arte Italica

Warm bay breezes and marvelous fresh produce have a certain way of inspiring cooks to create delicious Tuscan dishes. What better place to experience dining at its best than on a patio overlooking the beautiful bay. Uncork a bottle of wine or serve one of our fruity sangrias to round out a perfect meal.

Kiddie Sangria

1 quart (4 cups) orange juice, chilled
1¹/₂ cups unsweetened white grape juice or purple grape juice, chilled
1 liter ginger ale, chilled
2 cups ice
2 cups chopped fresh fruit, such as oranges, lemons, limes,
    pineapple and/or grapes

Combine the orange juice, grape juice and ginger ale in a large pitcher or punch bowl and mix gently. Add the ice and fresh fruit and mix gently. Pour into glasses or ladle into punch cups.

Makes 3 quarts

White Sangria

1¹/₂ Granny Smith apples, cut into thin wedges
1 peach, cut into wedges
2 lemons, cut into wedges
1 navel orange, cut into wedges
1 cup lemon-lime soda
2 tablespoons Grand Marnier
2 tablespoons Peach Pucker schnapps
2 tablespoons each peach schnapps, apricot brandy and amaretto
1 tablespoon Chambord
1 cinnamon stick
1 (750-milliliter) bottle light white wine, chilled

Place the apples, peach, lemons and orange in a large pitcher. Add the soda, Grand Marnier, schnapps, brandy, amaretto, Chambord and cinnamon stick to the pitcher and stir gently. Let stand at room temperature for 20 to 30 minutes.

Add the wine just before serving and mix gently. Discard the cinnamon stick. Pour the sangria into chilled wine glasses, adding some of the fruit to each glass.

Serves 6

A Fisherman's Paradise

St. Andrew Bay has lured visitors to its pristine waters and beautiful coastlines since the 1800s. Early literature promoted the area as "St. Andrews by the Sea," and featured beautifully clad women and children picking oranges from lush tropical fruit groves. Lots at this time sold for only $1.25 and were hard to get rid of.

Today, St. Andrew Bay is known as a sportsman's paradise, and on any given day you can view shrimp boats and sails of every color crossing the waterways. The St. Andrew Bay Yacht Club sits on the banks of the Cove area, and has always been a relaxing spot for both locals and visitors since 1933.

Bruschetta

Cut 2 crusty Italian or French bread loaves into ½-inch slices with a serrated knife. Arrange the slices on a grill rack 4 inches from the coals. Grill for 1 to 1½ minutes per side or until golden brown and crisp on the outside but soft inside, or broil the slices in batches 4 inches from the heat source for 1 to 1½ minutes per side or until golden brown. Rub the toasts on one side with the cut sides of 2 garlic cloves and lightly brush the same side with ½ cup olive oil. You may prepare up to 1 week in advance and store in an airtight container.

Bruschetta Bar

The crusty toasts above will serve as the basis for a Brushetta Bar, an easy appetizer idea, and one that guests will enjoy. Top or serve with Tomato and Feta Salata, Mozzarella with Greens and Garlic, Caponata, and/or the topping of Feta and Tomato Crostini and allow guests to sample and select their favorites.

Tomato and Feta Salata

2 large shallots, thinly sliced
1 tablespoon extra-virgin olive oil
2 cups chopped seeded vine-ripe tomatoes
salt and freshly ground pepper to taste
2 ounces feta cheese, crumbled
2 tablespoons minced fresh chives
2 teaspoons balsamic vinegar
Bruschetta (this page)

Cook the shallots in the olive oil in a small skillet over medium heat until tender. Stir in the tomatoes, salt and pepper. Cook for 30 seconds or just until heated through, stirring constantly. Toss the tomato mixture with the feta cheese, chives and vinegar in a bowl. Season with salt and pepper. Serve with Bruschetta.

Makes 3 cups

Mozzarella with Greens and Garlic

6 garlic cloves, minced
½ teaspoon coarse salt
2 tablespoons olive oil
1¼ pounds spinach, arugula or escarole, trimmed and coarsely chopped
salt and freshly ground pepper to taste
½ cup coarsely shredded mozzarella cheese
Bruschetta (this page)

Mash the garlic with ½ teaspoon coarse salt in a bowl. Cook the garlic paste in the olive oil in a large heavy skillet over low heat for 1 minute, stirring constantly. Add the spinach, salt and pepper to taste. Sauté over medium-high heat for 3 minutes or until the greens are tender; drain. Spoon into a bowl. Cool slightly. Stir in the cheese. Serve with Bruschetta.

Makes 2 cups

Feta and Tomato Crostini

3 (6-inch) French bread rolls, cut into halves
2 tablespoons olive oil
7 ounces feta cheese, crumbled
2 teaspoons garlic powder
3 small ripe tomatoes, chopped
1¹/₂ tablespoons balsamic vinegar
2 tablespoons chopped fresh mint
fresh mint leaves

Brush the cut side of each roll with olive oil. Arrange the roll halves cut side up on a baking sheet. Broil 6 inches from the heat source for 2 minutes or until light brown. Layer the cheese, garlic powder, tomatoes, vinegar and chopped mint in the order listed on the toasted side of the roll halves.

Broil for 2 minutes or until the cheese melts. Garnish each half with mint leaves. Serve immediately.

Serves 6

Caponata

¹/₄ cup olive oil
3¹/₂ cups (¹/₄-inch pieces) eggplant (about 1¹/₄ pounds)
³/₄ cup finely chopped onion
³/₄ cup finely chopped celery
3 plum tomatoes, cut into ¹/₄-inch pieces
¹/₃ cup chopped pitted green olives
¹/₄ cup red wine vinegar
3 tablespoons chopped rinsed drained capers
3 tablespoons golden raisins (optional)
3 tablespoons pine nuts, lightly toasted
1¹/₂ tablespoons sugar, or to taste
¹/₄ cup finely chopped fresh flat-leaf parsley
salt and freshly ground pepper to taste
Bruschetta (page 116)

Heat 2 tablespoons of the olive oil in a heavy skillet over medium-high heat until hot but not smoking. Sauté the eggplant in the hot olive oil for 3 to 5 minutes or until tender. Remove the eggplant to a bowl using a slotted spoon, reserving the pan drippings. Heat the remaining 2 tablespoons olive oil with the reserved pan drippings over medium heat. Stir in the onion and celery. Cook for 5 minutes, stirring frequently. Add the tomatoes, olives, vinegar, capers, raisins, pine nuts and sugar and mix well.

Cook, covered, for 5 to 10 minutes or until the mixture is cooked through and the celery is tender, stirring occasionally. Spoon the caponata into a bowl. Stir in the parsley. Let stand until cool. Chill, covered, for 8 to 10 hours. Taste and season with salt and pepper. Serve with Bruschetta.

Serves 15 to 20

Italian Sausage Soup

8 ounces sweet Italian sausage links
8 ounces hot Italian sausage links
1 cup chopped onion
2 carrots, peeled and chopped
2 garlic cloves, minced
12 ounces zucchini, chopped
1 green bell pepper, chopped
1 pound Italian plum tomatoes, peeled and chopped, or
    1 (16-ounce) can plum tomatoes
5 cups chicken broth
1 cup dry red wine
1 tablespoon chopped fresh basil, or
    2 teaspoons dried basil
1 teaspoon dried oregano
freshly ground pepper to taste
1/2 cup uncooked pastini, cavatelli or other tiny pasta

Brown the sausage links in a large heavy saucepan; remove the sausage and drain all but 1 tablespoon of the pan drippings. Cut the sausage into 1-inch slices and return to the saucepan. Add the onion, carrots and garlic and sauté for 5 minutes.

Stir in the zucchini, bell pepper, tomatoes, broth, wine, basil, oregano and pepper. Bring to a boil. Add the pasta and cook for 20 minutes, stirring occasionally. Serve with freshly grated Romano or Parmesan cheese and crusty Italian or French bread.

Serves 6 to 8

Cantaloupe Vinaigrette

1/2 cantaloupe, seeded
salt and freshly ground pepper to taste
2 teaspoons extra-virgin olive oil
2 teaspoons white wine vinegar
leaf lettuce leaves
2 teaspoons finely chopped fresh chives

Scoop 1-inch balls from the cantaloupe using a melon baller. Combine the melon balls, salt and pepper in a bowl. Add the olive oil and vinegar and toss gently to coat. Spoon the melon mixture onto a lettuce-lined serving platter. Sprinkle with the chives. Serve immediately.

Serves 4

Green Bean and Tomato Salad

Salad

1¼ pounds fresh green beans

salt to taste

2 ripe medium tomatoes, cut into wedges

Bacon and Pine Nut Dressing

½ cup pine nuts

6 ounces bacon, cut into ¼-inch pieces

3 tablespoons extra-virgin olive oil

3 tablespoons red wine vinegar

½ teaspoon salt

½ teaspoon sugar

⅛ teaspoon freshly ground pepper

For the salad, cook the green beans in boiling salted water in a saucepan for 5 minutes or just until tender-crisp, stirring once; drain. Plunge the beans into a bowl of ice water to stop the cooking process; drain. Arrange the beans on a serving platter. Surround the beans with the tomato wedges.

For the dressing, spread the pine nuts on a baking sheet. Toast at 375 degrees for 10 minutes or until golden brown, stirring frequently. Remove to a plate to cool.

Cook the bacon in a small skillet over low heat for 10 minutes or until crisp and golden brown. Drain, reserving 2 tablespoons of the bacon drippings. Add the olive oil to the reserved bacon drippings and mix well. Stir in the vinegar, salt, sugar and pepper. Bring to a boil; reduce the heat.

Simmer for 1 minute or until the sugar dissolves, stirring constantly. Stir in the pine nuts and bacon. Drizzle the hot dressing over the beans and tomatoes. Serve immediately.

Serves 4

Spicy Garlic Croutons

Combine 2 teaspoons olive oil, ¾ teaspoon Cajun seasoning and 1 minced garlic clove in a medium glass bowl. Microwave on High for 20 seconds. Add 2 cups ¾-inch sourdough bread cubes and toss gently to coat well. Spread in a single layer on a baking sheet and bake at 400 degrees for 15 minutes or until golden brown.

Garlic Bread

Slice a large loaf of French bread lengthwise. Melt 1 cup (2 sticks) butter in a small saucepan and add 4 to 6 minced garlic cloves, ⅔ cup grated Romano or Parmesan cheese and pepper to taste. Spread on both sides of the bread slices and reassemble the loaf. Wrap tightly in foil and bake at 350 degrees for 15 to 20 minutes or until heated through, turning once.

Pasta with Hot Bacon Vinaigrette

Hot Bacon Vinaigrette

12 ounces sliced bacon

1/3 cup olive oil

3 medium garlic cloves, minced

1/3 cup balsamic vinegar

1/4 cup red wine

1 cup thinly sliced fresh mushrooms

3 tablespoons chopped fresh chives

3 tablespoons chopped fresh flat-leaf parsley

freshly ground pepper to taste

Pasta

16 ounces spaghetti

1/2 cup freshly grated Parmesan cheese

For the vinaigrette, fry the bacon in a skillet until brown and crisp. Drain the bacon and crumble. Discard the bacon drippings from the skillet; do not wipe the skillet clean. Heat 3 tablespoons of the olive oil in the same skillet over medium heat.

Sauté the garlic in the hot oil for 3 minutes or until tender and golden brown. Stir in the vinegar and wine. Bring to a simmer, stirring occasionally and scraping the bottom of the skillet with a wooden spoon to loosen any browned bits. Add the mushrooms and mix well. Simmer for 4 to 5 minutes or until the mushrooms begin to soften, stirring frequently. Add the remaining olive oil, bacon, chives, parsley and pepper. Remove from the heat. Cover to keep warm.

For the pasta, cook the pasta using package directions until al dente; drain. Place the pasta in a large bowl. Add the warm vinaigrette and cheese and toss gently to coat. Serve with additional cheese.

Serves 6 to 8

Penne Italiano with Meat Sauce

4 ounces pancetta, thickly sliced and chopped

4 garlic cloves, crushed

1 fresh or dried bay leaf

olive oil

1 pound ground beef, pork and veal combination

8 ounces bulk hot Italian sausage

1 medium carrot, finely chopped

1 medium onion, chopped

1 rib celery, chopped

1 cup dry red wine

2 (32-ounce) cans chunky crushed tomatoes

1 cup beef stock

1 cup chopped flat-leaf parsley

1/4 teaspoon allspice or cinnamon

salt and pepper to taste

16 ounces penne rigate, cooked al dente and drained

grated Pecorino Romano cheese

Heat a large saucepan over medium-high heat. Add the pancetta, garlic, bay leaf and olive oil to the saucepan. Cook for 1 minute, stirring constantly. Add the ground meat mixture and sausage and mix well.

Cook for 5 minutes or until the ground meat mixture and sausage are brown and crumbly, stirring constantly. Stir in the carrot, onion and celery. Cook for 5 minutes, stirring frequently. Add the wine and mix well. Cook for 1 minute. Stir in the undrained tomatoes and stock. Add the parsley, allspice, salt and pepper and mix well. Bring the sauce to a boil; reduce the heat to medium-low.

Cook for 10 to 15 minutes or to the desired consistency, stirring occasionally. Discard the bay leaf. Toss the pasta in a large bowl with just enough of the sauce to coat. Spoon the remaining sauce over the top of the pasta and sprinkle with cheese. Serve with crusty Italian bread.

Serves 8

Tuscan-Style Lasagna

5 garlic cloves, minced
2 tablespoons olive oil
1 medium onion, minced
3 medium carrots, minced
2 ribs celery, minced
2 tablespoons chopped fresh sage
1 pound ground veal
1 pound ground lean pork
1 pound ground lean lamb
salt and freshly ground pepper
    to taste

2 cups dry red wine
2 cups beef stock or beef broth
1 (14-ounce) can chopped tomatoes,
    drained
2 tablespoons chopped fresh basil
1/2 cup heavy cream
White Sauce (this page)
16 lasagna noodles
salt to taste
1 to 2 cups freshly grated Parmesan
    cheese

Sauté the garlic with olive oil in a large saucepan or Dutch oven over medium-high heat for 1 to 2 minutes or until brown. Stir in the onion, carrots and celery. Cook for 10 minutes or until the vegetables are tender, stirring frequently. Add the sage and mix well. Cook for 1 minute. Add the ground veal, ground pork, ground lamb, salt and pepper and mix well.

Cook over high heat for 8 to 10 minutes or until the veal, pork and lamb are brown and crumbly, stirring frequently. Stir in the wine. Cook for 15 minutes or until the liquid is reduced by 1/2, stirring occasionally. Add the stock, tomatoes, basil, salt and pepper and mix well. Reduce the heat to medium-low.

Cook, partially covered, for 45 minutes or until the liquid is reduced by 1/2, stirring occasionally. Stir in the heavy cream. Cook for 10 minutes longer, stirring frequently. Remove from the heat.

Cook the pasta al dente in boiling salted water in a saucepan. Drain and rinse under cold water. Pat dry with paper towels. Spread 1/4 of the meat sauce over the bottom of a 9×13-inch baking dish sprayed with nonstick cooking spray. Layer with 4 of the noodles, 1/3 of the remaining meat sauce, 2/3 cup of the White Sauce and 1/4 of the cheese. Top with 4 of the remaining noodles, 1/2 of the remaining meat sauce, 2/3 cup of the White Sauce and 1/3 of the remaining cheese. Layer with 4 of the remaining noodles, remaining meat sauce, 2/3 cup of the White Sauce and 1/2 of the remaining cheese. The dish will be very full so gently pat down each layer before continuing to the next. Top with the remaining noodles, remaining white sauce and remaining cheese. Bake at 350 degrees for 35 to 45 minutes or until bubbly. Broil just until golden brown.

Serves 8

White Sauce

Melt 1/2 cup (1 stick) butter in a large saucepan. Whisk in 1/2 cup flour. Cook over medium-high heat for 2 to 3 minutes or until the mixture is golden brown, whisking constantly. Add 4 cups milk gradually, whisking constantly until blended. Cook over medium heat for 15 minutes or until thickened, stirring frequently. Whisk in 1/2 teaspoon freshly grated nutmeg and salt and pepper to taste.

Entertaining Italian-Style

Italian food is very versatile and makes entertaining easy to plan. Antipasti are great starters, easy to prepare, full of flavor, and pleasing to the eye. They can be as simple as prosciutto-wrapped breadsticks, grilled mixed vegetables, or stuffed and roasted vegetables.

Many baked pasta dishes can be prepared the day before and some are substantial enough not to need a second course, particularly if the antipasto course was filling. All you would need to complete the meal would be a selection of breads, some Italian wines, and an appealing dessert, such as Tiramisu with Raspberries (page 131).

Bow Tie Pasta with Asparagus and Prosciutto

8 ounces bow tie pasta
salt to taste
olive oil to taste
1½ pounds fresh asparagus, trimmed
1 (8-ounce) package sliced fresh mushrooms
⅓ cup finely chopped sweet onion
4 or 5 garlic cloves, minced
4 ounces prosciutto, finely chopped
1 cup heavy cream
freshly ground pepper to taste
freshly grated Parmesan cheese to taste

Cook the pasta in boiling salted water in a saucepan for 10 to 11 minutes or until al dente; drain. Toss the pasta with just enough olive oil to coat in a bowl.

Combine the asparagus with just enough water to cover in a saucepan. Bring to a boil. Boil for 3 minutes or until tender-crisp. Drain and cool slightly. Cut the tips from the spears and set aside. Process the remaining asparagus in a food processor until coarsely chopped.

Sauté the mushrooms, onion and garlic in olive oil in a large skillet or wok until the onion is tender. Stir in the prosciutto. Sauté for 3 to 4 minutes longer. Add the heavy cream and pepper and mix well. Bring to a boil.

Cook for 1 to 2 minutes or until slightly thickened, stirring frequently. Stir in the chopped asparagus. Cook just until heated through, stirring frequently. Add the pasta and mix well. Stir in the asparagus tips. Spoon into a serving bowl and sprinkle with cheese. You may top with sliced grilled chicken for a hearty main dish.

Serves 6 to 8 as side dish

Sausage-Stuffed Rigatoni

Sausage Stuffing
1 pound hot bulk pork sausage
¾ cup dry Italian bread crumbs with Romano cheese
⅓ cup milk
1 egg, lightly beaten

Rigatoni
16 ounces rigatoni
olive oil
Italian Tomato Sauce (this page)
1 (6-ounce) package shredded Parmesan cheese

For the stuffing, brown the sausage in a skillet, stirring until crumbly; do not drain. Stir in the bread crumbs, milk and egg. Spoon the sausage mixture into a bowl. Chill, covered, in the refrigerator.

For the rigatoni, cook the pasta using package directions until al dente; drain and rinse. Toss the pasta with just enough olive oil to coat in a bowl. Spray a 9×13-inch baking dish with nonstick cooking spray. Ladle just enough of the Italian Tomato Sauce over the bottom of the prepared dish to form a thin layer.

Shape the stuffing into several small logs to make the stuffing process easier. Stuff enough of the pasta shells with the stuffing for 2 complete layers, serving the leftover pasta with your favorite sauce. Arrange the stuffed pasta in rows in a single layer in the prepared baking dish. Ladle ½ of the remaining Italian Tomato Sauce over the pasta and sprinkle with ½ of the cheese. Layer with another row of the stuffed rigatoni. Top with the remaining Italian Tomato Sauce and sprinkle with the remaining cheese. Bake at 350 degrees for 1 hour. Let stand for 10 to 15 minutes before serving. You may prepare in advance and freeze, covered, for future use. Adjust the baking times as needed.

Serves 8 to 10

Italian Tomato Sauce

1 large onion, chopped
3 tablespoons olive oil
4 cups water
1 (28-ounce) can crushed Italian tomatoes
1 (14-ounce) can diced tomatoes
2 (6-ounce) cans tomato paste
1 tablespoon sugar
1 tablespoon salt
½ teaspoon pepper
½ teaspoon oregano
½ teaspoon basil

Sauté the onion in the olive oil in a Dutch oven until tender. Stir in the water, undrained tomatoes, tomato paste, sugar, salt, pepper, oregano and basil. Simmer, covered, for 1 hour, stirring occasionally.

Serves 8 to 10

Chicken and Spinach Italiano

4 boneless skinless chicken breasts
salt and pepper to taste
12 ounces fresh spinach, sautéed
1 red bell pepper, roasted, skinned, seeded and cut
    into quarters
12 ounces goat cheese, crumbled
8 ounces Parmesan cheese, grated
1/2 cup milk
2 eggs
8 ounces bread crumbs
2 ounces Romano cheese, grated
4 teaspoons chopped flat-leaf parsley
2 teaspoons granulated garlic
flour
3/4 cup olive oil

Pound the chicken between sheets of waxed paper until flattened. Sprinkle with salt and pepper. Layer each chicken breast equally with the spinach, roasted bell pepper, goat cheese and Parmesan cheese. Roll to enclose the filling and secure with wooden picks. Chill, covered, for 1 to 10 hours.

Whisk the milk and eggs in a bowl until blended. Mix the bread crumbs, Romano cheese, parsley, garlic, salt and pepper in a shallow dish. Coat the rolls lightly with flour. Dip in the milk mixture and coat with the bread crumb mixture.

Heat the olive oil in a large skillet over medium heat. Add the rolls. Sauté until golden brown on all sides. Remove the rolls to a baking dish. Bake at 350 degrees for 12 to 15 minutes or until the chicken is cooked through.

Serves 4

Spaghettini with Spicy Scallops

4 quarts water
salt to taste
16 ounces spaghettini, capellini, spaghetti or linguini
4 scallions
1/4 cup pine nuts
1/4 cup plus 2 tablespoons olive oil
6 large garlic cloves, minced
2 tablespoons coarsely chopped fresh flat-leaf parsley
1 teaspoon crushed red pepper
1 pound medium sea scallops, cut into quarters
1/2 teaspoon freshly ground black pepper
1/2 cup fresh whole flat-leaf parsley leaves

Bring the water and salt to a boil in a large saucepan. Add the pasta. Cook using package directions until al dente; drain. Cover to keep warm. Cut the scallions into thin slices, keeping the white and green parts separate.

Toast the pine nuts in a heavy skillet over medium-high heat for 2 to 3 minutes or until light brown. Remove the pine nuts to a small plate. Heat the olive oil in the same skillet used to toast the pine nuts over medium heat. Add the sliced scallion bulbs, garlic, chopped parsley and red pepper and mix well.

Cook for 3 to 4 minutes or until the scallions are tender, stirring frequently. Stir in the scallops. Cook over medium-high heat for 2 minutes or just until cooked through. Season with the black pepper and salt. Add the scallop mixture, scallion greens, pine nuts and parsley leaves to the pasta and toss to mix. Serve immediately.

Serves 4

Shrimp with Spinach and Pine Nuts

Lemon Butter Sauce

2 cups (4 sticks) lightly salted butter,
    cut into tablespoons
1 tablespoon minced shallots
1 tablespoon minced garlic
$1/2$ cup dry white wine
1 cup heavy cream
$1/2$ cup fresh lemon juice
$1/8$ teaspoon white pepper

Shrimp

$1^1/2$ tablespoons pine nuts
$1/4$ cup ($1/2$ stick) butter
2 tablespoons minced garlic
3 cups ($1/4$-inch slices) mushrooms
2 dozen jumbo shrimp, peeled and
    deveined
6 cups (about) fresh spinach leaves,
    trimmed
6 cups hot cooked vermicelli

For the sauce, melt 1 tablespoon of the butter in a large skillet over medium-high heat. Sauté the shallots and garlic in the butter until the shallots are tender. Stir in the wine.

Cook until the mixture is reduced by slightly more than $1/2$, whisking frequently. Add the heavy cream and mix well. Cook until reduced by $1/2$, whisking frequently. Stir in the lemon juice and white pepper. Reduce the heat to low. Add the remaining butter 2 tablespoons at a time, whisking constantly until blended. Continue to simmer until the sauce is just thick enough to coat the back of a spoon, stirring frequently. Remove from the heat and cover to keep warm.

For the shrimp, spread the pine nuts on a baking sheet. Place the baking sheet on the top oven rack. Roast at 350 degrees for 2 to 4 minutes or until golden brown. Remove the pine nuts to a plate to cool.

Heat the butter in a large skillet over medium-high heat. Sauté the garlic in the butter until tender. Stir in the mushrooms, shrimp and pine nuts. Sauté for several minutes or until the shrimp turn pink. Remove from the heat. Stir in the spinach gently. Spoon the warm pasta onto a serving platter with the shrimp mixture to the side. Drizzle the sauce over the pasta and lightly over the shrimp mixture.

Serves 6

Basil Pepper Boats

Cut 12 sweet banana peppers into halves lengthwise and discard the seeds. Place 1 large fresh basil leaf in each half. Brown 8 ounces mild sausage in a skillet, stirring until crumbly; drain. Stir in 4 ounces crumbled feta cheese. Spoon the sausage mixture into the pepper halves. Sprinkle with 8 ounces shredded mozzarella cheese and place in a baking pan. Bake at 375 degrees for 10 to 15 minutes or until bubbly.

Deep-Dish Pizza

Prepare your favorite pizza dough and roll to fit a deep pie dish. Trim and flute the edge and brush with olive oil. Spread with tomato purée and layer with kalamata olives, artichoke hearts, fresh mushrooms, sliced fresh mozzarella balls, crumbled bacon and herbes de Provence. Bake at 475 degrees for 8 to 10 minutes or until the crust is golden brown.

Timberland Pizza

Everyday Pizza Crust

1 tablespoon dry yeast

1 cup warm water

2½ cups bread flour

3 tablespoons semolina flour

2 tablespoons olive oil

1½ teaspoons sugar

½ teaspoon salt

olive oil

Pizza

¼ cup olive oil

2 tablespoons pesto

2 tomatoes, thinly sliced

4 canned water-pack artichoke hearts

¼ cup pine nuts, toasted

½ cup crumbled bleu cheese

For the crust, proof the yeast in the warm water in a bowl. Combine the bread flour, semolina flour, 2 tablespoons olive oil, sugar and salt in a food processor. Process until mixed. Add the yeast mixture and process until the mixture adheres.

Shape the dough into a ball and place in a floured bowl. Let rest, covered with damp paper towels, for 10 to 20 minutes. Knead on a lightly floured surface until an easily handled dough forms. Brush the bottom of a pizza pan or baking pan with olive oil. Pat the dough over the bottom and up the side of the prepared pan.

For the pizza, combine the olive oil and pesto in a bowl and mix well. Brush the pesto mixture over the crust. Layer with the sliced tomatoes, artichoke hearts, pine nuts and bleu cheese. Bake at 475 degrees for 8 to 10 minutes or until brown and bubbly.

Makes 1 pizza

Asparagus with Pine Nuts

1/4 cup pine nuts
1 1/2 pounds (6- to 7-inch) spears fresh asparagus
2 teaspoons salt
6 tablespoons unsalted butter
1 tablespoon lemon juice
1/4 cup rinsed drained capers
freshly ground pepper to taste
salt to taste
4 ounces Italian Parmesan cheese (preferably
    Parmigiano-Reggiano)

Toast the pine nuts in a heavy skillet over medium heat for 1 to 2 minutes or until fragrant, stirring constantly. Remove the pine nuts to a bowl to cool.

Snap off the woody ends of the asparagus spears and discard. Cut the spears to same length. Add enough water to measure 2 to 3 inches to a skillet large enough to accommodate the length of the asparagus lying flat. Arrange the asparagus in the skillet and bring to a boil over high heat. Add 2 teaspoons salt; reduce the heat slightly. Boil gently for 4 to 7 minutes or until tender; drain. Cover to keep warm.

Heat the unsalted butter in a saucepan over medium-low heat. Stir in the lemon juice, capers and pepper. Cook for 30 to 40 seconds, stirring gently. Taste and adjust the seasoning, adding pepper, salt to taste and/or additional lemon juice as desired.

Arrange the asparagus on a serving platter or individual plates. Spoon the caper sauce over the asparagus and sprinkle with the pine nuts. Shave paper-thin slices of the cheese over the asparagus using a vegetable peeler. Serve immediately.

Serves 4 to 6

Risotto Milanese

1 teaspoon saffron threads
1/4 cup warm water
1 cup (2 sticks) butter
2 small onions, chopped
freshly ground pepper to taste
1 cup dry white wine
4 cups arborio rice
salt to taste
10 cups beef broth
2 1/2 cups freshly grated Parmesan cheese
sprigs of flat-leaf parsley

Dissolve the saffron in the warm water. Heat 5 tablespoons of the butter in a heavy saucepan over medium-low heat. Cook the onions in the butter for 10 minutes or until tender, stirring occasionally. Season with pepper. Stir in the wine and bring to a boil.

Boil until the liquid evaporates, stirring frequently. Add the rice and stir until coated. Season with salt. Add 6 cups of the broth and saffron and mix well. Bring to a boil; reduce the heat. Simmer until the liquid is absorbed, stirring frequently. Continue simmering and adding enough of the broth 1 cup at a time until the rice is tender; the risotto should be creamy but not mushy. Remove from the heat. Stir in the remaining butter and 1/4 cup of the cheese.

Let stand for 1 minute. Spoon the risotto onto a serving platter. Garnish with parsley. Serve immediately with the remaining cheese.

Serves 12

Cheesy Artichoke Bread

1 loaf French bread
6 garlic cloves, minced
1 cup (2 sticks) margarine
2 (14-ounce) cans artichoke hearts, drained and chopped
2 cups (8 ounces) shredded Monterey Jack cheese
1 cup (4 ounces) shredded Cheddar cheese
1 cup sour cream
1/2 cup grated Parmesan cheese

Slice the loaf horizontally into halves. Remove the centers carefully from each half, leaving 2 shells. Cut the bread from the centers into small pieces. Sauté the garlic in the margarine in a skillet until tender. Let stand until cool.

Combine the garlic mixture, reserved bread pieces, artichoke hearts, Monterey Jack cheese, Cheddar cheese, sour cream and Parmesan cheese in a bowl and mix well. Mound the artichoke heart mixture in the bread shells. Cover each half with foil and place on a baking sheet. Bake at 375 degrees for 45 minutes; remove the foil. Bake for 8 minutes longer. Slice as desired.

Serves 6 to 8

Pesto and Pine Nut Bread

1 3/4 cups warm (105- to 110-degree) water
2 1/4 teaspoons dry yeast
1 teaspoon sugar
1/4 cup olive oil
1 1/2 teaspoons salt
2 garlic cloves, minced
4 1/2 cups (or more) bread flour
3/4 cup chopped fresh basil
3/4 cup freshly grated Parmesan cheese
3/4 cup pine nuts, toasted
1/2 teaspoon ground pepper

Combine the warm water, yeast and sugar in a large bowl and mix well. Let stand for 10 minutes or until foamy. Stir in the olive oil, salt and garlic. Add 2 1/2 cups of the bread flour and mix well. Stir in the basil, cheese, pine nuts and pepper. Add enough of the remaining bread flour to make a soft dough and mix well.

Knead the dough on a lightly floured surface for 5 minutes or until smooth and elastic, adding additional flour if needed to make an easily handled dough. Place the dough in an oiled bowl, turning to coat the surface. Let rise, covered with plastic wrap, in a warm place for 1 hour or until doubled in bulk.

Punch the dough down. Divide into 2 equal portions. Shape each portion into an 8-inch oval loaf. Arrange the loaves on a large baking sheet. Make 4 slits at equal intervals in the top of each loaf. Let rise, covered with a tea towel, for 30 minutes or until almost doubled in bulk. Bake at 375 degrees for 35 minutes or until the loaf makes a hollow sound when lightly tapped. Remove to a wire rack to cool. You may prepare and bake 1 day in advance and store, wrapped in foil, at room temperature.

Makes 2 loaves

Mascarpone Ice Cream

4 cups milk
1 vanilla bean, split lengthwise into halves
6 egg yolks
1¹/₄ cups sugar
2 cups mascarpone cheese
2 cups sliced fresh strawberries
¹/₄ cup Grand Mariner
1 tablespoon finely grated orange zest

Combine the milk and vanilla bean in a heavy saucepan. Bring just to the boiling point over medium heat. Whisk the egg yolks and sugar in a bowl until blended. Add the hot milk mixture to the egg yolk mixture gradually, whisking constantly. Return the egg yolk mixture to the saucepan.

Cook over medium-low heat for 7 minutes or until the mixture just barely coats the back of a spoon, stirring constantly. Remove from the heat. Scrape the seeds from the vanilla bean into the egg yolk mixture, discarding the bean. Add the cheese gradually and mix well. Chill, covered, for 2 hours or until completely cooled.

Toss the strawberries, liqueur and orange zest in a bowl and set aside. Pour the cooled custard into an ice cream freezer. Freeze using manufacturer's directions, adding the strawberry mixture about 20 minutes after the freezing process begins. Spoon the ice cream into a freezer container and freeze until firm.

Serves 6 to 8

Tiramisu Ice Cream

4 cups milk
1 vanilla bean, split lengthwise into halves
6 egg yolks
1¹/₄ cups sugar
2 cups mascarpone cheese
1 tablespoon instant espresso granules or instant
    coffee granules
¹/₄ cup coffee liqueur
¹/₂ cup shaved bittersweet chocolate

Combine the milk and vanilla bean in a heavy saucepan. Bring just to the boiling point over medium heat. Whisk the egg yolks and sugar in a bowl until blended. Add the hot milk mixture to the egg yolk mixture gradually, whisking constantly. Return the egg yolk mixture to the saucepan.

Cook over medium-low heat for 7 minutes or until the mixture just barely coats the back of a spoon, stirring constantly; do not boil. Remove from the heat. Scrape the seeds from the vanilla bean into the egg yolk mixture, discarding the bean. Add the cheese gradually and mix well. Chill, covered, for 2 hours or until completely cooled. Stir in the espresso granules. Pour the cooled custard into an ice cream freezer. Freeze using manufacturer's directions, stirring in the liqueur and chocolate after 20 minutes. Spoon the ice cream into a freezer container and freeze until firm.

Serves 6 to 8

Mediterranean Nuts

Pistachio Crust Amaretto Cheesecake incorporates pistachios in the crust and the flavor of almonds in the amaretto used in the filling. Both nuts have long been staples of the diet in the Mediterranean, where they grow naturally. They are a versatile and flavorful addition to the diet and are also easy to store and preserve.

Pistachios have been cultivated in the area for 3,000 years, coming to Italy originally from the Middle East; the word "pistachio" actually is the Italian version of the Persian word "pistah," meaning nut.

Pistachio Crust Amaretto Cheesecake

Pistachio Crust
1 cup finely ground pistachios
3/4 cup finely crushed graham
    cracker crumbs
1/3 cup butter, melted

Cheesecake
24 ounces cream cheese, softened
1 cup sugar

2 tablespoons flour
1 teaspoon vanilla extract
2 eggs
1 egg yolk
2 tablespoons each milk and amaretto
1 cup whipping cream
1/4 cup grated semisweet chocolate
finely chopped pistachios
sliced fresh strawberries

For the crust, grease the bottom and 1¼ inches up the side of a 9-inch springform pan. Combine the pistachios and graham cracker crumbs in a bowl and mix well. Stir in the butter. Pat the crumb mixture over the bottom and 1¼ inches up the side of the prepared pan. Chill, covered, in the refrigerator.

For the cheesecake, beat the cream cheese, sugar, flour and vanilla in a mixing bowl. Add the eggs and egg yolk. Beat at low speed until blended. Stir in the milk and amaretto. Spoon the filling into the prepared springform pan.

Bake at 375 degrees for 35 to 40 minutes or until the center is nearly set when gently shaken. Cool in the pan on a wire rack for 15 minutes. Run a sharp knife around the edge of the cheesecake to loosen the crust from the side of the pan. Cool for 30 minutes longer. Remove the side of the pan. Let stand until completely cool. Chill, covered, for 4 to 24 hours.

Beat the whipping cream in a mixing bowl until stiff peaks form. Sprinkle the top of the cheesecake with 3 tablespoons of the chocolate. Pipe the whipped cream over the top of the cheesecake and sprinkle with the remaining 1 tablespoon chocolate and pistachios. Arrange the sliced strawberries over the top.

Serves 10 to 12

Tiramisu with Raspberries

Zabaglione

8 egg yolks
1 cup sugar
$1/8$ teaspoon salt
$1^1/2$ cups marsala

Tiramisu

1 (16-ounce) sponge cake or pound cake
3 tablespoons crème de cassis
19 ounces cream cheese, softened
3 tablespoons sugar
1 teaspoon vanilla extract
1 cup sour cream
1 (10-ounce) package frozen raspberries, drained
$1/2$ cup whipping cream, whipped

For the zabaglione, combine the egg yolks, sugar and salt in a large metal bowl and beat until thickened and pale yellow. Whisk in the wine gradually. Place over a large saucepan of hot water. Cook over low heat for 15 minutes or until the mixture triples in volume and mounds from a spoon, whisking constantly. Spoon into another bowl and cool to room temperature. Chill, covered, for 2 to 8 hours.

For the tiramisu, trim the crust from the cake and cut into $1/2$-inch slices. Fit into a 9×12-inch dish. Brush with the crème de cassis.

Combine the cream cheese, sugar and vanilla in a mixing bowl. Beat for 3 to 4 minutes or until light and fluffy, scraping the bowl occasionally. Fold in $2/3$ of the zabaglione and sour cream. Spread evenly over the cake; sprinkle with the raspberries. Fold the remaining zabaglione into the whipped cream and spread over the raspberries. Freeze, covered, for 3 hours. Let stand in the refrigerator for a few minutes and cut into large squares.

Serves 12

Coconut Pecan Biscotti

$2^1/4$ cups flour
$1^1/2$ teaspoons baking powder
$1/4$ teaspoon salt
$1/2$ cup (1 stick) unsalted butter, softened
$3/4$ cup packed brown sugar
2 eggs
$1/2$ cup plus 2 tablespoons shredded sweetened coconut
1 cup chopped pecans

Mix the flour, baking powder and salt together. Beat the unsalted butter and brown sugar in a mixing bowl until creamy. Add the eggs 1 at a time, beating well after each addition. Beat in the coconut. Add the dry ingredients gradually, stirring constantly. Add the pecans and mix well. Chill, covered, for 30 minutes.

Line a baking sheet with baking parchment. Place the dough on a lightly floured surface. Divide into 2 equal portions. Shape each portion into a 2-inch-wide log. Arrange the logs on the prepared baking sheet.

Bake at 350 degrees for 35 minutes or until the logs are golden brown, firm to the touch and a wooden pick inserted in the center comes out clean. Cool the logs on the baking sheet for 20 minutes. Reduce the oven temperature to 325 degrees.

Remove the logs to a work surface, discarding the baking parchment. Cut each log diagonally into $1/2$-inch slices. Arrange the biscotti cut side down on the baking sheet. Bake for 15 minutes or until brown and crisp. Cool on baking sheet for 2 minutes. Remove to a wire rack to cool completely. You may prepare up to 2 weeks in advance and store in an airtight container at room temperature.

Makes 45 cookies

Spring
is in the
Air

MENU

White Rabbit Invites

Little girls are gifts that cannot be compared with any other. Some are shy, some prissy, some tomboys, and others are truly indescribable. We were such little girls in our own time, and a tradition with many was to celebrate with tea parties. Guest lists range from our favorite teddy or porcelain doll to our closest friends who share fond memories.

Apricot Tea

1 cup sweetened instant tea granules
1 cup orange instant breakfast drink mix
1 cup lemonade mix
1 package apricot gelatin
1 teaspoon ground cloves
1 teaspoon cinnamon
1 teaspoon nutmeg

Combine the instant tea, orange drink mix, lemonade mix, gelatin, cloves, cinnamon and nutmeg in a bowl and mix well. Store in an airtight container. To serve, place 2 teaspoons of the dry mixture in a cup of either hot or cold water and stir to dissolve. Add ice cubes if serving cold.

Makes 75 cups

Orange Dreamsicle Punch

4 cups orange juice, chilled
1 cup milk
3 tablespoons sugar
2 teaspoons grated orange zest
$1/2$ teaspoon nutmeg
1 cup sparkling water, chilled
1 quart orange sherbet

Combine the orange juice, milk, sugar, orange zest and nutmeg in a large pitcher and stir until the sugar dissolves. Your may prepare up to this point 3 days in advance and store, covered, in the refrigerator.

Pour the sparkling water into the orange juice mixture and mix well. Scoop the sherbet into a large glass punch bowl. Pour the punch over the sherbet. Ladle into punch cups.

Serves 12

The McKenzie House and Park

The historic McKenzie House is located across from McKenzie Park in downtown Panama City, Florida. It was originally built in 1909 and is one of the oldest homes in the area. The house has strong historical significance as the home of Robert Lee McKenzie, a pioneer in the creation and development of Bay County and Panama City. McKenzie served as a state legislator, the first mayor of Panama City, and the first chairman of the Board of County Commissioners of Bay County. The City of Panama City purchased the property from the McKenzie family and restored the house in the late 1990s. Restored to its original beauty, the home is now available for private functions and is often used for wedding receptions, tea parties, and many other special events. The historic atmosphere provides a charming setting for any occasion.

Raspberries in Rose Cream

1 cup heavy whipping cream
1 cup milk
1 teaspoon rose water or rose syrup
7 tablespoons sugar
4 egg yolks
2¹/₂ cups fresh raspberries
fresh pink tea rose petals

Heat the whipping cream, milk, rose water and sugar in a heavy saucepan just until warm, stirring constantly. Beat the egg yolks in a heatproof bowl until blended. Add the hot milk mixture to the egg yolks, whisking constantly. Return the milk mixture to the saucepan.

Cook over low heat for 10 minutes or until thickened, stirring constantly. Strain into a bowl. Chill, covered, in the refrigerator. Place some of the raspberries in the bottom of a serving bowl or in individual dessert goblets. Spoon the chilled custard over the raspberries and sprinkle with the remaining raspberries and rose petals.

Serves 4

Almond-Stuffed Strawberries

20 fresh large strawberries
3 ounces cream cheese, softened
2 tablespoons finely chopped pecans or walnuts
    (optional)
1¹/₂ tablespoons confectioners' sugar
¹/₂ teaspoon almond extract
18 slivered almonds

Finely chop 2 of the strawberries and drain on a paper towel. Remove the tops from the remaining strawberries. Cut a thin slice from the stem end of each strawberry to allow the strawberries to stand upright. Make 2 slits in the form of an "X" from the top of each strawberry (pointed end) cutting almost to the stem end.

Beat the cream cheese in a mixing bowl until light and fluffy. Stir in the chopped strawberries, pecans, confectioners' sugar and flavoring. Spoon the cream cheese mixture into a pastry bag fitted with a star tip. Pipe into the center of each strawberry and top with 1 slivered almond. You may prepare the cream cheese filling in advance and stored, covered, in the refrigerator. Do not stuff the strawberries more than 2 to 4 hours in advance, being sure to chill until serving time. Substitute 1 teaspoon Grand Marnier for the almond extract and finely grated orange zest for the almonds for variety.

Makes 18

Toasted Pecan Tea Sandwiches

12 ounces cream cheese, softened
1/2 cup ground toasted pecans
2 tablespoons finely minced fresh parsley
1 tablespoon finely minced onion
1 teaspoon fresh lemon juice
1/4 teaspoon freshly grated nutmeg, or to taste
salt and white pepper to taste
24 slices white bread
1/2 cup (1 stick) unsalted butter, softened

Combine the cream cheese, pecans and parsley in a bowl and mix well. Stir in the onion, lemon juice, nutmeg, salt and white pepper. Spread 1 side of each slice of bread lightly with unsalted butter.

Spread the buttered side of 12 slices of the bread with some of the cream cheese mixture. Top with the remaining bread slices butter side down. Trim the crusts from the sandwiches. Cut each sandwich diagonally into halves. Cut the halves into halves again.

Makes 1 dozen sandwiches

Scones

2 cups flour
2 tablespoons sugar
1 tablespoon baking powder
1/2 teaspoon salt
6 tablespoons butter
1/2 cup buttermilk or milk
1 egg white, lightly beaten

Combine the flour, sugar, baking powder and salt in a bowl and mix well. Cut in the butter until crumbly. Make a well in the center of the flour mixture. Add the buttermilk to the well and mix until the dough adheres and is slightly sticky.

Place the dough on a lightly floured surface and shape or cut as desired. Arrange the scones on a cookie sheet and brush the tops with the egg white. Bake at 425 degrees for 10 to 20 minutes or until light brown. Cool on cookie sheet for 2 minutes. Remove to a wire rack to cool completely.

Makes 12 scones

Easter Place Cards

Decorated Easter eggs make easy and simple place cards for Easter dinner. They can be personalized with a wax crayon before dying or with glue and glitter. Egg and bunny shaped cookies with the guests' names piped on them are both attractive place keepers and tasty treats. You can also tie the place names on the necks of chocolate bunnies with a pastel ribbon or pipe the names on with colored frosting.

Petits Fours

Petits Fours
3 cups sifted cake flour
3 tablespoons baking powder
¼ teaspoon salt
1 cup milk
1 teaspoon bourbon vanilla extract
2 cups sugar
1 cup (2 sticks) butter, softened

4 egg yolks
4 egg whites, stiffly beaten

Fondant Icing
7½ cups sifted confectioners' sugar
½ cup plus 3 tablespoons water
3 tablespoons light corn syrup
1 teaspoon bourbon vanilla extract

For the petit fours, line a 10×15-inch cake pan with baking parchment. Sift the cake flour, baking powder and salt together. Mix the milk and bourbon vanilla in a small bowl. Beat the sugar and butter in a mixing bowl until creamy, scraping the bowl occasionally. Add the egg yolks 1 at a time, beating well after each addition. Add the dry ingredients alternately with the milk mixture, beating well after each addition. Fold in the egg whites.

Spread the batter in the prepared pan. Bake at 350 degrees for 25 minutes. Cool in pan on a wire rack for 5 to 10 minutes. Invert the cake onto a large sheet of foil, discarding the baking parchment. Let stand until cool. Wrap the cooled cake in foil and return the cake to the cake pan; this will help keep the shape of the cake. Freeze until firm or for up to 6 months.

Trim the edges of the frozen cake. Using a ruler to measure the width, start with the center and cut the cake into halves and continue with each row until you have about 1-inch strips of cake. Cut each strip into halves and continue dividing the strips to form 1-inch squares that would fit into miniature baking cups. Trim a thin layer from the top of each square.

For the icing, combine the confectioners' sugar, water, corn syrup and bourbon vanilla in a medium saucepan and mix well. Cook over low heat until the mixture registers 110 degrees on a candy thermometer, stirring constantly. Remove from the heat. Cool slightly. Dip the cake squares into the icing and arrange on a flat surface. Let stand until set. Place the petit fours in miniature baking cups. Reheat the icing to 110 degrees if the mixture becomes too cool and thick to work with.

Makes 8 dozen petits fours

Candied Flowers and Berries

small rose petals, violets or pansies
small fresh mint leaves
small raspberries, blueberries, blackberries or wild
    strawberries
11 cups confectioners' sugar
1 tablespoon meringue powder
1/3 cup water
1 cup superfine sugar

Rinse the flowers, mint leaves and berries and pat dry with paper towels. Combine the confectioners' sugar, meringue powder and water in a mixing bowl. Beat at low speed until blended. Beat at high speed for 4 to 5 minutes or until fluffy, scraping the bowl occasionally.

Brush the meringue mixture over the surface of the fruit, mint and berries and sprinkle with the sugar. Dry on wire racks for 8 to 10 hours.

Servings variable

Dainty Rose Macaroons

4 cups flaked coconut
1 (14-ounce) can sweetened condensed milk
1 (3-ounce) package strawberry gelatin
1/2 teaspoon almond extract

Combine the coconut, condensed milk, gelatin and flavoring in a bowl and mix well. Chill, covered, for 2 hours or longer.

Shape the coconut mixture into 1-inch balls and arrange 2 inches apart on a greased cookie sheet. Bake at 350 degrees for 8 to 10 minutes or until light brown around the edges. Cool on the cookie sheet for 5 minutes. Remove to a wire rack to cool completely. The cookies have a soft texture.

Makes 4 dozen cookies

Macaroon Kiss Cookies

1½ cups flour
2 teaspoons baking powder
¼ teaspoon salt
¾ cup sugar
⅓ cup butter, softened
3 ounces cream cheese, softened
1 egg yolk
2 teaspoons almond extract
2 teaspoons orange juice
1 (14-ounce) package flaked coconut
1 (9-ounce) package milk chocolate kisses

Mix the flour, baking powder and salt. Beat the sugar, butter and cream cheese in a mixing bowl until light and fluffy. Add the egg yolk, flavoring and orange juice and beat until smooth. Add the flour mixture gradually, beating constantly until blended. Stir in 3 cups of the coconut. Chill, covered, for 1 hour or until firm.

Shape the dough into 1-inch balls and coat with the remaining coconut. Arrange 2 inches apart on an ungreased cookie sheet. Bake at 350 degrees for 10 to 12 minutes or until light brown. Immediately press 1 chocolate kiss in the top of each cookie. Cool on the cookie sheet for 2 minutes. Remove to a wire rack to cool completely.

Makes 4½ dozen cookies

Melt-Away Cookies

1 cup (2 sticks) butter, softened
6 tablespoons confectioners' sugar
1 teaspoon vanilla extract
2 cups sifted flour
½ cup chocolate chips
chopped pecans (optional)
confectioners' sugar to taste

Beat the butter in a mixing bowl until creamy. Add 6 tablespoons confectioners' sugar and vanilla and beat until blended. Stir in the flour, chocolate chips and pecans.

Shape the dough into 1-inch balls. Arrange 2 inches apart on a cookie sheet. Bake at 350 degrees for 15 minutes. Cool on the cookie sheet for 2 minutes. Remove to a wire rack to cool completely. Coat with confectioners' sugar to taste. Store in an airtight container.

Makes 2 dozen cookies

Dainty Lemon Tarts

Tart Shells

1¼ cups flour

½ cup (1 stick) margarine, frozen
    and cut into pieces

1 teaspoon sugar

½ teaspoon salt

¼ to ⅓ cup water

Lemon Filling

½ cup sugar

2½ tablespoons cornstarch

1 to 2 tablespoons grated lemon zest

⅛ teaspoon salt

¾ cup water

¼ cup lemon juice

2 egg yolks, beaten

1 tablespoon butter

Meringue

2 egg whites

¼ teaspoon salt

¼ cup sugar

For the shells, combine the flour, margarine, sugar and salt in a food processor fitted with a steel blade. Pulse to a coarse consistency. Add the water gradually, pulsing constantly until the mixture adheres. Roll the pastry on a lightly floured surface and cut with a 2-inch cutter. Fit the rounds into miniature muffin cups. Bake at 425 degrees for 8 to 10 minutes or until light brown.

For the filling, combine the sugar, cornstarch, lemon zest, salt, water and lemon juice in a saucepan and mix well. Bring to a boil over medium heat, stirring occasionally. Remove from the heat. Stir 1 to 2 tablespoons of the hot mixture into the egg yolks. Stir the egg yolk mixture into the hot mixture. Add the butter and mix well. Cook until the butter melts, stirring constantly. Spoon the filling into the baked shells.

For the meringue, beat the egg whites and salt in a mixing bowl until soft peaks form. Add the sugar gradually, beating constantly until stiff peaks form. Spread the meringue over the filling, sealing to the edge. Bake at 400 degrees for 5 to 8 minutes or until light brown.

Makes 8 tarts

Pulled Mints

Combine 2 cups sugar, 1 cup hot water and ¼ cup (½ stick) butter in a saucepan. Cook until the mixture registers 260 degrees on a candy thermometer, hard-ball stage. Mix in 2 drops of food coloring and 8 drops of oil of peppermint. Pour onto a marble slab. Cool slightly.

Pull the candy mixture until smooth and firm. Divide into long strips and cut into small pieces with scissors. Store in an airtight container; do not stack. Do not substitute peppermint extract for the oil of peppermint.

MENU

A Mother's Wish

One of the beautiful antebellum-style homes along scenic Beach Drive is the location of our Mother's Day luncheon, for it captures the hint of spring in the air. Select a special outdoor setting and recruit the children to help with the tables. Use your best china and linens, and create a menu that will let Mother know how special she is.

Raspberry Champagne Punch

2 (10-ounce) packages frozen red
    raspberries in syrup, thawed
1/2 cup sugar
1/3 cup thawed frozen concentrated
    lemon juice

1 (750-milliliter) bottle red rosé,
    chilled
1 quart raspberry sherbet
1 (750-milliliter) bottle Champagne,
    chilled

Process the undrained raspberries in a blender until puréed. Combine the puréed raspberries, sugar, lemon juice and wine in a punch bowl and stir until the sugar dissolves. Scoop the sherbet into the punch bowl and stir in the Champagne just before serving. Ladle into punch cups.

Makes 3 quarts

Strawberry Tossed Salad

Poppy Seed Dressing
3/4 cup sugar
1/3 cup mild wine vinegar
1/3 cup canola oil
1/3 cup minced onion
3 tablespoons poppy seeds

Salad
2 heads romaine, torn
2 cups sliced strawberries
2/3 cup chopped pecans, toasted
4 ounces sliced bacon, crisp-cooked
    and crumbled

For the dressing, process the sugar, vinegar, canola oil and onion in a blender until blended. Add the poppy seeds and process until mixed.

For the salad, toss the lettuce, strawberries, pecans and bacon in a salad bowl. Add the dressing and mix until coated. Serve immediately. You may substitute commercially prepared poppy seed dressing for the homemade dressing.

Serves 10 to 12

The Azalea Trail

Originating in Mobile, Alabama, the Azalea Trail has been a Bay County tradition since 1967, when local Garden Club members introduced the pageant to Panama City as a way of celebrating the beauty of springtime in the area. The pageant features young ladies dressed in antebellum attire as hostesses for the event, and the Azalea Trail Queen and her court are chosen from this bevy of beauties. Along the trail, the ladies stand poised gracefully and wave at passersby as they ride through enjoying the breathtaking natural beauty of vibrant azaleas and fragrant magnolias.

Lemon Chicken with Scallions

4 boneless skinless chicken breasts
salt and pepper to taste
3 tablespoons flour
2 teaspoons (or more) olive oil
1/4 cup finely chopped scallions
2 garlic cloves, minced
1/2 cup chicken broth
1/4 cup dry white wine
1 tablespoon lemon juice
1/4 cup chopped fresh parsley
grated zest of 1 lemon
1 lemon, cut into 8 wedges

Pound the chicken 1/2 inch thick between sheets of plastic wrap. Sprinkle with salt and pepper and coat with the flour. Heat 1 1/2 teaspoons of the olive oil in a large skillet over medium-high heat. Brown the chicken breasts 2 at a time on both sides in the hot olive oil until cooked through, adding additional olive oil if needed. Remove the chicken to a platter, reserving the pan drippings; cover.

Heat the remaining 1/2 teaspoon olive oil with the reserved pan drippings. Sauté the scallions and garlic in the hot olive oil mixture for 2 minutes or until tender. Add the broth and wine, stirring to deglaze the skillet. Stir in the lemon juice and 2 tablespoons of the parsley. Increase the heat to high.

Cook for 3 minutes or until the sauce is slightly reduced, stirring frequently. Stir in the lemon zest and season with salt and pepper. Return the chicken to the skillet and turn to coat. Cook just until heated through, stirring occasionally. Sprinkle servings with the remaining 2 tablespoons parsley and top with the lemon wedges.

Serves 4

Pork Medallions with Tarragon Sauce

2 pork tenderloins, trimmed
freshly ground pepper to taste
1/4 cup (about) Dijon mustard
2 tablespoons butter
2/3 cup beef broth
4 teaspoons chopped fresh tarragon
1 cup heavy whipping cream
salt to taste

Cut each tenderloin into 8 equal medallions. Pound the medallions between sheets of waxed paper or plastic wrap to flatten slightly. Sprinkle 1 side with pepper and brush with 1/2 of the Dijon mustard. Heat the butter in a large heavy skillet over medium heat. Arrange the medallions in batches mustard side down in the skillet. Sprinkle with pepper and brush with the remaining Dijon mustard. Cook for 5 minutes per side or until cooked through. Remove the medallions to a platter using a slotted spoon, reserving the pan drippings. Cover to keep warm.

Add the broth to the reserved pan drippings, scraping the browned bits from the bottom of the skillet with a wooden spoon. Bring to a boil, stirring occasionally. Stir in the tarragon. Boil for 2 minutes, stirring occasionally. Add the whipping cream and mix well. Boil until the sauce is thickened and reduced by 1/2, stirring frequently. Season with salt and pepper. Drizzle the sauce over the pork.

Serves 6 to 8

Wine and Cheese Omelet

1 large loaf French bread, torn into bite-size pieces
6 tablespoons unsalted butter, melted
12 ounces Swiss cheese, shredded
8 ounces Monterey Jack Cheese, shredded
9 thin slices Genoa salami, chopped
16 eggs
3¼ cups milk
½ cup dry white wine
1 tablespoon Dijon mustard
¼ teaspoon black pepper
⅛ teaspoon red pepper
4 large green onions, chopped
1½ cups sour cream
⅔ cup grated Parmesan cheese

Spread the bread over the bottom of 2 buttered 9×13-inch baking dishes and drizzle with the butter. Sprinkle with the Swiss cheese, Monterey Jack cheese and salami. Whisk the eggs, milk, wine, Dijon mustard, black pepper and red pepper in a bowl until blended. Stir in the green onions.

Pour the egg mixture over the prepared layers. Chill, covered with foil, for 10 to 24 hours. Let stand at room temperature for 30 minutes. Bake, covered, at 350 degrees for 1 hour or until set; remove the foil. Spread with the sour cream and sprinkle with the Parmesan cheese. Bake for 10 minutes longer or until light brown.

Serves 12 to 15

Marinated Asparagus

4 pounds fresh asparagus spears
salt to taste
1 cup olive oil
⅓ cup tarragon vinegar
3 tablespoons chopped fresh parsley
3 tablespoons sweet pickle relish
1 (2-ounce) jar chopped pimento, drained
1½ tablespoons chopped fresh chives
1 teaspoon salt
½ teaspoon pepper
2 hard-cooked eggs, grated
sprigs of fresh parsley

Snap off the woody ends of the asparagus spears. Remove the scales from the stalks with a sharp knife. Cook the asparagus in boiling salted water in a saucepan for 6 minutes or until tender-crisp; drain. Arrange the spears in a shallow dish.

Combine the olive oil, vinegar, chopped parsley, pickle relish, pimento, chives, 1 teaspoon salt and pepper in a jar with a tight-fitting lid and seal tightly. Shake to mix. Pour the olive oil mixture over the asparagus, turning to coat. Marinate, covered, in the refrigerator for 2 hours or longer; drain. Arrange the asparagus on a serving platter. Sprinkle with the eggs and top with sprigs of parsley.

Serves 16

Tomato and Basil Pie

3 large tomatoes, peeled and sliced
1 baked (9-inch) pie shell
1/2 cup mayonnaise
1/2 cup (2 ounces) grated Parmesan cheese
1 garlic clove, crushed
6 fresh basil leaves, chopped, or 1 teaspoon dried basil
1/4 teaspoon pepper
1/4 cup butter cracker crumbs
2 teaspoons unsalted butter

Arrange the tomato slices in the pie shell. Combine the mayonnaise, cheese, garlic, basil and pepper in a bowl and mix well. Spread the mayonnaise mixture over the tomatoes. Sprinkle with the cracker crumbs and dot with the unsalted butter. Bake at 425 degrees for 20 to 25 minutes.

Serves 6 to 8

Wild Rice with Mushrooms

3 tablespoons butter
3 tablespoons olive oil
1 1/2 cups chopped celery
1 1/2 cups chopped onions
3 cups thinly sliced mushrooms
3 garlic cloves, chopped
6 tablespoons soy sauce
3 cups assorted uncooked wild, brown and black rice, cooked

Heat the butter and olive oil in a large sauté pan over medium heat. Sauté the celery and onions in the butter mixture for 5 minutes or just until the vegetables begin to soften. Stir in the mushrooms. Sauté for 5 minutes or until the celery and onions are tender and the mushrooms begin to soften. Add the garlic and mix well. Cook for 1 minute, stirring frequently. Stir in the soy sauce. Simmer until the liquid is absorbed, stirring occasionally. Remove from the heat. Combine the mushroom mixture and rice in a bowl and mix well.

Serves 20

Anadama Rolls

$^1/_2$ cup milk
$^1/_2$ cup water
salt to taste
$^1/_4$ cup yellow cornmeal
$^1/_4$ cup light molasses
3 tablespoons unsalted butter
$1^1/_2$ teaspoons dry yeast
$^1/_4$ cup warm water
$2^1/_2$ cups flour
sesame seeds (optional)
Orange Zest Butter (this page)

Bring the milk, $^1/_2$ cup water and salt to a boil in a saucepan. Add the cornmeal gradually, whisking constantly. Cook until thickened, stirring frequently. Whisk in the molasses and 1 tablespoon unsalted butter. Spoon the cornmeal mixture into a bowl. Let stand until cool.

Proof the yeast in $^1/_4$ cup warm water. Stir the yeast mixture into the cornmeal mixture. Add the flour gradually, mixing until the dough pulls from the side of the bowl. Knead the dough on a lightly floured surface until smooth and shape into a ball. Coat a bowl with $1^1/_2$ teaspoons of the remaining unsalted butter. Add the dough, turning to coat. Let rise, covered, until doubled in bulk. Punch the dough down. Let rest, covered with plastic wrap, for a few minutes.

Brush two 9-inch baking pans with some of the remaining unsalted butter. Shape the dough into 18 balls. Arrange 9 balls in each prepared pan. Let rise, covered, until doubled in bulk. Preheat the oven to 400 degrees. Brush the tops of the rolls with the remaining unsalted butter and sprinkle with sesame seeds. Reduce the oven temperature to 350 degrees. Bake for 20 to 25 minutes or until golden brown. Serve with Orange Zest Butter. Decrease the size of the dough balls for smaller rolls.

Makes (about) 1 dozen rolls

Orange Zest Butter

Combine 2 cups (4 sticks) butter, 3 tablespoons confectioners' sugar, $^1/_4$ cup orange juice, 1 tablespoon Cognac and the grated zest of 1 orange in a 2-quart saucepan. Bring to a boil, stirring frequently. Remove from the heat. Let stand for 5 minutes or until cool. Fill a plastic squeeze bottle with the melted butter and squirt into your favorite butter molds. Chill for 15 minutes or until firm. If you prefer not to use butter molds, allow the butter to harden in a small bowl or shape the butter mixture into logs. You may store the butter in the refrigerator for up to 3 months. Microwave for a few seconds to soften.

Mother's Day

Ana Jarvis of Philadelphia began a campaign to establish a national day for mothers in 1907. Ms. Jarvis persuaded her mother's church in Grafton, West Virginia, to celebrate Mother's Day on the second anniversary of her mother's death—the second Sunday in May. By the next year, Mother's Day was also celebrated in Philadelphia. Ms. Jarvis and her supporters began to write to ministers, businessmen, and politicians in their effort to establish a national day. The day was being celebrated in almost every state by 1911, and President Woodrow Wilson made the day official in 1914.

Herb and Buttermilk Breadsticks

$^1/_3$ cup warm (105 to 115 degrees) water
1 tablespoon honey
1 envelope dry yeast
1 cup buttermilk
3 tablespoons vegetable oil
1 teaspoon salt
1 teaspoon minced fresh parsley, or $^1/_2$ teaspoon dried parsley, crumbled
1 teaspoon minced fresh oregano, or $^1/_2$ teaspoon dried oregano, crumbled
1 teaspoon minced fresh basil, or $^1/_2$ teaspoon dried basil, crumbled
$3^1/_4$ cups unbleached flour
1 teaspoon olive oil
$^1/_2$ cup cornmeal
6 medium garlic cloves, crushed
$^1/_3$ cup olive oil
coarse salt to taste

Combine the warm water and honey in a medium bowl. Sprinkle the yeast over the top of the honey mixture and stir until dissolved. Let stand for 5 minutes. Stir in the buttermilk, vegetable oil, 1 teaspoon salt, parsley, oregano and basil. Add enough of the flour $^1/_2$ cup at a time to make a soft dough and mix well. Knead the dough on a lightly floured surface for 5 minutes or until smooth and elastic. Coat the bottom and side of a large bowl with 1 teaspoon olive oil. Add the dough, turning to coat the surface. Chill, covered, for 2 hours or until doubled in bulk.

Line 3 large baking sheets with baking parchment and sprinkle evenly with the cornmeal. Punch the dough down. Knead the dough on a lightly floured surface until smooth. Divide the dough into 24 equal portions.

Roll each portion between your palm and work surface to form a 10-inch-long rope. Arrange $1^1/_2$ inches apart on the prepared baking sheets. Mix the garlic and $^1/_3$ cup olive oil in a bowl. Brush the garlic mixture over the breadsticks and sprinkle lightly with coarse salt. Bake at 400 degrees for 15 to 20 minutes or until golden brown. Cool slightly on a wire rack. Serve warm or at room temperature.

Makes 2 dozen breadsticks

Chocolate Silk

6 tablespoons sugar
3 eggs
1 tablespoon rum
1/8 teaspoon salt
18 ounces semisweet chocolate chips (preferably
    Ghirardelli double chocolate chips)
2 1/4 cups half-and-half
Raspberry Coulis (this page)
Almond Cream (this page)
fresh raspberries
fresh mint leaves
sliced almonds

Combine the sugar, eggs, rum and salt in a blender.
Process for 10 seconds. Add the chocolate chips. Scald the
half-and-half in a saucepan. Add the hot half-and-half to
the blender. Let stand for 1 minute.

Holding a hand firmly on the blender lid, process on
high for 1 minute. Remove the lid carefully to allow the
steam to escape. Let stand for 5 to 10 minutes. Pour into a
large glass serving bowl. Chill, covered, for 4 to 10 hours.
You may prepare up to 2 days in advance and store, covered,
in the refrigerator.

Spoon onto dessert plates. Drizzle the Raspberry
Coulis around the chocolate. Top each serving with a
dollop of Almond Cream. Garnish with fresh raspberries,
mint leaves and almonds.

To avoid uncooked eggs that may carry salmonella,
we suggest using an equivalent amount of pasteurized egg
substitute.

Serves 10 to 12

Raspberry Coulis

1 pint raspberries
1/2 cup sugar
1/2 cup water
2 tablespoons Grand Marnier

Bring the raspberries, sugar, water and Grand Marnier to
a boil in a medium saucepan. Boil for 1 minute, stirring
occasionally. Process in a blender until puréed. Remove
the lid carefully to allow the steam to escape. Strain several
times through a fine sieve into a bowl, discarding the seeds.
Chill, covered, for 4 to 10 hours. You may prepare up to
2 days in advance and store, covered, in the refrigerator.

Serves 10 to 12

Almond Cream

1 cup heavy whipping cream
1 to 2 tablespoons sugar, or to taste
1/2 teaspoon almond extract

Beat the whipping cream in a mixing bowl until soft
peaks form. Add the sugar and flavoring and mix until
blended. Cover and chill if not using immediately. You
may prepare several hours in advance and store, covered,
in the refrigerator. Rewhip if necessary.

Serves 10 to 12

Milk Chocolate Candy Bar Cake

1 (2-layer) package Swiss chocolate cake mix
8 ounces cream cheese, softened
1 cup confectioners' sugar
½ cup sugar
10 (1.5-ounce) milk chocolate candy bars with almonds
12 ounces frozen whipped topping, thawed

Prepare the cake using package directions in 3 greased and floured 8-inch cake pans. Bake at 325 degrees for 20 to 25 minutes or until a wooden pick inserted in the center comes out clean. Cool in pans on a wire rack for 10 minutes. Invert onto a wire rack to cool completely.

Beat the cream cheese, confectioners' sugar and sugar in a mixing bowl at medium speed until creamy, scraping the bowl occasionally. Chop finely 8 of the candy bars. Fold the cream cheese mixture and chopped candy bars into the whipped topping in a bowl.

Spread the cream cheese mixture between the layers and over the top and side of the cake. Chop finely the remaining 2 candy bars. Sprinkle ½ of the chopped candy over the top of the cake. Pat the remaining candy along the bottom edge of the cake.

Serves 12

Apricot Macaroon Crust

¼ cup packed dried apricots
¼ cup water
⅓ cup sugar
2 egg whites
2¼ cups shredded unsweetened coconut, toasted

Bring the apricots and water to a boil in a small heavy saucepan. Remove from the heat. Let stand, covered, for 30 minutes or until the apricots are soft. Drain and pat dry with paper towels.

Combine the apricots, sugar and egg whites in a food processor. Process until the mixture is thick and fluffy and the apricots are minced, scraping the bowl occasionally. Add ½ cup of the coconut. Process until the coconut is minced. Spoon the apricot mixture into a bowl. Stir in the remaining coconut. Freeze, covered, for 20 minutes or until firm.

Wrap heavy-duty foil around the bottom and side of a 9-inch springform pan with 2¾-inch side. Spoon the coconut mixture into the prepared pan. Wrap plastic wrap around fingers and press the coconut mixture over the bottom and 2 inches up the side of the pan. Bake at 350 degrees for 15 minutes or until light brown. Remove the pan to a wire rack.

Makes 1 crust

Fresh Strawberry Cheesecake

Strawberry Sauce

3 pints fresh strawberries, cut into halves

1/2 cup sugar

2 tablespoons fresh lemon juice

Filling and Garnishes

24 ounces cream cheese, softened

1 1/4 cups sugar

1/4 teaspoon salt

3/4 cup sour cream

1 tablespoon dark rum

1 tablespoon fresh lemon juice

2 teaspoons vanilla extract

3 eggs

Apricot Macaroon Crust (page 150)

1 1/2 pints fresh strawberries with tops, cut lengthwise into halves

sprigs of fresh mint

For the sauce, bring the strawberries, sugar and lemon juice to a boil in a heavy saucepan over medium heat. Reduce the heat to medium-low. Simmer for 1 hour or until the mixture is of a syrupy consistency, stirring occasionally. Let stand until cool. Chill, covered, for up to 2 days.

For the filling, beat the cream cheese, sugar and salt in a mixing bowl until smooth, scraping the bowl occasionally. Add the rum, lemon juice and vanilla and beat until blended. Add the eggs 1 at a time, beating well after each addition. Spoon the cream cheese mixture into the Apricot Macaroon Crust in the springform pan.

Bake at 350 degrees for 1 hour or until brown, puffed and firm in the center. Cool on a wire rack for 10 minutes. Run a sharp knife around the edge of the pan to loosen the crust. Let stand until completely cool. Chill, covered, for 8 to 10 hours.

To serve, run a sharp knife around the side of the pan to loosen the crust and remove the side of the pan. Arrange the strawberry halves cut side down with green tops pointing toward the outside around the outer edge of the cheesecake. Garnish each slice with a sprig of fresh mint and serve with the sauce.

Serves 10 to 12

Cookie Magic

Dainty cookies can be used for so many occasions and add a special touch that children and adults alike will love. They can be served for bridal showers or luncheons and small afternoon wedding receptions as well as tea parties and open houses. You can pack them into a pretty tin for a special gift for Mother, an anniversary gift, or a special treat to send off with newly married couples on their special trip.

Sunny Day Punch

Combine 3 cups unsweetened pineapple juice, one 6-ounce can thawed frozen orange juice concentrate, one 6-ounce can thawed frozen lemonade concentrate and 4 cups water in a large container and mix well. Chill in the refrigerator. Pour into a punch bowl and pour 2 bottles chilled club soda or Champagne gently down the side of the bowl. Garnish with orange slices, lemon slices and mint leaves.

MENU

Puss in Boots

Every couple awaits the arrival of a new baby with a glow of anticipation. All of us wish to celebrate the birth of a child with warm wishes for the happy parents. To help make this time unforgettable, we hosted a luncheon to show our support for the growing family. We decorated with pastels, from the punch to the pillows, to carry the theme.

Tropical Fruit Sun Tea

2 ounces fruit tea leaves
zest of 1 lemon
zest of 1 orange
2 cinnamon sticks

2 large pieces candied ginger
5 quarts spring water
sliced fresh fruit

Combine the tea leaves, lemon zest, orange zest, cinnamon sticks and ginger in cheesecloth and secure with kitchen twine. Pour the spring water into a large container and add the tea bag. Steep in the sun for several hours. Pour the tea over ice in glasses. Garnish each serving with sliced fresh fruit.

Makes 20 servings

Walnut and Brie Tartlets with Grape Salsa

1 cup seedless red grapes,
    cut into halves
1/4 teaspoon salt
9 tablespoons finely chopped green
    onion tops
1 tablespoon balsamic vinegar
2 teaspoons walnut oil

1/4 teaspoon chopped fresh rosemary
1/4 teaspoon finely minced garlic
1/8 teaspoon pepper
48 miniature phyllo shells
1/2 cup chopped walnuts, toasted
8 ounces Brie cheese, rind removed

Process the grapes and salt in a food processor until coarsely chopped. Drain the grape mixture in a colander for 10 minutes. Pat dry with a paper towel. Combine the green onion tops, vinegar, walnut oil, rosemary, garlic and pepper in a bowl and mix well. Stir in the grapes.

Arrange the phyllo shells on a baking sheet. Fill each with 1/2 teaspoon of the walnuts, 1/2 teaspoon of the Brie and 1/2 teaspoon of the grape mixture. Bake at 350 degrees for 5 minutes or until the cheese melts. Serve immediately.

Makes 4 dozen tartlets

The Development of Bay County

The 1970s brought a huge home-building boom to Panama City, and subdivisions began sprouting up all over Bay County. One very popular section was Pretty Bayou in North Bay County; others were North Shore and Baywood Shores. A new trend of "moving into the country" also began with areas of Bayou George and Deer Point Lake being developed. In addition to other subdivisions, two condominiums began going up on the beach.

Panama City Beach was established on August 12, 1970, when numerous small communities and unincorporated beach areas were united. The municipalities of Long Beach Resort, Edgewater Gulf Beach, Old Panama City Beach, and West Panama City Beach then became one municipality, a merger thought to benefit future promotion of the beach. Condominiums continued to take shape, and tourism was on its way to becoming the thriving industry it is today.

Savory Ham Cheesecake

Parmesan Crust

2 cups (8 ounces) grated Parmesan cheese
2 cups fresh bread crumbs
1 cup (2 sticks) unsalted butter, softened

Filling

2 cups chopped onions
2 cups chopped green, red and yellow bell peppers
2 tablespoons olive oil
2 teaspoons salt
pepper to taste
3 1/2 pounds cream cheese, softened
8 eggs
1 cup heavy cream
2 cups (8 ounces) shredded smoked Gouda cheese
2 pounds cooked ham, chopped
Green Onion Coulis (this page)

For the crust, combine the cheese, bread crumbs and unsalted butter in a bowl and mix well. Pat the crumb mixture over the bottom of two 9-inch springform pans.

For the filling, sauté the onions and bell peppers in the olive oil in a skillet until the vegetables are tender. Season with the salt and pepper. Beat the cream cheese and eggs in a mixing bowl for 4 minutes or until light and fluffy, scraping the bowl occasionally. Stir in the heavy cream and Gouda cheese. Add the sautéed vegetables and ham and mix well.

Spoon the cream cheese mixture evenly into the 2 prepared pans. Bake at 350 degrees for 1 1/4 hours or until set. Cool on a wire rack. Remove the sides of the pans and slice with a warm knife. Top each serving with Green Onion Coulis.

Serves 24

Green Onion Coulis

1 1/2 cups chopped green onions
1 cup chopped fresh parsley
2 tablespoons chopped garlic
2 tablespoons chopped shallots
1 cup sour cream
1/4 cup fresh lemon juice
1/2 teaspoon salt
1/2 teaspoon pepper
3 cups extra-virgin olive oil

Process the green onions, parsley garlic and shallots in a food processor until puréed. Add the sour cream, lemon juice, salt and pepper. Process until combined. Add the olive oil gradually, processing constantly until incorporated.

Serves 24

Pickled Radish and Cucumber Triangles

3/4 cup rice wine vinegar
1 cup thinly sliced radishes
2/3 cup goat cheese, softened
1/3 cup cream cheese, softened
1/8 teaspoon white pepper
12 slices buttermilk bread or white bread, crusts trimmed
1 English seedless cucumber, thinly sliced and cut into
    halves

Pour the vinegar over the radishes in a bowl. Marinate, covered, in the refrigerator for 1 to 10 hours; drain. Pat dry with paper towels. Combine the goat cheese, cream cheese and white pepper in a bowl and mix well.

Spread about 1 tablespoon of the cheese mixture on each slice of bread. Cut each slice into 4 triangles. Fan 3 cucumber slices on each triangle. Fold the radish slices into halves and arrange on top of the cucumber slices.

Makes 4 dozen triangles

Asparagus and Cheese Pie

1 1/2 pounds fresh asparagus spears
2 refrigerator pie pastries
1 tablespoon butter or margarine
1 large onion, finely minced
2 1/2 tablespoons Dijon mustard
8 ounces Monterey Jack cheese blend, shredded
1 1/2 cups half-and-half
2 eggs
1/2 teaspoon salt
1/2 teaspoon freshly grated pepper

Snap off the woody ends of the asparagus spears. Blanch the asparagus in boiling water in a saucepan for 30 seconds. Drain and plunge into a bowl of ice water to stop the cooking process; drain. Reserve 9 of the spears. Coarsely chop the remaining spears. Unfold the pie pastries and stack on a lightly floured surface. Roll the pastries into a 14-inch circle. Fit the pastry into a 9 1/2-inch pie plate, trimming the excess dough. Line the pastry with foil and fill with pie weights or dried beans. Arrange the pie plate on a baking sheet. Bake at 425 degrees for 10 minutes; remove the weights and foil. Bake for 4 minutes longer. Cool on a wire rack. Reduce the oven temperature to 375 degrees.

Heat the butter in a skillet over medium-high heat. Sauté the onion in the butter for 5 minutes or until tender. Brush the bottom and side of the baked layer with the Dijon mustard. Layer 1/2 of the cheese, chopped asparagus, onion and remaining cheese in the pastry-lined pie plate. Arrange the reserved spears in a spoke pattern over the top. Whisk the half-and-half, eggs, salt and pepper in a bowl until blended. Pour the egg mixture over the prepared layers. Bake for 25 minutes or until set and golden brown. Let stand for 15 minutes before serving.

Serves 6 to 8

Not-Your-Mother's Baby Shower

If you would like to give a baby shower that is just a little different, you might try one of the following themes:

- *A Baby Safety Shower, with presents of a nature to make baby safe and the house and car safe for baby*
- *A Mom's Shower, with gifts to pamper the expectant or new mom*
- *A Couples Shower, which both the expectant couple and friend of both attend*
- *A Nursery Theme Shower, based on the theme of a nursery rhyme*
- *A Dad's Shower, with gifts for dad, such as Tylenol, coffee, etc.*

Seafood Crepes Mornay

8 ounces small shrimp, peeled and deveined
1 tablespoon butter
1 tablespoon olive oil
salt and pepper to taste
herbes de Provence to taste
8 ounces lump crab meat, shells and cartilage removed
1/4 cup madeira
5 tablespoons butter
5 tablespoons flour
1 cup whipping cream
1 cup half-and-half
1/3 cup shredded Gruyère cheese
1/4 cup dry white wine
1/2 teaspoon Worcestershire sauce
nutmeg to taste
1 teaspoon tomato paste
12 crepes
1 bunch fresh asparagus spears, blanched and drained
1/2 cup slivered almonds, toasted

Reserve a few of the shrimp for the garnish. Heat 2 tablespoons butter and olive oil in a medium sauté pan over medium-high heat. Add the remaining shrimp, salt, pepper and herbes de Provence and mix well. Stir in the crab meat. Cook for 4 minutes or until the shrimp turn pink, stirring frequently. Stir in the madeira. Let stand until cool.

Heat 5 tablespoons butter in a 2 1/2-quart saucepan over medium heat. Whisk in the flour until blended. Cook until a soft paste forms, whisking constantly. Add the whipping cream and half-and-half gradually, whisking constantly until smooth. Cook until slightly thickened, stirring frequently. Stir in the cheese. Add the white wine and mix well. Cook until thickened, stirring frequently. Season with salt, pepper, Worcestershire sauce and generously with nutmeg. Combine 1/3 cup of the sauce with the tomato paste in a bowl and mix well. Keep both sauces warm.

To serve, layer each crepe with 2 asparagus spears, some of the shrimp mixture and some of the mornay sauce and roll to enclose the filling. Arrange the crepes in a baking dish and warm to serving temperature in a 350-degree oven. Remove to a serving platter and drizzle with the tomato paste sauce. Sprinkle with the almonds and reserved shrimp.

Serves 6

Exotic Chicken Salad

3 cups mayonnaise
2 tablespoons soy sauce
2 tablespoons lemon juice
1 tablespoon curry powder
2 quarts chopped cooked chicken
1 (20-ounce) can water chestnuts, drained and chopped
2 pounds seedless green grapes, whole or cut into halves
2 cups sliced celery
1½ cups slivered almonds, toasted
1 (16-ounce) can pineapple chunks, drained
1½ cups pecan pieces, toasted

Combine the mayonnaise, soy sauce, lemon juice and curry powder in a bowl and mix well. Stir in the chicken. Chill, covered, for 8 to 10 hours. Add the water chestnuts, grapes, celery, almonds, pineapple and pecans just before serving and mix well. Spoon the chicken salad onto a lettuce-lined serving platter.

Serves 20

Tea Rice Salad with Shrimp

Lemon Vinaigrette
3 tablespoons vegetable oil
3 tablespoons fresh lemon juice
2 tablespoons rice vinegar
1 teaspoon sesame oil
1 teaspoon soy sauce
¼ to ½ teaspoon hot sauce, or to taste

Salad
1½ cups water
2 regular bags black tea
¾ cup white uncooked rice
¼ teaspoon each salt and sugar
4 ounces snow peas, trimmed and strings removed
8 to 16 ounces peeled steamed small shrimp
1 small cucumber, cut lengthwise into quarters and cut into ¼-inch slices
1 carrot, coarsely grated
1 green onion, thinly sliced

For the vinaigrette, whisk the oil, lemon juice, vinegar, sesame oil, soy sauce and hot sauce in a bowl until blended.

For the salad, bring the water to a boil in a medium saucepan. Remove from the heat. Add the tea bags to the boiling water. Steep for 5 minutes; discard the tea bags. Bring the tea to a boil. Stir in the rice, salt and sugar. Cook, covered, for 20 minutes.

Cut the snow peas diagonally into thirds. Blanch the snow peas in boiling water in a saucepan for 30 seconds; drain. Combine the rice, snow peas, shrimp, cucumber, carrot and green onion in a bowl and mix gently. Add the vinaigrette and toss to coat. Chill, covered, until serving time.

Serves 4

Useful Baby Presents

Modern mothers appreciate useful baby presents as well as the traditional keepsake presents, especially for second and third babies. Good friends can sign up for a meal every few days for a couple of weeks to ensure that all food offerings do not arrive on the same day. Diapers are always welcome, and in different sizes. Free gifts, such as a coupon book for free babysitting and housecleaning, might just be the most welcome presents for the busy new mom. Since babies outgrow clothing well before it gets much wear, gifts of used clothing from other moms is an inexpensive way to share in the happy time.

Spinach Pie

1 refrigerator pie pastry
1 (10-ounce) package frozen chopped spinach, thawed and drained
2 tablespoons butter or margarine
1 small onion, chopped
1 small red bell pepper, chopped
2 ribs celery, chopped
4 garlic cloves, minced
2 tablespoons flour
4 ounces feta cheese, crumbled
3 eggs, lightly beaten
1 tablespoon parsley flakes
1/2 teaspoon dill weed
1/2 teaspoon salt
1/2 teaspoon pepper
1/4 cup grated Parmesan cheese

Fit the pastry into a 9-inch pie plate and crimp the edge. Bake at 400 degrees for 7 minutes. Remove to a wire rack to cool. Decrease the oven temperature to 350 degrees.

Press excess moisture from the spinach between layers of paper towels. Heat the butter in a large skillet over medium heat. Add the onion, bell pepper, celery and garlic and mix well. Sauté for 5 minutes or until the vegetables are tender. Stir in the flour. Cook for 1 minute, stirring constantly. Remove from the heat. Stir in the spinach, feta cheese, eggs, parsley flakes, dill weed, salt and pepper.

Spoon the spinach mixture into the prepared pie plate. Bake for 25 minutes. Sprinkle with the Parmesan cheese. Bake for 5 minutes longer or until set. Let stand for 10 minutes before serving.

Serves 8

Miniature Cheese Biscuits

2 cups self-rising flour
1 teaspoon baking powder
1 teaspoon sugar
¹/₃ cup shortening
³/₄ cup (3 ounces) shredded Cheddar cheese
1 cup buttermilk

Combine the self-rising flour, baking powder and sugar in a bowl and mix well. Cut in the shortening until crumbly. Stir in the cheese. Add the buttermilk and stir just until moistened.

Drop the dough by teaspoonfuls onto a greased baking sheet. Bake at 425 degrees for 12 to 15 minutes or until light brown. Serve immediately.

Makes 12 to 14 miniature biscuits

Sweet Bow Tie Rolls

2 tablespoons dry yeast
2 cups warm water
3 cups bread flour
¹/₂ cup sugar
¹/₃ cup shortening
1 teaspoon salt
1 egg, lightly beaten
2 cups bread flour
1 tablespoon water
1 egg

Dissolve the yeast in the warm water. Let stand for 5 to 10 minutes or until bubbly. Combine 3 cups flour, sugar, shortening and salt in a food processor and pulse several times. Process until blended. Remove the flour mixture to a large bowl. Mix the yeast mixture, 1 egg and 2 cups flour in a bowl and mix well. Add the yeast mixture to the shortening mixture and mix until a soft dough forms. Shape the dough into a ball. Let stand, covered with a tea towel, until doubled in bulk.

Divide the dough into 4 equal balls. Working with 1 ball at a time, cut each into 8 portions. Roll each portion into a 5- to 6-inch long rope. Shape each into a bow tie on a baking sheet. Repeat the process with the remaining dough balls. Let rise until doubled in bulk. Whisk the water and 1 egg in a bowl until blended. Brush the tops of the rolls with the egg wash. Bake at 350 degrees for 10 to 12 minutes or until golden brown.

Makes 32 rolls

Lemon Sorbet with Blackberry Sauce

Lemon Sorbet

3 cups sugar

1 cup fresh lemon juice or lime juice

1 teaspoon lemon extract

grated zest of 4 lemons or limes

¹/₂ gallon 2% milk, chilled

Blackberry Sauce

1 pound frozen unsweetened blackberries

5 tablespoons sugar

For the sorbet, combine the sugar, lemon juice, flavoring and lemon zest in a heavy saucepan and mix well. Cook over medium heat until the sugar dissolves, stirring constantly. Let stand until cool. Pour the lemon mixture into an ice cream freezer container. Stir in the 2% milk. Freeze using manufacturer's directions. Spoon the ice cream into a freezer container. Freeze, covered, until firm.

For the sauce, place the frozen blackberries in a large bowl. Sprinkle with the sugar. Let stand for 1 hour or just until the blackberries thaw but are still cold. Coarsely mash the blackberries with a fork and mix well. Chill, covered, in the refrigerator. Serve with the sorbet.

Serves 10

Lemon Butter Cookies

³/₄ cup (1¹/₂ sticks) butter, softened

²/₃ cup sugar

2 tablespoons finely grated lemon zest

1 egg

1 teaspoon vanilla extract

¹/₄ teaspoon salt

2 cups flour

confectioners' sugar to taste

Beat the butter in a mixing bowl until light and fluffy. Add the sugar and lemon zest and beat until combined. Beat in the egg, vanilla and salt. Add the flour 1 cup at a time, beating just until blended after each addition.

Shape the dough into a ball and divide the ball into 2 equal portions. Flatten each portion into a disk. Chill, wrapped in plastic wrap, for 30 minutes or until firm. Roll each disk ¹/₄ inch thick on a lightly floured surface and cut with a 2¹/₂- to 2³/₄-inch cookie cutter. Arrange the rounds 2 inches apart on an ungreased cookie sheet.

Bake at 375 degrees for 8 minutes or until golden brown around the edges. Cool on the cookie sheet for 2 minutes. Remove to a wire rack to cool completely. Sift confectioners' sugar over the top of each cookie.

Makes 3 dozen cookies

Lemon and Orange Tart

1½ cups sugar
½ cup orange juice
½ cup lemon juice
¼ cup heavy cream
4 eggs
grated zest of 1 orange
grated zest of 1 lemon
Easy Tart Shell (this page)
fresh raspberries, strawberries or blueberries
whipped cream

Combine the sugar, orange juice, lemon juice, heavy cream, eggs, orange zest and lemon zest in a bowl with a pouring spout and whisk until combined. Chill, covered, in the refrigerator.

Place the prepared tart shell on a baking sheet and return the baking sheet to the oven with the oven rack extended out. Whisk the chilled filling and pour into the tart pan. Bake for 25 to 30 minutes or until the tart is barely set; do not overbake. Serve at room temperature or chilled, garnished with fresh berries and whipped cream.

Makes 1 tart

Easy Tart Shell

1¼ cups plus 2 tablespoons flour
1 tablespoon plus 1 teaspoon sugar
⅛ teaspoon salt
½ cup (1 stick) chilled butter, cut into pieces
1 egg yolk
1 tablespoon milk
1 egg white, lightly beaten

Combine the flour, sugar and salt in a food processor. Pulse until combined. Add the butter. Pulse at 1 second intervals until crumbly. Whisk the egg yolk and milk lightly in a bowl. Add the egg yolk mixture to the flour mixture. Pulse until combined; the mixture will be crumbly.

Press the crumb mixture over the bottom and up the side of a 10½-inch tart pan. Line the pastry with foil and fill with pie weights or dried beans. Bake at 350 degrees for 20 minutes; remove the foil and weights. Bake for 10 minutes longer or until golden brown. Brush immediately with the egg white to seal.

Dark-colored pans require less baking time. Be sure to check crusts earlier if using a dark-colored pan.

Makes 1 tart shell

Beach Buddies

MENU

Anderson's Pier

Not everyone can pack a boat with a complete table setup and a dinner for six, but you can use your imagination to come as close as possible. We found a deserted dock and did just that. Decorate with natural touches such as tin buckets and vases full of sand and shells. Prepare food ahead of time to best enjoy the beauty of the setting and the camaraderie of friends.

Electric Lemonade

2 cups sugar
2 cups water
1 cup fresh lemon juice
2 large sprigs of mint, finely chopped

8 ounces lemon-flavor vodka
1 cup lemon-lime soda
1 tablespoon grated lemon zest
sprigs of fresh mint

Bring the sugar and water to a boil in a saucepan, stirring occasionally. Boil for 3 minutes. Let stand until cool. Combine 1 cup of the cooled syrup, lemon juice and half the chopped mint in a bowl and mix well. Pour into an ice cube tray. Freeze for 1 hour.

Combine the frozen cubes, vodka, soda and remaining chopped mint in a blender. Process until blended. Pour into chilled glasses. Garnish with the lemon zest and sprigs of mint.

Serves 4 to 6

Banana Punch

7 cups water
1/2 cup sugar
5 bananas, mashed
1 (6-ounce) can frozen orange juice
    concentrate, thawed

1 (6-ounce) can frozen lemonade
    concentrate, thawed
1 (46-ounce) can pineapple juice
1 quart ginger ale
vodka (optional)

Combine the water and sugar in a saucepan and boil for 5 minutes. Cool to room temperature. Add the bananas, orange juice concentrate, lemonade concentrate and pineapple juice. Pour into a freezer container and freeze until solid.

Remove from the freezer 2 to 3 hours before serving and let stand until slushy. Pour into a large punch bowl and add the ginger ale and vodka. Ladle into punch cups.

Serves 20 to 25

Shell Island

In the early 1900s, shipping in St. Andrews Bay was on the rise. By 1934, the Corps of Engineers was charged with dredging a new pass into St. Andrews Bay, thereby creating a new island. This island became known as Shell Island after the "shelling parties" hosted by a local Captain operating tours to the island. Even prior to becoming an island, the beaches of this area were popular with locals and tourists alike. As early as 1908 and on through the late 1920s, the Gulf Beach Pavilion, located on what is now the east end of Shell Island, offered beachgoers an amusement center with bathing attire rentals, bathhouses, and refreshments. Eventually, amenities also included a second floor for dancing and roller skating....The Pavilion is no longer on Shell Island. However, as in the past, visitors to the island today primarily disembark from anchored boats on the Bay side of the island and walk the short distance across the island to the Gulf side to enjoy the real Shell Island experience—warm sunshine, beautiful emerald waters, and a long stretch of white sandy beaches.

—Along the Bay, Marlene Womak, 1994

Puff Pastry Shells

Fold 2 sheets of puff pastry into thirds and roll each sheet into a $^1/_8$-inch-thick rectangle on a lightly floured surface. Place on a baking sheet and cover with waxed paper. Freeze for 15 minutes or until firm. Cut the pastry into eight $4^1/_2×6$-inch rectangles. Arrange 1 inch apart on a baking sheet. Brush the tops with a lightly beaten egg, being careful not to allow the egg to drip down the sides of the rectangles. Chill for 20 minutes. Brush the tops again with the egg. Cut a $^1/_2$-inch border around each rectangle, cutting about halfway through the pastry. Bake at 425 degrees for 15 minutes or until the pastry is puffed and golden brown. Remove to a wire rack immediately. Lift out the center of each rectangle and remove any moist dough inside to form pastry boxes, reserving the tops.

Seafood Treasure Chests

2 tablespoons unsalted butter
4 ounces mushrooms, sliced
1 (8-ounce) bottle clam juice
1 cup dry white wine
1 small onion, minced
2 tablespoons minced fresh parsley
$^1/_2$ teaspoon thyme
2 cups heavy cream
1 large carrot, cut into 2-inch strips and blanched
2 ounces fresh snow peas, julienned lengthwise and blanched
1 teaspoon cornstarch
2 tablespoons cold water
$^1/_8$ teaspoon freshly ground pepper
2 tablespoons unsalted butter
$1^1/_2$ pounds small shrimp, peeled and deveined
$1^1/_2$ pounds bay scallops
$^1/_4$ teaspoon salt
$^1/_8$ teaspoon pepper
1 medium tomato, seeded and chopped
8 Puff Pastry Shells (this page)

Heat 2 tablespoons unsalted butter in a large skillet over medium heat. Cook the mushrooms in the butter for 5 minutes, stirring frequently. Stir in the clam juice, wine, onion, parsley and thyme. Cook for 5 minutes, stirring frequently. Remove from the heat. Strain through a fine sieve into a skillet, discarding the solids. Bring to a boil over high heat. Boil for 8 minutes or until reduced to 1 cup. Stir in the heavy cream. Bring to a boil. Boil for 10 minutes or until reduced to 2 cups, stirring occasionally. Remove from the heat. Cover to keep warm.

Wrap the carrot and snow peas in foil and place on a baking sheet. Arrange the puff pastry boxes and lids on the baking sheet. Bake at 300 degrees for 10 minutes or until heated through. Bring the cream sauce to a simmer over medium heat. Dissolve the cornstarch in the cold water in a small bowl and mix well. Whisk into the sauce. Cook for 1 minute or until thickened, stirring constantly. Season with $^1/_8$ teaspoon pepper. Keep warm over low heat. Heat 2 tablespoons unsalted butter over medium-high heat until the foam subsides. Stir in the shrimp and scallops. Cook for 2 minutes or until the shrimp turn pink and the scallops are tender, stirring frequently. Season with the salt and $^1/_8$ teaspoon pepper; drain.

To serve, place 1 warm Puff Pastry Shell on each of 8 heated appetizer plates or salad plates. Spoon the shrimp mixture evenly into the pastry chests. Sprinkle the carrot mixture over the shrimp mixture and top with the tomato. Replace the lids and serve immediately.

Serves 8

Island Salad

Balsamic Vinaigrette

1/4 medium Vidalia onion or any sweet onion, coarsely
    chopped
1 large shallot, coarsely chopped
3 tablespoons balsamic vinegar
1 1/2 tablespoons soy sauce
1 teaspoon minced fresh gingerroot
3 tablespoons extra-virgin olive oil
1 tablespoon finely chopped fresh cilantro
salt and freshly ground pepper to taste

Salad

16 ounces mixed baby salad greens or mesclun salad mix
1 Hass avocado, thinly sliced
1/2 mango, thinly sliced
1 red bell pepper, thinly sliced
1/2 medium cucumber, peeled and thinly sliced

For the vinaigrette, combine the onion, shallot, vinegar,
soy sauce and gingerroot in a blender. Process until
puréed. Add the olive oil and process until smooth. Pour
the vinaigrette into a small bowl. Stir in the cilantro, salt
and pepper.

    For the salad, toss the salad greens, avocado,
mango, bell pepper and cucumber in a large salad bowl.
Add the vinaigrette and mix gently. Mound the salad on
individual salad plates. Serve immediately.

    Serves 6

Portobello and Red Pepper Salad

Rosemary Dressing

1 tablespoon red wine vinegar
1 tablespoon chopped fresh rosemary
1 garlic clove
1/3 cup olive oil
salt and pepper to taste

Salad

7 large portobello mushrooms, stemmed (about 2 pounds)
1/3 cup olive oil
2 large red bell peppers
salt and pepper to taste
1 (4- to 5-ounce) package mixed baby salad greens

For the dressing, combine the vinegar, rosemary and
garlic in a food processor. Process until blended. Add the
olive oil gradually, processing constantly until
incorporated. Season with salt and pepper.

    For the salad, brush both sides of the mushrooms
with the olive oil. Arrange the mushrooms and whole
bell peppers on a grill rack over medium heat. Grill the
mushrooms for 20 minutes or until tender, turning
occasionally. Grill the bell peppers for 25 minutes or until
charred and blistered on all sides, turning occasionally.
Place the bell peppers in a brown paper bag. Let stand
for 10 minutes. Peel, seed and cut the bell peppers into
1/2-inch strips. Cut the mushrooms into 1/2-inch strips.
Sprinkle the mushrooms and bell peppers with salt
and pepper.

    To serve, arrange the salad greens on a large platter.
Top with the mushroom strips and bell pepper strips and
drizzle with the dressing. Serve immediately.

    Serves 8

Rosemary-Grilled Flank Steak

3 cups dry red wine
1 small onion, coarsely chopped
3 tablespoons olive oil
4 sprigs each of fresh rosemary and thyme
2 bay leaves
4 garlic cloves, coarsely chopped
1 (2-pound) flank steak
salt and freshly ground pepper to taste

Combine the wine, onion, olive oil, rosemary, thyme, bay leaves and garlic in a shallow dish and mix well. Add the steak and turn to coat. Marinate, covered, in the refrigerator for 4 to 10 hours, turning occasionally.

Drain the steak, discarding the marinade. Sprinkle with salt and pepper. Grill over hot coals for 6 to 7 minutes per side or to the desired degree of doneness. Let stand for 5 minutes. Cut across the grain into thin slices.

Serves 4

Texas-Style Steak on Toast

1 teaspoon chili powder
1/2 teaspoon dark brown sugar
1 1/2 pounds (1-inch-thick) top sirloin steak, trimmed
salt and pepper to taste
1 cup coarsely chopped seeded fresh tomatoes
1/2 cup pitted kalamata olives
5 tablespoons plus 2 teaspoons extra-virgin olive oil
2 teaspoons red wine vinegar
2 tablespoons minced red onion
8 (1-inch-thick) slices French bread
2 bunches watercress, thick stems removed

Mix the chili powder and brown sugar in a small bowl. Rub the chili powder mixture over both sides of the steak. Sprinkle with salt and pepper. Combine the tomatoes, olives, 2 tablespoons of the olive oil and vinegar in a food processor. Pulse just until the olives are coarsely chopped. Remove the tomato mixture to a bowl. Stir in the onion. Season with salt and pepper. You may prepare the steak as well as the tomato relish up to 6 hours in advance and store, covered, in the refrigerator.

Heat 2 teaspoons of the olive oil in a large heavy skillet over medium-high heat. Cook the steak in the hot olive oil for 3 minutes per side for medium-rare or to the desired degree of doneness. Remove the steak to a platter. Let stand for 5 minutes. Wipe the skillet with a paper towel. Brush 1 side of each bread slice with the remaining 3 tablespoons olive oil. Heat the skillet over medium heat. Add the bread oil side down to the skillet. Cook for 2 minutes per side or until golden brown.

Cut the steak across the grain into 1/4-inch slices. Spread the tomato relish generously over the oiled side of 4 of the toasted bread slices. Layer with the watercress, steak, tomato relish and remaining toasted bread slices.

Serves 4

Greek Isle Chicken Packets

1 (10-ounce) package frozen chopped spinach, thawed and drained
4 (6-ounce) boneless skinless chicken breasts
2 tablespoons extra-virgin olive oil
2 teaspoons Italian seasoning
1 teaspoon salt
1/2 teaspoon pepper
1 cup thinly sliced yellow onion
1 cup chopped drained oil-pack sun-dried tomatoes
1/2 cup dry white wine
1/2 cup kalamata olives, pitted and cut into halves
2 tablespoons minced garlic
2 tablespoons chopped fresh basil
1/2 teaspoon minced fresh thyme
1/2 teaspoon salt
1/4 teaspoon pepper
4 ounces goat cheese or feta cheese, crumbled

Cut four 12×15-inch sheets of heavy-duty foil. Fold each sheet crosswise into halves to crease, then unfold. Press any excess moisture from the spinach. Place 1/4 of the spinach in the center of the bottom half of each sheet of foil. Coat both sides of the chicken lightly with the olive oil and sprinkle with the Italian seasoning, 1 teaspoon salt and 1/2 teaspoon pepper. Arrange 1 chicken breast on each mound of spinach.

Combine the onion, sun-dried tomatoes, wine, olives, garlic, basil, thyme, 1/2 teaspoon salt and 1/4 teaspoon pepper in a bowl and mix gently. Spread the tomato mixture evenly over the chicken, allowing any liquid to puddle around the chicken. Sprinkle with the cheese.

Fold the top of the foil over the chicken. Starting at the corner, fold the edges of the foil over to seal tightly, each fold overlapping the previous one. Arrange the packets on a grill rack. Grill over hot coals for 15 minutes or until the chicken is cooked through. Cut the tops of the packets open with a small sharp knife. Serve immediately in the packet or remove the chicken and toppings to serving plates. You may bake in a 500-degree oven for 12 minutes or until the packets puff and the chicken is cooked through.

Serves 4

Fresh Herb and Lemon Marinade

Combine 1/2 cup finely mixed fresh herbs, such as thyme, summer savory, sage, oregano and/or parsley in a nonreactive bowl. Add 2 tablespoons finely grated lemon zest, 1/4 cup safflower oil, 1/4 cup olive oil, 3 tablespoons fresh lemon juice, 2 teaspoons dry mustard and 1/2 teaspoon salt; mix well. Store, tightly covered, in the refrigerator for up to 1 week.

Rosemary and Orange Marinade

Combine 1/3 cup fresh orange juice, 1 1/2 tablespoons finely grated orange zest, 3 tablespoons safflower oil, 1 tablespoon chopped fresh rosemary, 1/2 teaspoon salt and 1 tablespoon crushed green peppercorns in a nonreactive bowl and mix well. Store, tightly covered, in the refrigerator for up to 1 week. Use as a marinade for beef, pork, and duck.

Beach Parties

Beach Parties are a natural part of summer fun along the Gulf Coast. You need to start with a great location: a beach with a calm surf, restrooms nearby, and an area with picnic tables. Then add delicious summer foods and drinks, a shady place to keep everything cool, some music by the Beach Boys, and you are set to party!

For invitations, write all the party details on inflatable beach balls and mail them folded to the guests with instructions to bring the beach ball to the party. That will provide a built-in activity to get the party "rolling." Since beach parties are a good way to include guests of all ages, be sure to include activities for the younger set. Island limbo, water balloon toss, and sandcastle building are activities that all ages can enjoy.

Grilled Grouper with Florida Fruit Salsa

Florida Fruit Salsa
1 cup chopped pineapple
1 cup chopped red bell pepper
1 cup chopped red onion
sections of 4 oranges
1 bunch fresh cilantro, coarsely chopped
¹/₄ cup olive oil
¹/₄ cup red wine vinegar
1 teaspoon sea salt
¹/₂ teaspoon freshly ground pepper

Grouper
6 (6- to 8-ounce) grouper fillets or other firm-flesh fish, 1-inch thick
¹/₂ cup olive oil
sea salt and freshly ground pepper to taste
lemon wedges (optional)

For the salsa, combine the pineapple, bell pepper, onion, oranges and cilantro in a bowl and mix gently. Stir in the olive oil, vinegar, sea salt and pepper. Cover and set aside.

For the grouper, brush both sides of the fillets with the olive oil and sprinkle with the sea salt and pepper. Grill over medium-high heat for 5 minutes per side or until the fillets flake easily. Serve immediately with the salsa or lemon wedges. You may arrange the fillets on a baking sheet and broil for 5 minutes per side or until the fillets flake easily, turning the baking sheet as needed for even cooking.

Serves 6

Orzo with Fresh Spinach

4 quarts water
1 cup orzo
½ teaspoon salt
2 tablespoons olive oil
1 tablespoon butter
2 tablespoons coarsely chopped shallots
1 tablespoon minced garlic
2 cups slivered fresh spinach
salt and freshly ground pepper to taste

Bring the water to a boil in a medium saucepan or stockpot. Add the orzo and salt and mix well. Return to a boil. Boil for 9 minutes or until the orzo is al dente; drain. Toss the orzo with 1 tablespoon of the olive oil in a bowl.

Heat the remaining 1 tablespoon olive oil and butter in a skillet over medium heat until the butter melts. Sauté the shallots and garlic in the butter mixture for 2 minutes or just until the shallots are tender. Stir in the spinach. Sauté for 4 minutes. Season with salt and pepper. Remove from the heat. Add the orzo and toss until combined.

Serves 6

Herbed Sesame Twist Bread

1 tablespoon yeast
1 cup warm water
2½ cups flour
¼ cup grated asiago cheese
2 tablespoons sugar
2 tablespoons lemon savory
2 tablespoons lemon herbes de Provence
2 tablespoons olive oil
1 egg
1 to 2 tablespoons water
white sesame seeds
½ cup (1 stick) butter, melted
1 tablespoon pesto paste

Dissolve the yeast in the warm water in a large bowl and mix well. Let stand for 5 to 10 minutes or until bubbly. Combine the flour, cheese, sugar, lemon savory and lemon herbes de Provence in a bowl and mix well. Stir in the yeast mixture and olive oil. Let rise, covered with a tea towel, for 15 to 20 minutes. Punch the dough down and shape into a ball.

Knead the dough on a lightly floured surface until smooth and elastic. Divide the dough into 4 equal portions. Divide one of the dough portions into 8 equal portions. Divide the 8 portions into 16 portions. Roll each portion into a 6- to 8-inch rope. Twist 2 of the ropes together and tuck the ends under. Repeat this process with the remaining 14 ropes.

Arrange the twists on an ungreased baking sheet. Whisk the egg and water in a bowl. Brush the tops of the twists with the egg wash and sprinkle with sesame seeds. Repeat this process with the remaining 3 large dough portions. Bake at 350 degrees for 12 to 15 minutes or until golden brown. Brush a mixture of the melted butter and pesto paste over the hot twists.

Makes 32 twists

Frozen Tropical Gingersnap Dessert

1¼ cups gingersnap cookie crumbs
   (about twenty-five 2-inch cookies)
¼ cup (½ stick) butter, melted
1 pint vanilla ice cream, softened
14 (2-inch) gingersnaps
1 pint mango sorbet
Tropical Fruit Salsa (this page)
½ cup shredded coconut, toasted

Combine the cookie crumbs and butter in a bowl and
mix well. Press the crumb mixture over the bottom and
½ inch up the side of a 9-inch springform pan. Freeze for
10 minutes. Spread the ice cream in the prepared pan,
pressing firmly with the back of a spoon to level. Arrange
the cookies in a single layer over the ice cream. Freeze,
covered, for 1 hour or until firm.

   Soften the sorbet in the refrigerator for 30 minutes.
Spread over the prepared layers and press firmly with the
back of a spoon to level and smooth the surface. Freeze,
covered, for 3 hours.

   To serve, slice the cake and top each serving with
Tropical Fruit Salsa and sprinkle with the coconut. Store
the leftovers, covered, in the freezer.

   Serves 8

Tropical Fruit Salsa

2 kiwifruit, chopped
1 papaya, peeled, seeded, chopped
1 cup chopped fresh strawberries
2 tablespoons fresh lime juice
1 tablespoon honey
1 teaspoon grated fresh lime zest

Combine the kiwifruit, papaya, strawberries, lime juice,
honey and lime zest in a bowl and toss gently.

   Serves 8

Recipe for this photograph on facing page.

Florida Citrus Pie

Macadamia Crust

1 (7-ounce) jar roasted macadamia
    nuts
3/4 cup vanilla wafer crumbs
1/4 cup packed dark brown sugar
2 tablespoons melted butter

Grapefruit filling

2 cups fresh pink grapefruit juice
1/4 cup sugar
1 1/4 teaspoons unflavored gelatin
1/4 cup fresh lime juice

9 ounces imported white chocolate,
    chopped
1/4 cup whipping cream
1 1/4 cups whipping cream, chilled
1 tablespoon sugar

Florida Topping

1 cup whipping cream, chilled
2 tablespoons sugar
7 thin lime slices, cut into halves
8 ounces imported white chocolate,
    shaved into curls (optional)

For the crust, process the macadamia nuts in a food processor until finely chopped. Add the cookie crumbs, brown sugar and butter. Pulse until moist crumbs form. Press over the bottom and side of a 10-inch deep-dish pie plate. Bake at 350 degrees for 10 minutes or until golden brown. Let stand until cool.

For the filling, boil the grapefruit juice and 1/4 cup sugar in a heavy saucepan over high heat for 15 minutes or until reduced to 3/4 cup, stirring frequently. Sprinkle the unflavored gelatin over the lime juice in a bowl. Let stand for 10 minutes. Whisk the gelatin mixture, white chocolate and 1/4 cup whipping cream into the grapefruit mixture. Whisk over low heat until the white chocolate melts and the gelatin dissolves. Pour into a large bowl. Chill for 2 hours or until cool but not set, whisking occasionally and scraping the side of the bowl.

Beat 1 1/4 cups chilled whipping cream in a mixing bowl until soft peaks form. Add 1 tablespoon sugar and beat until blended. Fold the whipped cream into the grapefruit mixture. Spoon the filling into the prepared pie plate. Chill, covered, for 4 to 10 hours or until set.

For the topping, beat the whipping cream and sugar in a mixing bowl until stiff peaks form. Spoon the whipped cream into a pastry bag fitted with a large star tip. Pipe 15 rosettes around the edge of the pie. Arrange 1 lime slice round side up between each rosette. Fill the center with white chocolate curls. You may add the topping up to 4 hours in advance and store, covered, in the refrigerator.

Serves 8

Key Lime Pie

Mix 1 cup cinnamon cracker crumbs, 1/2 cup chocolate cracker crumbs and 1/4 cup sugar in a bowl. Stir in 1/3 cup softened butter. Press over the bottom and up the side of a 9-inch pie plate. Whisk 1 can sweetened condensed milk, 1/2 cup lime juice or Key lime juice, 2 teaspoons grated lime zest and 2 egg yolks in a bowl until thickened. Fold in 2 stiffly beaten egg whites. Spoon into the prepared pie plate. Bake at 325 degrees for 15 to 20 minutes or just until firm. Cool on a wire rack. Chill, covered, for 4 hours or longer. Spread sweetened whipped cream around the edge of the pie and garnish with lime slices.

Menu

Star-Spangled

Panama City has its own version of tailgating; it's called boatgating! The Fourth of July is the perfect time for this special kind of summer entertaining. Just take the boat out and invite friends to join you on the water. Ask everyone to bring a favorite dish that can be enjoyed in boats. Save room for dessert as the fireworks light the sky.

Fresh Raspberry Lemonade

2 pints fresh raspberries
1 cup sugar
4 cups water
2 cups fresh lemon juice

1/2 cup sugar
fresh raspberries to taste
sprigs of fresh mint

Purée 2 pints raspberries and 1 cup sugar in a blender or food processor. Strain in 4 batches into a large pitcher, mashing against the strainer and discarding the seeds. Stir in the water, lemon juice and 1/2 cup sugar. Pour the lemonade over ice in glasses. Garnish with fresh raspberries and sprigs of mint.

Serves 8 to 12

Missionary's Downfall

1/2 ounce fresh whole mint
    leaves
4 cups cracked ice

1 (16-ounce) can frozen lemonade
    concentrate
2 cups vodka, or to taste

Reserve 1/4 ounce of the mint. Process the remaining ingredients in a blender on high until slushy. Serve in mint julep cups garnished with the reserved mint leaves.

Serves 8

Red-White-Blue Hawaiian

1/2 cup curaçao
1/2 cup cream of coconut
1 cup white rum

1 cup pineapple juice
16 maraschino cherries
4 pineapple wedges

Process the curaçao, cream of coconut, rum and pineapple juice in a blender and fill the blender with ice. Process until nearly smooth. Place 3 cherries into each of 4 tall glasses and fill with the cocktail mixture. Garnish the rim of each glass with a pineapple wedge and 1 of the remaining cherries on a wooden pick.

Serves 4

Tyndall Air Force Base

Initially known only as Tyndall Field, Tyndall Air Force Base has occupied the eastern peninsula of Bay County since December, 1941, when the United States government condemned the land to open a gunnery school in preparation for the impending World War.

Tyndall Air Force Base and the men and women stationed there continue to make a mark on our nation. Today, Tyndall sprawls across 29,102 acres and employs about 6,460 military and civilian personnel. Tyndall is currently home to the 325th Fighter Wing, which provides combat readiness training for air defense. Flying F-15 Eagles, the 325th Fighter Wing pilots train for worldwide assignment. Members of these squadrons have been deployed to some of the fiercest combat in history, including the Gulf War and the war against terrorism in Afghanistan.

Although residents and visitors to Panama City are accustomed to the daily roar of F-15s flying overhead, they are treated once a year to a special display of the pilots' skills at the Tyndall Air Show, which is usually held every April.

Smoked Oyster Roll

8 ounces cream cheese, softened
1 tablespoon mayonnaise
1 teaspoon Worcestershire sauce
1 teaspoon chopped shallots
1/8 teaspoon hot sauce
garlic powder to taste
lemon dill to taste
1 (4-ounce) can smoked oysters
chopped fresh parsley

Line a baking sheet with foil. Combine the cream cheese, mayonnaise, Worcestershire sauce, shallots, hot sauce, garlic powder and lemon dill in a bowl and mix well. Pat the cream cheese mixture into a 1/2-inch-thick rectangle on the foil. Mash the oysters in a bowl with a fork. Spread the oysters over the rectangle. Chill, covered, in the refrigerator. Roll as for a jelly roll and coat with parsley. Serve with assorted party crackers.

Serves 8

Bacon and Tomato Bites

16 to 20 cherry tomatoes
1 pound sliced bacon, crisp-cooked and crumbled
1/2 cup mayonnaise
1/3 cup chopped green onions
3 tablespoons grated Parmesan cheese
2 tablespoons snipped fresh parsley

Cut a thin slice from the top of each tomato and discard. Carefully remove the pulp and seeds with a melon baller and discard. Invert the tomato shells onto a wire rack or paper towels to drain.

Combine the bacon, mayonnaise, green onions, cheese and parsley in a bowl and mix well. Spoon the bacon mixture into the tomato shells. Chill, covered, for several hours before serving.

Makes 16 to 20 appetizers

Marinated Tomatoes with Field Pea Vinaigrette

Field Pea Vinaigrette

2 ounces country ham, julienned
¼ cup peanut oil
2 ribs celery, finely chopped
1 medium carrot, finely chopped
1 small onion, finely chopped
1 small green bell pepper, chopped
1 small red bell pepper, chopped
1 tablespoon minced garlic
1 bay leaf
⅛ teaspoon crushed red pepper
1½ pounds fresh field peas
3 cups chicken stock
1½ teaspoons salt, or to taste
½ cup peanut oil
½ cup cider vinegar

2 tablespoons chopped fresh parsley
2 tablespoons chopped fresh basil
salt and freshly ground pepper
   to taste

Marinated Tomatoes

1 shallot, minced
splash of red wine vinegar
¼ cup olive oil
1 tablespoon chopped fresh parsley
1 tablespoon chopped fresh basil
½ teaspoon chopped fresh thyme
freshly ground pepper to taste
1 pound ripe red tomatoes
1 pound ripe yellow tomatoes
green tops of 3 scallions, thinly sliced

For the vinaigrette, sauté the ham in ¼ cup peanut oil in a large skillet over medium heat for 5 minutes or until crisp. Remove to a paper towel to drain using a slotted spoon and reserving the pan drippings. Add the celery, carrot and onion to the reserved pan drippings and mix well. Sauté for 5 minutes or until tender. Stir in the bell peppers, garlic, bay leaf and red pepper. Sauté for 2 minutes. Add the field peas and stock and mix well. Bring to a boil over medium-high heat; reduce the heat. Simmer for 10 to 30 minutes or until tender, stirring occasionally. Discard the bay leaf. Drain the peas and season with the salt. Whisk ½ cup peanut oil into the vinegar in a bowl. Whisk in the parsley and basil. Add the warm peas to the vinaigrette and mix gently. Set the bowl over a larger bowl of ice water. Let stand until cool, stirring occasionally. Stir in the ham, salt and pepper. Chill, covered, for 6 to 10 hours. Bring to room temperature before serving.

For the tomatoes, combine the shallot and vinegar in a bowl. Whisk in the olive oil. Stir in the parsley, basil, thyme and pepper. Arrange the tomatoes in slightly overlapping circles on a large serving platter. Drizzle with the shallot mixture. Marinate, covered, at room temperature for 3 hours.

To serve, spoon any accumulated tomato juices and marinade over the tomatoes and drizzle with the vinaigrette. Sprinkle with the scallion tops.

Serves 8

Clark Gable at Tyndall Air Force Base

One of the more famous fighters to earn his silver wings at Tyndall Field was the legendary Clark Gable. Gable arrived at Tyndall Field on October 27, 1942 and received his wings on January 6, 1943. Of his time at Tyndall Field, Gable remarked, "I am proud of the wings I won here and what they signify. The aerial gunners will make a mark for themselves—they have already done it."

   —Along the Bay, Marlene Womak, 1994

Deviled Eggs with Sun-Dried Tomatoes

1 (4-ounce) jar oil-pack sun-dried tomatoes, drained
6 hard-cooked eggs, cut into halves
1/4 cup mayonnaise
3 tablespoons sour cream
1/2 teaspoon white wine vinegar
salt and pepper to taste

Reserve 2 whole sun-dried tomatoes. Mince the remaining sun-dried tomatoes. Remove the yolks to a bowl, reserving the whites. Mash the yolks with a fork until smooth. Stir in the minced sun-dried tomatoes. Add the mayonnaise, sour cream and vinegar and mix well. Season with salt and pepper.

Spoon the yolk filling into a pastry bag fitted with a 1/2-inch decorative tip. Pipe the yolk filling into the whites, mounding in the center. Arrange the deviled eggs on a serving platter. Chop the reserved sun-dried tomatoes and sprinkle over the tops of the eggs. Chill, covered, until serving time.

Makes 12 deviled eggs

Boiled Peanut Salad

4 ears fresh corn, silk and husks removed
1/4 cup olive oil
1/4 cup cider vinegar
1 1/2 cups shelled boiled peanuts
1 small onion, finely chopped
1/2 each red and green bell pepper, finely chopped
1 tablespoon each minced garlic and finely chopped
    fresh basil, or 1 teaspoon dried basil
salt and pepper to taste

Arrange the corn on a lightly oiled baking sheet. Roast at 400 degrees for 15 to 25 minutes or until tender; cool.

Whisk the olive oil and vinegar in a bowl until blended. Stir in the peanuts, onion, bell peppers, garlic and basil. Cut the tops of the corn kernels into the bowl containing the peanut mixture and mix well. Season with salt and pepper. Chill, covered, for 1 hour or up to 10 hours, stirring occasionally. The flavor of the salad is enhanced if allowed to marinate overnight.

Serves 4

Antipasto Picnic Pie

1 (12-inch) loaf Tuscan French Bread (this page), or
  other round and crusty bread
1 (14- to 16-ounce) jar giardiniera pickles, drained
8 ounces provolone cheese, thinly sliced
1 (14- to 16-ounce) jar roasted red peppers
1 (14-ounce) can water-pack quartered artichoke
  hearts, drained
12 ounces any variety mixed salad greens
1/2 cup fresh flat-leaf parsley leaves
15 to 20 fresh basil leaves, chopped
extra-virgin olive oil
1/3 pound Genoa salami, sliced
1/3 pound sweet soppressata, sliced
1/3 pound capocolla, sliced (hot cured pork shoulder)
1/4 red onion, thinly sliced
1 ripe tomato, thinly sliced
coarse salt and pepper to taste
8 hot or sweet pickled cherry peppers

Cut the top from the bread loaf and reserve. Remove
the center carefully, leaving a 1/2-inch shell. Chop the
giardiniera in a food processor. Spread over the bottom of
the bread shell. Layer with some of the cheese, roasted
peppers and artichoke hearts, pressing each layer lightly.

Toss the salad greens, parsley and basil in a bowl.
Add a thin layer of the salad greens mixture over the
prepared layers and drizzle with olive oil. Top with the
salami, soppressata, capocolla, remaining cheese, some
of the remaining salad green mixture, onion and sliced
tomato. Drizzle with olive oil and sprinkle with salt
and pepper. Cut into wedges and garnish with cherry
pepper skewers.

Serves 8

Tuscan French Bread

1 tablespoon dry yeast
1/2 cup warm (105 to 115 degrees) water
3 cups flour
2 tablespoons olive oil
1 tablespoon salt
1 tablespoon sugar
olive oil
cracked pepper to taste
lemon savory seasoning to taste

Dissolve the yeast in the warm water in a bowl. Let stand
for 5 to 10 minutes or until bubbly. Combine the yeast
mixture, flour, 2 tablespoons olive oil, salt and sugar in a
food processor. Process until the mixture forms a ball.
Place the dough in a floured bowl, turning to coat the
surface. Let rest, covered with a tea towel, for 10 minutes.
Shape the dough into a 12-inch round or oval loaf on a
lightly floured surface.

Arrange the loaf on a baking sheet coated with
additional olive oil. Let rise, covered with a tea towel,
for 5 to 10 minutes. Brush with additional olive oil and
sprinkle with cracked pepper and lemon savory seasoning.
Bake at 425 degrees for 15 to 20 minutes, covering with foil
if needed to prevent overbrowning. Remove the loaf to a
wire rack to cool.

Serves 8

Oven-Roasted Pulled Pork

2 (2½- to 3-pound) pork shoulder blade Boston roasts
1 tablespoon salt
1 tablespoon freshly ground black pepper
1 tablespoon mustard seeds
2 teaspoons red pepper flakes
1 cup apple cider
1 cup cider vinegar
4 yellow onions, thinly sliced
1 green bell pepper, thinly sliced
1 red bell pepper, thinly sliced
4 garlic cloves, chopped
12 sandwich buns
Southern Barbecue Sauce (this page)

Arrange the roasts in a large roasting pan sprayed with nonstick cooking spray. Combine the salt, black pepper, mustard seeds and red pepper flakes in a bowl and mix well. Pat the spice mixture over the surface of the roasts. Pour the cider and vinegar around the roasts and scatter the onions, bell peppers and garlic over and around the roasts.

Roast, covered with foil, at 300 degrees for 3 hours; remove the foil. Roast for 1 hour longer. Remove the roasts to a serving platter, reserving the vegetables. Let stand for 1 hour. Remove the vegetables to a bowl using a slotted spoon.

Shred the pork by pulling with 2 forks, discarding the fat. Add the reserved vegetables to the pork if desired or spoon the vegetables over the pork on the buns.

Mix the Southern Barbecue Sauce with the pork or serve separately with the pork sandwiches.

Serves 12

Southern Barbecue Sauce

1 (14-ounce) can diced tomatoes
¼ cup (½ stick) butter
2 medium sweet onions, thinly sliced
2 tablespoons chopped fresh gingerroot
¾ cup molasses
½ cup bourbon
½ cup cider vinegar
⅓ cup coarse-ground Dijon mustard
⅓ cup ketchup
2 tablespoons Worcestershire sauce
2 tablespoons lemon juice
1 teaspoon Tabasco sauce
salt and pepper to taste

Process the undrained tomatoes in a food processor until puréed. Heat the butter in a large saucepan over medium heat. Stir in the onions and gingerroot. Cook for 5 minutes or until tender, stirring frequently.

Add the puréed tomatoes, molasses, bourbon, vinegar, Dijon mustard, ketchup, Worcestershire sauce, lemon juice, Tabasco sauce, salt and pepper to the onion mixture and mix well. Reduce the heat to low. Simmer for 2 hours or until thickened, stirring occasionally.

Serves 12

Molasses-Barbecued Spareribs

3 pounds spareribs, cut into serving pieces
1/2 cup prepared mustard
1/3 cup molasses
1/4 cup soy sauce
3 tablespoons vinegar
2 tablespoons Worcestershire sauce
2 teaspoons Tabasco sauce

Arrange the spareribs in a large baking pan. Bake at 350 degrees until almost cooked through; drain. Combine the prepared mustard, molasses, soy sauce, vinegar, Worcestershire sauce and Tabasco sauce in a bowl and mix well.

Spoon the mustard mixture over the ribs. Bake for approximately 1 hour longer or until the spareribs are glazed and cooked through, turning occasionally. The flavor of the ribs is enhanced if prepared on the grill.

Serves 3 to 4

Peach-Glazed Chicken Thighs

2 large peaches, peeled and chopped
6 chicken thighs
1/2 teaspoon salt
1/2 teaspoon freshly ground pepper
2 teaspoons olive oil
2 teaspoons honey
1 tablespoon red wine vinegar
1 large peach, peeled and sliced
2 tablespoons sliced scallions

Mash 2 peaches in a bowl with a fork. Add the chicken and toss to coat. Chill, covered, for 2 to 6 hours, stirring occasionally. Bring the chicken to room temperature; drain. Pat the chicken dry with paper towels and sprinkle with the salt and pepper.

Heat the olive oil in a large ovenproof skillet over high heat. Cook the chicken skin-side down in the hot olive oil for 5 minutes or until brown and crisp; turn the chicken. Bake at 350 degrees for 15 minutes or until cooked through; drain.

Heat the chicken in the skillet over high heat until the chicken begins to sizzle. Add the honey and toss to coat. Cook for 1 minute or until the honey begins to brown and stick to the bottom of the skillet, stirring constantly. Add the vinegar and peach slices and stir to loosen any browned bits.

Cook for 1 1/2 minutes or until the chicken is glazed. Remove the chicken to a serving platter. Spoon the peaches in the center of the platter and sprinkle with the scallions. Serve immediately.

Serves 2 to 3

Coastal Systems Station

The first Naval Section Base was established in 1942 on the site of a small Indian village that contained large amounts of various seashells. A few years later, workers cut the winding entrance road from U.S. 98 around the thick swamps and pines which were full of alligators and wild hogs. A unique feature to the base has always been its natural operating environment and close proximity to the Gulf of Mexico. Today, Coastal Systems Station is the Navy's premier research and development organization focused on littoral and expeditionary warfare, and the waters of our area continue to provide the perfect setting for training and experimentation.

Queen Mama's Barbecued Chicken

Barbecue Sauce
2 cups ketchup
1/2 cup tomato sauce
1/2 cup water
1/2 cup corn syrup
1/2 cup cola
1/4 cup cider vinegar
1/4 cup (1/2 stick) butter or margarine
1/4 cup steak sauce
2 tablespoons soy sauce

1 1/2 teaspoons sugar
1 teaspoon seasoned salt
1 teaspoon hot pepper sauce
1/2 teaspoon garlic powder
1/2 teaspoon onion powder
1/2 teaspoon liquid smoke

Chicken
1 (3 1/2-pound) chicken, cut up

For the sauce, combine the ketchup, tomato sauce, water, corn syrup, cola, vinegar, butter, steak sauce and soy sauce in a 2-quart saucepan and mix well. Stir in the sugar, seasoned salt, hot pepper sauce, garlic powder, onion powder and liquid smoke. Bring to a boil; reduce the heat. Simmer for 1 hour, stirring frequently. Reserve 1 cup of the sauce. Store the remaining sauce, covered, in the refrigerator for future use.

For the chicken, grill, covered, over medium-low heat for 40 minutes or until almost cooked through. Brush the chicken with the reserved sauce. Grill for 5 minutes longer. Brush with the reserved sauce and turn. Grill the chicken until the juices run clear when pierced with a fork.

Serves 4 to 5

Grilled Red Potato Salad

4 pounds new potatoes
1/4 cup olive oil
salt and freshly ground pepper to taste
12 ounces sliced smoked bacon
1 large red onion, thinly sliced
1/4 cup plus 2 tablespoons white wine vinegar
1/4 cup olive oil
1 tablespoon sugar
1/4 cup coarsely chopped flat-leaf parsley
1 cup crumbled bleu cheese or feta cheese

Combine the potatoes with enough water to cover in a saucepan. Bring to a boil. Boil until almost tender; drain. Cool slightly and cut the potatoes into halves. Toss the potatoes with 1/4 cup olive oil in a bowl. Season with salt and pepper. Grill cut side down over hot coals for 3 minutes; turn. Grill for 2 to 3 minutes longer. Remove the potatoes to a large bowl.

Heat a medium skillet on the stove top or grill until almost smoking. Add the bacon. Cook until golden brown and crisp, turning occasionally. Remove the bacon to a plate lined with paper towels to drain, reserving the bacon drippings. Let stand until cool and crumble.

Drain the skillet, reserving 2 tablespoons of the bacon drippings. Cook the onion in the reserved bacon drippings for 5 to 6 minutes or until tender. Stir in the vinegar, 1/4 cup olive oil and sugar. Cook until the sugar dissolves, stirring frequently. Spoon the onion mixture over the potatoes. Add the bacon and parsley and toss to mix. Season with salt and pepper. Spoon the potato salad onto a large serving platter. Sprinkle with the cheese.

Serves 10 to 12

Pea Salad with Cashews and Bacon

2 (10-ounce) packages frozen baby peas
1 cup chopped celery
3/4 cup whole cashews
2 green onions, minced
1/2 cup sour cream
1/2 teaspoon oregano
1/4 teaspoon garlic salt
salt and pepper to taste
6 slices bacon, crisp-cooked

Thaw the peas in a colander. Combine the peas, celery, cashews and green onions in a bowl and mix well. Stir in the sour cream, oregano, garlic salt, salt and pepper. Crumble the bacon over the salad. Chill, covered, until serving time.

Serves 6

Fourth of July

The first official Fourth of July celebration, as affirmed by a legislative act, occurred in Massachusetts in 1781. By the mid 1800s, it became a United States custom to commemorate Independence Day in states and territories. Today, we celebrate with parades, picnics, and fireworks to honor our country's fight for freedom.

Lemon Blueberry Cake with White Chocolate Frosting

Cake

3¹/₂ cups cake flour

¹/₂ teaspoon salt

¹/₂ teaspoon baking powder

¹/₂ teaspoon baking soda

³/₄ cup (1¹/₂ sticks) butter, softened

2 cups sugar

¹/₃ cup lemon juice

2 teaspoons grated lemon zest

¹/₂ teaspoon lemon extract

4 eggs

1 cup plus 2 tablespoons buttermilk

2¹/₂ cups fresh blueberries

White Chocolate Frosting and Assembly

1 pound white chocolate, finely chopped

16 ounces cream cheese, softened

1 cup (2 sticks) unsalted butter, softened

3 tablespoons fresh lemon juice

¹/₄ teaspoon lemon extract

lemons, thinly sliced

fresh blueberries

For the cake, coat two 9-inch cake pans with 2-inch sides or two 9-inch springform pans with butter and dust lightly with flour. Line the bottoms with baking parchment. Sift the cake flour, salt, baking power and baking soda together. Beat the butter in a mixing bowl until light and fluffy. Add the sugar gradually, beating constantly until blended and scraping the side of the bowl occasionally. Add the lemon juice, lemon zest and flavoring and mix well. Add the eggs 1 at a time, beating well after each addition. Add the flour mixture in 4 equal batches alternately with the buttermilk, beating well after each addition. Fold in the blueberries. Spoon the batter into the prepared cake pans. Bake at 350 degrees for 40 minutes or until a wooden pick inserted in the centers comes out clean. Cool in pans on a wire rack.

For the frosting, heat the chocolate in a heavy saucepan over low heat until almost melted, stirring occasionally. Remove from the heat and stir until smooth. Let stand until lukewarm. Beat the cream cheese and unsalted butter in a mixing bowl until blended, scraping the bowl occasionally. Beat in the lemon juice and flavoring. Stir in the chocolate until blended.

To serve, remove the layers from the cake pans and discard the baking parchment. Slice each layer horizontally into halves creating 4 layers. Arrange 1 layer flat side up on a cake plate. Spread with some of the frosting. Repeat the process with the remaining layers. Spread the remaining frosting over the top and side of the cake. Garnish with lemon slices and fresh blueberries.

Serves 10 to 12

Raspberry Pound Cake

2¹/₂ cups flour
1 teaspoon baking powder
¹/₂ teaspoon salt
1²/₃ cups sugar
5 eggs
1¹/₄ cups (2¹/₂ sticks) butter, softened and cut into pieces
2 tablespoons Chambord, kirsch or framboise
3 cups fresh raspberries (about 1¹/₂ pints)
confectioners' sugar (optional)

Reserve 2 tablespoons of the flour. Mix the remaining flour, baking powder and salt together. Beat the sugar and eggs in a mixing bowl at medium speed until the mixture is pale yellow in color. Add the butter and liqueur. Beat until light and fluffy. Add the flour mixture and beat until blended.

Toss the raspberries with the reserved 2 tablespoons flour in a bowl. Fold the raspberries into the batter. Spoon the batter into a buttered and floured 9-inch bundt pan.

Bake at 325 degrees for 1 hour or until a wooden pick inserted in the center comes out clean. Cool in pan on a wire rack for 20 to 30 minutes. Invert onto a serving platter. Let stand until cool. Dust with confectioners' sugar.

Serves 10 to 12

Fourth of July Blueberry Pie

14 pecan sandies, crumbled
2 tablespoons (about) butter, softened
8 ounces cream cheese, softened
²/₃ cup sugar
3 eggs
1 teaspoon vanilla extract
1¹/₂ pints fresh blueberries

Combine the cookie crumbs with just enough of the butter in a bowl until the mixture adheres and mix well. Pat the crumb mixture over the bottom of an 8-inch pie plate. Beat the cream cheese and sugar in a mixing bowl until light and fluffy. Add the eggs 1 at a time, beating well after each addition. Beat in the vanilla.

Spoon the cream cheese mixture into the prepared pie plate. Sprinkle with the blueberries. Bake at 350 degrees for 25 minutes. Let stand until cool. Chill, covered, for 2 to 10 hours.

Serves 6

MENU

Carl's Cook Shack

Seafood is plentiful in these parts, and nothing is more enjoyable than a backyard cookout with lots of crab and shrimp and plenty of side dishes. Have the grill and steam pot ready to prepare the sea's bounty for hungry guests. Dress casually and be prepared to get messy; we all know it is worth every morsel.

Frozen Peacharitas

4 cups frozen chopped peaches
1 cup orange juice
$^{1}/_{2}$ cup tequila
$^{1}/_{2}$ cup peach schnapps
1 tablespoon fresh lime juice
1 teaspoon grenadine
4 fresh peach slices or lime slices

Combine the frozen peaches, orange juice, tequila, peach schnapps, lime juice
and grenadine in a blender. Add enough ice to fill the blender and process until
smooth. Pour the cocktail mixture into margarita glasses or wine glasses. Garnish
the rim of each glass with a fresh peach slice or lime slice. Serve immediately.

Serves 4

Fruit Slush

1 fifth whiskey
1 (46-ounce) can pineapple juice
28 ounces lemon-lime soda
1 (16-ounce) jar maraschino cherries, drained and cut into halves
1 (6-ounce) can frozen orange juice concentrate
1 cup sugar
1 cup hot water

Combine the whiskey, pineapple juice, soda, cherries, orange juice concentrate,
sugar and hot water in a freezer container and mix well. Freeze until firm,
stirring frequently.

Serves 12 to 14

Boat Building and the Port of Panama City

*In order to understand the history of the
Port and boat building in the area, you must
go back to the opening of the Wainwright
Shipyard, which opened in 1942. The yard was
located near the east end of Hathaway Bridge
and was the location for building the sturdy
Liberty ships that were used to transport
cargo during World War II.*

*Because of the depth of the harbor
entrance channel into St. Andrews Bay, which
allows for navigation of deep-water vessels
into the waters, the Port of Panama City has
had steady growth and development over the
years. Ships moving with their cargos through
Port Panama City have had a significant
impact on the economy of Bay County and
play a significant role in international trade
in the United States.*

Cook Shack Crab Dip

2 ounces cream cheese, softened
¼ cup sour cream
1 tablespoon mayonnaise
1 tablespoon butter, softened
¼ teaspoon seasoned salt
⅛ teaspoon paprika
6 ounces fresh crab meat, shells and cartilage removed
¼ cup shredded mozzarella cheese
4 teaspoons minced onion
4 teaspoons minced green bell pepper
chopped green onions
chopped fresh parsley

Combine the cream cheese, sour cream, mayonnaise and butter in a bowl and mix until smooth. Stir in the seasoned salt and paprika. Add the crab meat, cheese, minced onion and bell pepper and mix well.

Spoon the crab meat mixture into a lightly greased small shallow baking dish. Bake at 350 degrees for 15 minutes or until bubbly. Sprinkle with green onions and parsley. Serve with unsalted tortilla chips.

Serves 4

Recipe for this photograph on facing page.

Crab Meat West Indies

1 pound fresh jumbo lump crab meat
salt and pepper to taste
1 cup vegetable oil
½ cup apple cider vinegar
½ cup white vinegar
¼ to ⅓ teaspoon Tabasco sauce
1 medium white onion, chopped

Rinse the crab meat with cold water and drain, discarding any shells or cartilage. Place the crab meat in a plastic container. Season lightly with salt and pepper. Add the oil, cider vinegar, white vinegar and Tabasco sauce and mix well. Stir in the onion.

Marinate, covered, in the refrigerator for 8 to 10 hours, stirring occasionally. Serve with saltine crackers. You may store, covered, in the refrigerator for up to 1 week, stirring once every day. The quality is best if served within 2 to 5 days. Add chopped fresh tomatoes, lettuce and olives for a great salad.

Serves 20

Coconut Shrimp with Orange Ginger Sauce

Orange Ginger Sauce

1 (10-ounce) jar orange marmalade
3 tablespoons prepared horseradish
3 tablespoons Creole mustard
$^1/_4$ to $^1/_2$ teaspoon ground ginger

Shrimp

2 pounds fresh medium shrimp
$1^1/_2$ cups flour
$^1/_2$ teaspoon baking powder
$^1/_2$ teaspoon paprika
$^1/_2$ teaspoon curry powder
$^1/_4$ teaspoon salt
$^1/_4$ teaspoon cayenne pepper
1 (12-ounce) can beer
$^1/_2$ cup flour
1 (14-ounce) package shredded coconut
vegetable oil for frying

For the sauce, combine the marmalade, prepared horseradish, mustard and ginger in a bowl and mix well. Set aside.

For the shrimp, peel and devein the shrimp, leaving the tails intact. Combine $1^1/_2$ cups flour, baking powder, paprika, curry powder, salt and cayenne pepper in a bowl and mix well. Stir in the beer.

Holding the shrimp by the tails, coat with $^1/_2$ cup flour and dip in the beer batter. Roll in the coconut. Fry the shrimp in hot oil in a deep heavy skillet until golden brown on both sides; drain on paper towels. Serve with the sauce.

Serves 6

Grilling Seafood

Seafood can be difficult to grill and has a tendency to stick to the grill. The grill must be clean and lightly oiled before starting to grill seafood. Contrary to popular wisdom, fish actually cook better when done quickly over high heat; it sears the outside and cooks the center. Long slow cooking is more likely to result in dry fish that falls apart. It is best to leave the fish fillet or steak on the grill long enough for the skin or exterior to brown and begin to pull away from the grill before trying to turn it. This will make flipping the fish easier.

Shrimp Fritters

2 cups flour
1 teaspoon baking soda
1 cup water
1/2 cup finely chopped scallions
1/3 cup minced red bell pepper
1 garlic clove, minced
1/4 teaspoon Worcestershire sauce
Tabasco sauce to taste
8 ounces chopped peeled cooked shrimp
vegetable oil for frying
salt to taste
Spicy Tartar Sauce (this page)
lemon wedges

Combine the flour and baking soda in a bowl and mix well. Whisk in the water. Add the scallions, bell pepper, garlic, Worcestershire sauce and Tabasco sauce and mix well. Add the shrimp and stir until coated. Let stand, covered, at room temperature for 1 hour.

Add enough oil to a deep heavy saucepan or deep-fat fryer to measure 3 inches. Heat to 325 degrees. Drop the batter by spoonfuls into the hot oil. Fry until golden brown on all sides, turning once. Drain the fritters on a baking sheet lined with paper towels. Sprinkle with salt. Keep warm in a 200-degree oven. Serve with Spicy Tartar Sauce and lemon wedges.

Serves 8

Spicy Tartar Sauce

3/4 cup mayonnaise
3 tablespoons minced fresh cilantro
2 tablespoons Dijon mustard
2 to 4 tablespoons lemon juice
2 tablespoons minced fresh parsley
2 tablespoons minced pickled jalapeño chiles
2 tablespoons minced red onion
salt to taste
cayenne pepper or Tabasco sauce to taste

Combine the mayonnaise, cilantro, Dijon mustard, lemon juice, parsley, jalapeño chiles, onion, salt and cayenne pepper in a bowl and mix well. Chill, covered, until serving time.

Serves 8

Stone Crab Claws with Mustard Sauce

1 cup mayonnaise
3 tablespoons sour cream
2 tablespoons half-and-half
3½ teaspoons dry mustard
2 teaspoons Worcestershire sauce
1½ teaspoons prepared yellow mustard
1 teaspoon steak sauce
⅛ teaspoon salt
⅛ teaspoon pepper
4 pounds fresh Florida stone crab claws, cooked and
    cracked

Combine the mayonnaise, sour cream, half-and-half, dry mustard, Worcestershire sauce, prepared mustard, steak sauce, salt and pepper in a food processor. Process until smooth. Chill, covered, for 1 hour or longer. Serve with crab claws or steak.

Serves 4

Boiled Blue Crabs

1 cup salt
½ cup cayenne pepper
½ cup freshly ground white pepper
½ cup freshly ground black pepper
crab boil to taste
2 lemons, cut into quarters
12 live blue crabs

Fill a large stockpot ⅓ full of water. Add the salt, cayenne pepper, white pepper, black pepper, crab boil and lemons and cover. Bring to a boil over high heat. Boil for 10 minutes. Add the crabs and cover. Return to a boil.

Watch for the steam to escape from under the cover. Boil for 15 minutes longer from this point. Remove from the heat. Let stand, covered, for 10 minutes longer. Remove the crabs to a colander. Let stand until cool and clean. If blue crabs are not available substitute with other small to medium crabs.

Serves 4 to 6

Chilled Spiced Shrimp

1½ cups cider vinegar
½ cup water
¼ cup fresh lemon juice
3 garlic cloves, crushed
2 teaspoons shrimp and crab boil
2 teaspoons sugar
½ teaspoon whole black peppercorns
½ teaspoon salt
¼ teaspoon celery seeds
3 bay leaves
1 pound large shrimp (21 to 25 count)
Spicy Marinade (this page)

Combine the vinegar, water, lemon juice, garlic, shrimp and crab boil, sugar, peppercorns, salt, celery seeds and bay leaves in a medium nonreactive saucepan. Bring to a boil over high heat; reduce the heat. Simmer for 10 minutes.

Return the heat to high. Add the shrimp. Cook for 2 minutes or until the shrimp are pink and firm, stirring occasionally. Remove the shrimp to a colander, reserving ½ cup of the cooking liquid for the marinade. Rinse the shrimp with cool water until cool. Peel the shrimp and devein if desired, leaving the tails intact. Add the shrimp to the Shrimp Marinade and mix to coat. Marinate, covered, in the refrigerator for 6 to 36 hours, stirring occasionally.

To serve, drain the shrimp, reserving the marinade. Arrange on a serving platter with wooden picks and napkins. Or, hang the shrimp around the edge of a bowl filled with some of the reserved marinade. Serve with toasted slices of French bread to sop up the juices.

Serves 4

Spicy Marinade for Shrimp

½ cup reserved cooking liquid from the
    shrimp (this page)
⅓ cup mild olive oil
1 tablespoon Dijon mustard
1 teaspoon prepared horseradish
½ medium onion, thinly sliced
½ lemon, thinly sliced
¼ cup chopped fresh parsley

Strain the reserved cooking liquid into a nonreactive bowl. Whisk in the olive oil, Dijon mustard and prepared horseradish. Stir in the onion, lemon and parsley.

Makes 2 cups

Green Chile Casserole

1 pound Monterey Jack cheese, coarsely shredded
1 pound Cheddar cheese, coarsely shredded
2 (4-ounce) cans green chiles, drained and chopped
4 egg yolks
2/3 cup evaporated milk
1 tablespoon flour
1 teaspoon salt
1/2 teaspoon pepper
4 egg whites, stiffly beaten
2 large red and/or yellow tomatoes, sliced

Combine the Monterey Jack cheese, Cheddar cheese and green chiles in a bowl and mix well. Spread the cheese mixture in a greased 2-quart baking dish. Whisk the egg yolks and evaporated milk in a bowl until blended. Stir in the flour, salt and pepper. Fold in the egg whites.

Pour the egg mixture over the prepared layer, using a fork to insure the egg mixture penetrates the cheese layer. Bake at 325 degrees for 30 minutes. Arrange the tomato slices over the baked layers. Bake for 30 minutes longer.

Serves 8 to 10

Layered Tangy Coleslaw

1 head cabbage, thinly sliced
1 large green bell pepper, cut into rings
2 small onions, sliced
1 cup sugar
1 cup white vinegar
3/4 cup vegetable oil
1 tablespoon salt
2 teaspoons sugar
1 teaspoon dry mustard
1 teaspoon celery seeds
1 cup cherry tomatoes, cut into halves

Layer the cabbage, bell pepper and onions in a large glass bowl with a straight side. Sprinkle with 1 cup sugar.

Combine the vinegar, oil, salt, 2 teaspoons sugar, dry mustard and celery seeds in a saucepan and mix well. Bring to a boil, stirring frequently. Pour the vinegar mixture over the cabbage mixture. Chill, covered, for 4 hours or longer. Add the tomatoes just before serving and toss to mix.

Serves 8

Famous Cheese Biscuits

2 cups buttermilk baking mix
2/3 cup milk
1/2 to 1 cup (2 to 4 ounces) shredded mild Cheddar cheese
1/4 cup (1/2 stick) margarine, melted
1 tablespoon parsley flakes
1/2 teaspoon garlic powder

Combine the baking mix, milk and cheese in a bowl and mix until a soft dough forms. Beat vigorously for 30 seconds. Drop the dough by spoonfuls onto a baking sheet. Bake at 450 degrees for 10 minutes or until light brown.

Mix the margarine, parsley flakes and garlic powder in a bowl. Brush the margarine mixture over the warm biscuits. Serve immediately.

Makes 1 dozen biscuits

Rum Pineapple Boats

1 pineapple
1/3 cup butter, melted
1/4 cup packed brown sugar
3 tablespoons dark rum
1/2 teaspoon cinnamon
1/8 teaspoon ground cloves
Freshly grated nutmeg

Cut the pineapple through the leaves from the top to the bottom into 4 wedges. Remove the core and discard. Make vertical slits in the top of each wedge; do not slice through. Slice between the fruit and rind to detach the rind, but keep the wedges on the rind to create the look of a boat.

Combine the butter, brown sugar, rum, cinnamon and cloves in a saucepan and mix well. Cook until the brown sugar dissolves and the mixture is of a sauce consistency, stirring frequently. Remove from the heat. Brush each boat with some of the sauce. Wrap only the green tops of the pineapple wedges with foil and arrange the boats rind side down on a grill rack. Grill over medium-hot coals for 15 minutes or until heated through, basting frequently with the sauce. Sprinkle with nutmeg before serving.

Serves 4

White Chocolate Dream Cookies

2¼ cups flour
¾ teaspoon baking soda
½ teaspoon salt
1 cup (2 sticks) butter, softened
⅔ cup packed light brown sugar
½ cup sugar
1 egg
1 tablespoon grated orange zest
2 teaspoons orange extract
2 cups white chocolate morsels

Mix the flour, baking soda and salt together. Beat the butter, brown sugar and sugar in a mixing bowl until creamy, scraping the bowl occasionally. Add the egg, orange zest and flavoring and beat until mixed. Add the flour mixture gradually, beating constantly until blended. Stir in the white chocolate morsels.

Drop the dough by rounded tablespoonfuls onto an ungreased cookie sheet. Bake at 350 degrees for 10 to 12 minutes or until light brown. Cool on the cookie sheet for 2 minutes. Remove to a wire rack to cool completely.

Makes 3½ dozen cookies

Glazed Key Lime Cake

Cake
2 cups flour
1⅓ cups sugar
1 (3-ounce) package lime gelatin
1 teaspoon baking powder
⅔ teaspoon salt
½ teaspoon baking soda
1⅓ cups vegetable oil
¾ cup orange juice
5 eggs
1 teaspoon lemon extract
½ teaspoon vanilla extract

Key Lime Glaze
⅓ cup Key lime juice
⅓ cup confectioners' sugar

For the cake, combine the flour, sugar, gelatin, baking powder, salt and baking soda in a mixing bowl and mix well. Add the oil, orange juice, eggs and flavorings. Beat until blended.

Spoon the batter into a greased and floured tube pan. Bake at 350 degrees for 55 minutes. Pierce the top of the warm cake with a skewer or fork. Cool in the pan on a wire rack. Remove to a cake plate.

For the glaze, mix the lime juice and confectioners' sugar in a bowl until blended. Drizzle over the cooled cake.

Serves 12

Mermaid Lagoon

What better way to entertain a group of friends than a luau along the waterfront or beside the swimming pool. Lots of tiki torches and flowers everywhere create a spirit of Aloha no matter where you may be. Ask guests to dress in tropical clothing and provide them with leis as they enter the door.

Hawaiian Lady

1½ ounces melon liqueur
1 ounce tequila
3 ounces grapefruit juice
2 ounces pineapple juice
1 maraschino cherry and pineapple chunk skewer

Combine the liqueur, tequila, grapefruit juice and pineapple juice in a measuring cup and mix well. Strain into a glass filled with finely crushed ice. Garnish with the skewer.

Serves 1

Islander Cocktail

1 ounce light rum
½ ounce orange curaçao
¼ ounce strawberry liqueur
2 dashes angostura bitters
3 ounces ice
1 strawberry skewer

Process the rum, curaçao, liqueur, bitters and ice in a blender until smooth. Pour into a glass and garnish with a strawberry skewer.

Serves 1

The Legend of Mermaid Lagoon

In the early 1900s, anglers often ventured into the waters of North Bay in search of the elusive tarpon, then considered the finest of American game fish. With its silvery scales and size, the tarpon displayed a dazzling show once it was hooked and often leapt high in the air to seek freedom from its captor.

Legend has it that mermaids swam these waters and meandered into the many bayous and lagoons in search of sailors and fishermen. Maybe stories from the tarpon fishermen are the origin of the mermaid tales, but one thing is for sure, the legend still exists today, to which the hostess of this party will attest. Who knows? Maybe the sightings were simply the silvery tarpon sliding through the crystal waters and avoiding the anxious anglers above.

Ice Rings

Ice Rings are a beautiful addition to a luau punch. To make them, combine 2 cups orange juice and 2 cups pineapple juice in each of 2 ring molds. Add orange slices, lime slices, cherries and pineapple chunks equally to the molds and stir. Freeze, covered, until firm. Fill the molds the rest of the way with a mixture of orange juice and pineapple juice and freeze for 8 to 10 hours.

Red-Headed Mermaid

1½ ounces lime juice
1 ounce vodka
½ ounce light rum
⅓ ounce grenadine

3 ounces crushed ice
pineapple juice
maraschino cherry

Mix the lime juice, vodka, rum and grenadine with the ice in a wine glass. Add enough pineapple juice to fill the glass and stir. Garnish with a cherry.
Serves 1

Sea Horse

1½ ounces vodka
½ ounce Pernod
2½ ounces cranapple juice

½ ounce lime juice
3 ounces ice
1 cherry umbrella

Combine the vodka, Pernod, cranapple juice and lime juice in a cocktail shaker and mix well. Strain the cocktail mixture into a 5½-ounce cocktail glass filled with the ice. Garnish with a cherry umbrella.
Serves 1

Ship Ahoy

2 ounces fresh pineapple chunks
1 ounce light rum
½ ounce lime juice
½ ounce peach liqueur

½ ounce honey
fresh mint leaves
1 pineapple cherry skewer

Process the pineapple chunks, rum, lime juice, liqueur, honey and mint in a blender until puréed. Pour the cocktail mixture over crushed ice in a 9-ounce glass. Garnish with a pineapple cherry skewer.
Serves 1

Bacon-Wrapped Pineapple Chunks

1 cup ketchup
¼ cup dark corn syrup
1 tablespoon Worcestershire sauce
1 tablespoon prepared horseradish
⅛ teaspoon hot sauce
1 (15-ounce) can pineapple chunks, drained
1 pound sliced bacon, cut crosswise into halves
1 (11-ounce) can mandarin oranges, drained (optional)

Combine the ketchup, corn syrup, Worcestershire sauce, prepared horseradish and hot sauce in a saucepan and mix well. Bring to a boil; reduce the heat. Simmer for 10 minutes, stirring frequently. Remove from the heat.

Wrap each pineapple chunk in bacon and secure with wooden picks. Arrange the bacon-wrapped pineapple in a single layer in a shallow roasting pan. Bake at 400 degrees for 15 minutes; baste with the sauce. Bake for 15 to 20 minutes longer or until the bacon is cooked through. Secure a mandarin orange to the bottom of each pineapple chunk before serving.

Makes 35 to 40 appetizers

Fresh Pineapple Salsa

2 cups chopped fresh pineapple
½ cup finely chopped red bell pepper
½ cup finely chopped red onion
¼ cup finely chopped fresh mint leaves
¼ cup finely chopped cilantro leaves
¼ cup finely chopped green bell pepper
2 tablespoons thawed frozen orange juice concentrate
2 tablespoons fresh lime juice
1 garlic clove, crushed
¼ teaspoon crushed red pepper
¼ to ½ teaspoon grated fresh gingerroot

Combine the pineapple, red bell pepper, onion, mint, cilantro, green bell pepper, orange juice concentrate, lime juice, garlic, red pepper and gingerroot in a bowl and mix well. Chill for 3 to 10 hours. Serve with grilled fish, pork or chicken.

Makes 4 cups

Luau

You don't have to be in the islands to share in the spirit of aloha. A luau is a fabulous way to bring family and friends together to celebrate a birth, marriage, graduation, new home, life! All you need is a warm summer day, a yard or lanai, delicious food, delightful Hawaiian music, and the laughter of those around you.

Egg Rolls

Sweet-and-Sour Sauce

2 cups pineapple juice

1/2 cup ketchup

2 tablespoons brown sugar

2 tablespoons cornstarch

Egg Rolls

8 ounces ground pork, ground turkey or ground chicken

1 cup finely chopped carrots

1 cup finely chopped celery

1 cup water chestnuts, chopped

1/2 cup finely chopped spring onions

1/4 cup minced garlic

2 eggs, lightly beaten

1/2 teaspoon soy sauce

1/2 teaspoon salt

1/2 teaspoon pepper

30 to 35 Filipino lumpia wrappers or egg roll wrappers

vegetable oil for frying

For the sauce, combine the pineapple juice, ketchup, brown sugar and cornstarch in a saucepan and mix well. Bring to a boil, stirring constantly. Let stand until cool.

For the egg rolls, combine the ground pork, carrots, celery, water chestnuts, spring onions and garlic in a bowl and mix well. Add the eggs, soy sauce, salt and pepper and mix well.

Spoon about 1 1/2 tablespoonfuls of the pork mixture at 1 end of each wrapper and roll to enclose the filling. Brush the edge with water to seal. Deep-fry the egg rolls in oil in a skillet until golden brown on all sides; drain. Serve with the sauce.

Makes 30 to 35 egg rolls

Sweet-and-Sour Meatballs

1½ pounds ground lean pork
1 pound ground cooked ham
2 cups cracker crumbs
2 eggs, beaten
1 cup milk
1 teaspoon minced onion
salt to taste
seasoned salt to taste
Sweet-and-Sour Sauce (this page)

Combine the pork and ham in a bowl and mix well. Stir in the cracker crumbs, eggs, milk, onion, salt and seasoned salt. Shape the pork mixture into balls using a melon baller.

Arrange the balls in a single layer on a baking sheet with sides. Bake at 350 degrees for 10 minutes; drain on paper towels. Place the sausage balls in a 9×13-inch baking dish and drizzle with the Sweet-and-Sour Sauce. Bake for 15 minutes. Remove the sausage balls and sauce to a chafing dish to serve.

Serves 12

Sweet-and-Sour Sauce

1¼ cups packed brown sugar
1½ teaspoons dry mustard
½ cup cider vinegar
½ cup hot water
¼ cup golden raisins

Combine the brown sugar and dry mustard in a bowl and mix well. Stir in the vinegar and hot water. Add the raisins and mix well.

Makes 3 cups

Hot Macadamia Dip

11 ounces cream cheese, softened
2 tablespoons milk
1 (2-ounce) jar sliced dried beef, chopped
$^1/_3$ cup each finely chopped onion and green bell pepper
1 garlic clove, minced
$^1/_2$ teaspoon freshly ground pepper
$^1/_4$ teaspoon ginger
$^3/_4$ cup sour cream
$^1/_2$ cup chopped macadamia nuts
1 tablespoon butter or margarine, melted

Combine the cream cheese and milk in a mixing bowl.
Beat at medium speed until creamy. Stir in the dried beef,
onion, bell pepper, garlic, pepper and ginger. Fold in the
sour cream. Spoon the cream cheese mixture into an
ungreased 8×8-inch baking dish.

Sauté the macadamia nuts in the butter in a small
skillet over medium heat until light brown. Sprinkle the
macadamia nuts over the prepared layer. Bake at 350
degrees for 20 to 25 minutes or until heated through. Serve
hot with assorted party crackers.

Makes 4 cups

Spicy Peanut Dip

2 cups roasted peanuts, chopped
3 large garlic cloves
1 (2-inch) piece fresh gingerroot
$^1/_4$ cup water
$^1/_4$ cup dark sesame oil
3 tablespoons soy sauce
2 tablespoons Chinese rice wine or sake
$1^1/_2$ tablespoons sugar
$1^1/_2$ tablespoons Chinese black vinegar
1 teaspoon hot chili paste

Combine the peanuts, garlic and gingerroot in a food
processor fitted with a steel blade. Process for 2 minutes,
scraping the bowl halfway through the process. Add the
water, sesame oil, soy sauce, rice wine, sugar, vinegar and
chili paste.

Process until blended. Serve with fresh snow peas,
carrot and celery sticks and red bell pepper strips.

Makes 2$^1/_3$ cups

Thai Noodle Salad

Thai Salad Dressing

$^{1}/_{4}$ cup peanut butter

$^{1}/_{4}$ cup chicken broth

1 scallion, sliced

2 garlic cloves, minced

2 tablespoons soy sauce

2 tablespoons sherry

2 tablespoons lemon juice

$1^{1}/_{2}$ tablespoons vegetable oil or peanut oil

1 teaspoon sugar

1 teaspoon grated fresh gingerroot

1 teaspoon dark Asian sesame oil

$^{1}/_{2}$ teaspoon chili powder

Salad

16 ounces thin spaghetti

1 cucumber, peeled

1 cup shredded carrots

1 red bell pepper or green bell pepper, julienned

$^{1}/_{3}$ cup chopped scallions

$^{1}/_{3}$ cup chopped roasted peanuts

For the dressing, combine the peanut butter, broth, scallion, garlic, soy sauce, sherry, lemon juice, vegetable oil, sugar, gingerroot, sesame oil and chili powder in a blender or food processor. Process until smooth.

For the salad, cook the pasta using package directions; drain. Slice the cucumber horizontally into halves. Remove the seeds and cut into thin slices. Toss the pasta, cucumber, carrots, bell pepper and scallions in a bowl. Add the dressing and mix until coated. Sprinkle with the peanuts.

Serves 10 to 12

Luau Planning Hints

- *Light tiki torches all around the pool area.*
- *Serve the food buffet-style.*
- *Cover tables with cloths in bright tropical patterns.*
- *Decorate with as much greenery and flowers as possible.*
- *Float gardenias or flower-shaped gardenia-scented candles in bowls of water.*

Lime Vinaigrette

Combine ⅓ cup olive oil, ¼ cup fresh lime juice, 3 tablespoons white balsamic vinegar, 1 tablespoon Maggi liquid seasoning, 1 tablespoon white wine vinegar, ½ teaspoon salt and ½ teaspoon pepper in a jar with a tight-fitting lid and seal tightly. Shake to mix. Chill until serving time.

Salpicon

Beef and Vegetables

1 (7-ounce) can chipotle chiles in
  adobo sauce
1 (2-pound) beef chuck roast
1 teaspoon each salt and pepper
1 teaspoon adobo seasoning with
  pepper (optional)
3 tablespoons olive oil
1 medium onion, chopped
1 cup dry red wine
1 (10-ounce) can beef broth
½ cup water
¼ cup red wine vinegar
1 teaspoon garlic paste

¼ teaspoon liquid smoke
1 tablespoon chopped fresh rosemary
1 tablespoon chopped fresh thyme
2 bay leaves
6 to 8 small red potatoes, cut into
  quarters
1 red onion, thinly sliced

Salpicon Salad

1 to 2 heads romaine, chopped
1 ripe avocado, chopped
3 radishes, thinly sliced
8 ounces pepper Jack cheese, chopped
Lime Vinaigrette (this page)

For the beef and vegetables, drain and chop the chipotle chiles, reserving the sauce. Season the roast on both sides with the salt, pepper and adobo seasoning. Brown the roast in the olive oil in a Dutch oven for 4 minutes per side. Remove from the heat.

Combine 1 teaspoon reserved chipotle chile sauce, or more if a hotter taste is desired, chopped onion, wine, broth, water, vinegar, garlic paste, liquid smoke, rosemary, thyme and bay leaves in a bowl and mix well. Spoon the onion mixture over the roast. Bake, covered, at 275 degrees for 2 hours or until the roast is fork-tender. Add the potatoes and sliced red onion.

Bake for 20 to 30 minutes longer or just until the potatoes are tender. Remove the potatoes to a bowl and cover loosely with plastic wrap. Cool the roast in the broth for 1 hour. Shred the roast and return the shredded roast to the broth in the Dutch oven. Let stand until cool. Discard the bay leaves.

For the salad, arrange the lettuce on a large serving platter. Drain the shredded roast, reserving the broth. Gently toss the shredded roast with the avocado, radishes, cheese and chipotle chiles in a bowl. Spoon the avocado mixture over the lettuce. Top with the reserved potatoes. Shake the Lime Vinaigrette and drizzle over the top of the salad. Drizzle with a small amount of the reserved broth if desired, or reserve the broth for another use.

Serves 8

Luau Shrimp and Fruit Salad

Banana Chutney Dressing

1 ripe banana
1/2 cup mayonnaise
2 tablespoons chutney
1 tablespoon fresh lemon juice

Salad

crisp lettuce leaves
1 cantaloupe, peeled and sliced into 4 rings
1 pound small shrimp, cooked and peeled
2 firm bananas, sliced
1 orange, peeled and sliced
1 pound red grapes, separated into small clusters

For the dressing, process the banana in a food processor or blender until puréed. Add the mayonnaise, chutney and lemon juice. Process until smooth. Chill, covered, in the refrigerator.

For the salad, line 4 salad plates with lettuce. Arrange 1 cantaloupe ring on each lettuce-lined salad plate. Fill the center of the rings with the shrimp. Arrange the sliced banana, sliced orange and grape clusters around the cantaloupe. Serve with the dressing.

Serves 4

Chicken Coconut Curry

1 1/2 pounds boneless skinless chicken breasts, cut into
   bite-size pieces
salt and pepper to taste
chili powder to taste
1/4 cup vegetable oil
2 carrots, chopped
1 red bell pepper, chopped
1 cup chicken stock
2 plum tomatoes, chopped
2 garlic cloves, minced
2 tablespoons curry powder
1 tablespoon soy sauce
1 (12-ounce) can coconut milk
6 scallions, chopped
1 bunch cilantro, coarsely chopped

Season the chicken with salt, pepper and chili powder. Heat 2 tablespoons of the oil in a medium saucepan. Brown the chicken on all sides in the hot oil. Remove the chicken to a platter with a slotted spoon, reserving the pan drippings. Add the remaining 2 tablespoons oil to the reserved pan drippings.

Sauté the carrots and bell pepper in the hot oil mixture for 5 minutes. Stir in the stock, tomatoes, garlic, curry powder and soy sauce. Simmer for several minutes, stirring occasionally. Add the chicken and any collected juices to the tomato mixture and mix well.

Simmer, covered, for 10 minutes, stirring occasionally. Stir in the coconut milk. Increase the heat slightly. Cook for 10 minutes, stirring occasionally. Spoon into a serving bowl. Sprinkle with the scallions and cilantro.

Serves 4 to 6

Turkey Burgers

1 pound ground turkey
1/2 cup fresh bread crumbs
1/3 cup finely chopped flat-leaf parsley
1 egg, lightly beaten
3/4 teaspoon salt
1/2 teaspoon freshly ground pepper
1 small onion, finely chopped
1 tablespoon safflower oil
1 small garlic clove, minced
Fresh Plum Sauce (this page)
4 hamburger buns, grilled or toasted

Combine the ground turkey, bread crumbs, parsley, egg, salt and pepper in a bowl and mix well. Chill, covered, in the refrigerator. Sauté the onion in the safflower oil in a small skillet for 3 to 4 minutes or until the onion begins to brown. Stir in the garlic. Remove from the heat. Cool to room temperature. Add the onion mixture to the turkey mixture and mix well.

Shape the turkey mixture into 4 patties. Arrange the patties on an oiled grill rack. Grill over hot coals for 6 minutes per side or until a meat thermometer registers 165 degrees. Serve the burgers with the Fresh Plum Sauce on the hamburger buns.

Serves 4

Fresh Plum Sauce

1 1/2 pounds ripe purple plums, cut into 1-inch pieces
1/3 cup balsamic vinegar
1/2 cup shredded fresh basil
1/2 teaspoon freshly ground pepper
1/4 teaspoon salt

Combine the plums and vinegar in a medium nonreactive saucepan. Bring to a boil over high heat; reduce the heat. Cook, covered, over medium-low heat for 10 minutes or until the plums are tender, stirring frequently. Process the plum mixture in a food processor until puréed. Strain the purée into a nonreactive bowl. Stir in the basil, pepper and salt. Let stand until cool. Store, covered, in the refrigerator for up to 1 week.

Serves 4

Grilled Crab Burgers

6 ounces fresh crab meat, shells and cartilage removed
1 cup fresh white bread crumbs
1/2 cup chopped green onions
2 tablespoons mayonnaise
1 teaspoon Old Bay seasoning or other seafood seasoning
1 egg yolk, beaten
1/2 cup fresh white bread crumbs
2 1/2 tablespoons mayonnaise
1 1/2 tablespoons Dijon mustard
4 slices French bread

Combine the crab meat, 1 cup bread crumbs, green onions, 2 tablespoons mayonnaise, Old Bay seasoning and egg yolk in a bowl and mix well. Shape the crab meat mixture into four 2 1/2-inch patties. Coat the patties with 1/2 cup bread crumbs. Combine 2 1/2 tablespoons mayonnaise and Dijon mustard in a small bowl and mix well.

Arrange the patties on an oiled grill rack. Grill over medium-high heat for 4 minutes per side or until golden brown. Grill the bread slices for 1 minute per side or until light brown. Spread 1 side of each bread slice with the mustard mixture and top with a crab burger. Serve immediately. You may broil the patties if a grill is not available.

Serves 2

Seared Tuna with Citrus Relish

Citrus Relish
2 teaspoons sherry vinegar or white wine vinegar
2 teaspoons soy sauce
1/2 teaspoon grated fresh gingerroot
1 tablespoon olive oil
sections of 1 medium grapefruit, cut into thirds
sections of 1 medium orange, cut into halves
2 tablespoons finely chopped red onion
2 tablespoons snipped fresh cilantro

Tuna
2 teaspoons olive oil
4 (4-ounce) tuna steaks, 3/4 inch thick
salt and pepper to taste
sprigs of fresh cilantro (optional)

For the relish, mix the vinegar, soy sauce and gingerroot in a bowl. Whisk in the olive oil. Stir in the grapefruit, orange, onion and cilantro.

For the tuna, heat the olive oil in a large skillet over medium-high heat. Add the tuna. Cook for 6 to 9 minutes or until the fish flakes easily, turning once. Sprinkle with salt and pepper. Garnish each serving with a sprig of cilantro and serve with the relish.

Serves 4

Caramelized Bananas with Vanilla Cream

1/2 cup sugar
3 1/2 tablespoons cornstarch
2 cups milk
4 egg yolks
1 vanilla bean, split lengthwise
Phyllo Dessert Cups (this page)
3 large firm ripe bananas, diagonally sliced
sugar to taste
chocolate sorbet

Mix the sugar and cornstarch in a heavy saucepan. Add the milk, whisking constantly. Whisk in the egg yolks. Scrape the seeds from the vanilla bean into the milk mixture and add 1/2 of the vanilla bean, reserving the remaining vanilla bean half for another recipe.

Cook over medium heat until the mixture thickens and comes to a boil, whisking constantly. Strain into a small bowl, discarding the solids. Press plastic wrap directly onto the surface of the cream. Chill for 3 hours or until cold. You may store, covered, in the refrigerator for up to 2 days.

To serve, arrange the phyllo cups on a small baking sheet. Spoon 1/3 cup of the cream into each cup. Overlap 5 or 6 banana slices over the top of each. Sprinkle with sugar to taste. Broil for 2 minutes or until the sugar caramelizes, turning the baking sheet for even browning. Arrange 1 phyllo cup on each dessert plate. Scoop sorbet alongside.

Serves 6

Phyllo Dessert Cups

9 (13×17-inch) phyllo pastry sheets
1/2 cup (1 stick) unsalted butter, melted
7 1/2 tablespoons sugar

Coat every other muffin cup in a 12-cup muffin pan generously with butter. Stack the pastry sheets and cut crosswise into halves, forming eighteen 8 1/2×13-inch rectangles. Place 1 pastry rectangle on a work surface, covering the remaining rectangles with a damp tea towel to prevent drying out.

Brush the rectangle with some of the melted butter and sprinkle with 1 1/2 teaspoons of the sugar. Top with a second phyllo rectangle. Brush with melted butter and sprinkle with 1 1/2 teaspoons sugar. Repeat this process 3 more times. Top with 1 more pastry rectangle and brush with melted butter.

This will make a stack of 6 rectangles. Using a small sharp knife and one 6-inch plate as a guide, cut out two 6-inch round stacks. Press each stack into a prepared muffin cup. Repeat the entire process 2 more times with the remaining pastry rectangles, remaining melted butter and remaining sugar, for a total of 6 phyllo cups.

Makes 6

Coconut Macadamia Pound Cake

Cake

3 cups sugar

1½ cups (3 sticks) butter, softened

8 ounces cream cheese, softened

6 eggs, at room temperature

3 cups sifted flour

7 to 10 ounces shredded coconut, lightly toasted

1½ to 2 cups macadamia nuts, lightly toasted, or
    honey-roasted macadamia nuts, coarsely chopped

Rum Glaze

¾ cup sugar

¼ cup water

¼ cup amber rum or dark rum

For the cake, beat the sugar and butter in a mixing bowl until creamy, scraping the bowl occasionally. Beat in the cream cheese until blended. Add the eggs 1 at a time, beating well after each addition. Add the flour gradually, beating constantly until blended. Fold in the coconut and macadamia nuts.

Spoon the batter into a greased and floured tube pan. Bake at 325 degrees for 1 to 1½ hours or until the cake tests done.

For the glaze, bring the sugar and water to a boil in a saucepan. Boil until the sugar dissolves, stirring constantly. Remove from the heat. Stir in the rum. Drizzle the warm glaze over the warm cake.

Serves 16

Toasted Coconut Brownies

Coconut Topping

½ can sweetened coconut

1 tablespoon sugar

2 teaspoons butter, melted

Brownies

⅔ cup sifted flour

½ teaspoon baking powder

¼ teaspoon salt

2 ounces unsweetened chocolate

⅓ cup butter

2 eggs

1 cup sugar

½ can sweetened coconut

1 teaspoon vanilla extract

For the topping, combine the coconut, sugar and butter in a bowl and mix well.

For the brownies, sift the flour, baking powder and salt together. Heat the chocolate and butter in a saucepan until blended, stirring frequently. Remove from the heat.

Place the eggs in a mixing bowl. Add the sugar gradually, beating constantly until blended. Add the chocolate mixture and beat until smooth. Add the flour mixture and mix well. Stir in the coconut and vanilla.

Spoon the batter into a baking pan. Spread with the topping. Bake at 350 degrees for 30 minutes. Cool in the pan on a wire rack. Cut into bars.

Makes 1½ to 2 dozen brownies

Culinary Bouquets

MENU

Breakfast in Bed

Begin a special day together as you wake up your Valentine with the perfect meal. Whether it is your anniversary, a honeymoon, or "just because," serving breakfast in bed is one of the most romantic things you can do for that sweet someone. Add lots of fluff with a morning cocktail served with a scrumptious plateful of extras.

Florida Citrus Fizz

25 ice cubes
½ cup vodka
½ cup whipping cream
½ cup club soda
¼ cup frozen lemonade concentrate
¼ cup frozen limeade concentrate
3 tablespoons frozen orange juice concentrate
3 tablespoons confectioners' sugar
nutmeg to taste
lemon zest twists or lime zest twists
lemon slices

Process the ice cubes, vodka, whipping cream, club soda, lemonade concentrate, limeade concentrate, orange juice concentrate, confectioners' sugar and nutmeg in a blender until smooth. Pour the cocktail mixture into 4 glasses. Garnish with lemon or lime zest twists and lemon slices.

You may prepare in advance and store, covered, in the freezer. Thaw slightly before serving.

Serves 4

Peach Bellini

2 ounces peach juice or peach nectar
4 ounces Champagne, chilled
⅛ teaspoon grenadine
fresh peach slice

Pour the peach juice into a Champagne flute or wine glass. Add the Champagne, and mix gently. Stir in the grenadine. Garnish the rim of the glass with a peach slice.

Serves 1

Romantic Destinations

Northwest Florida beckons and all highways lead to the mecca of vacationers: Panama City Beach. Nestled in the gentle westward curve of Florida's panhandle lies the beach area that has been affectionately named the "World's Most Beautiful Beach." This area has attracted millions of visitors, and year after year they return because it has some kind of effect that can't be duplicated. It is romantic!

Attracted by the natural beauty of the sugar-white sands and azure waters, today's vacationers can find accommodations ranging from cozy bed-and-breakfast lodgings to luxurious condominiums to large houses that sleep up to 25 guests. Nothing is better than waking up to the smell of salt air and knowing that coffee and orange juice will be served overlooking the Gulf of Mexico.

Hash Brown Casserole

3 cups frozen O'Brien hash brown potatoes
1 cup chopped cooked ham or Canadian bacon
1/4 cup sliced green onions
3/4 cup (3 ounces) shredded Monterey Jack cheese with
    jalapeño chiles
1 (12-ounce) can low-fat evaporated milk
4 eggs, beaten
1/4 teaspoon pepper
1/8 teaspoon salt
1/2 teaspoon Tabasco sauce, or to taste

Spread the potatoes in a greased 8×8-inch baking dish. Layer with the ham, green onions and cheese. Whisk the evaporated milk, eggs, pepper, salt and Tabasco sauce in a bowl until blended. Pour the evaporated milk mixture over the prepared layers. You may chill, covered, at this point for 2 to 10 hours.

Bake at 350 degrees for 40 to 45 minutes or until the center is set, covering with foil 15 minutes before the end of the baking process to prevent overbrowning. Let stand for 5 minutes before serving. Increase the baking time to 55 to 60 minutes if chilled.

Serves 6

Broiled Portobellos with Scrambled Eggs

6 (4- to 5-inch) portobello mushrooms
olive oil to taste
3 garlic cloves, minced
salt and pepper to taste
12 eggs
2 tablespoons grated Parmesan cheese
1 1/2 teaspoons chopped fresh rosemary
3/4 teaspoon salt
1/2 teaspoon ground pepper
6 tablespoons butter
2 tablespoons grated Parmesan cheese

Line a large baking sheet with foil. Remove and discard the mushroom stems. Scoop out and discard the tough centers where the mushroom stems were attached. Brush both sides of the mushrooms generously with olive oil.

Arrange the mushrooms gill side up on the prepared baking sheet. Sprinkle the mushrooms with the garlic, salt and pepper. Broil 5 inches from the heat source for 5 minutes or until the mushrooms begin to soften; turn. Broil for 7 minutes longer or until tender when pierced with a sharp knife. Cover to keep warm.

Whisk the eggs, 2 tablespoons cheese, rosemary, 3/4 teaspoon salt and 1/2 teaspoon pepper in a bowl until blended. Heat 5 tablespoons of the butter in a large heavy skillet over medium-low heat. Add the egg mixture to the hot butter. Stir gently in a circular motion with a wooden spoon, releasing the cooked eggs from the bottom of the skillet and allowing the uncooked portion of the eggs to flow underneath. Cook for 4 minutes or until the eggs are set but soft. Dot with the remaining 1 tablespoon butter.

To serve, arrange the hot portobello mushrooms gill side up on individual serving plates. Top each mushroom with an equal portion of the scrambled eggs. Sprinkle with 2 tablespoons cheese. Serve immediately.

Serves 6

Eggs Morning Glory

2 slices white or whole wheat bread
5 tablespoons butter
3 tablespoons flour
¾ cup (about) milk
salt and pepper to taste
2 hard-cooked eggs, sliced

Spread each slice of the bread with 1 tablespoon of the butter. Arrange the slices on a baking sheet. Toast until light brown on both sides, turning once.

Heat the remaining 3 tablespoons butter in a saucepan. Stir in the flour. Cook until smooth and bubbly, stirring constantly. Add the milk gradually, stirring constantly. Cook until slightly thickened, stirring constantly. Season with salt and pepper.

To serve, arrange 1 slice of the toast on each of 2 serving plates. Top each with 1 sliced egg and drizzle with the sauce. Serve immediately.

Serves 2

Bacon and Mushroom Quiche

1 tablespoon butter
1 cup thinly sliced fresh mushrooms
4 eggs
¾ teaspoon Worcestershire sauce
15 slices bacon, crisp-cooked and crumbled
1 cup sour cream
1 cup (4 ounces) shredded Swiss cheese
½ cup chopped green onions (white and pale green parts)
1 (3-ounce) can French-fried onions
1 baked (9-inch) pie shell

Heat the butter in a skillet over medium heat. Sauté the mushrooms in the butter for 7 minutes or until tender. Remove from the heat.

Whisk the eggs and Worcestershire sauce in a bowl. Stir in the bacon, sour cream, cheese, green onions, French-fried onions and mushrooms. Spoon into the pie shell. Bake at 350 degrees for 30 minutes.

Serves 6 to 8

Roasted Asparagus with Bacon

6 slices bacon
2 pounds fresh medium asparagus spears
2 tablespoons olive oil
salt and pepper to taste
1 (3½- to 4-ounce) log soft goat cheese, crumbled
2 teaspoons lemon juice
2 teaspoons olive oil
1 teaspoon grated lemon zest

Fry the bacon in a large heavy skillet over medium heat until brown and crisp; drain on paper towels. Crumble the bacon.

Snap off the tough woody ends of the asparagus. Arrange the asparagus in a single layer on a large baking sheet with sides. Drizzle with 2 tablespoons olive oil and sprinkle generously with salt and pepper. Place the baking sheet on the middle oven rack. Roast at 500 degrees for 7 minutes or until tender-crisp.

Arrange the asparagus in a single layer on a serving platter. Sprinkle with the goat cheese and bacon. Drizzle with the lemon juice and 2 teaspoons olive oil. Sprinkle with the lemon zest. You may prepare 1 hour in advance and let stand, covered, at room temperature.

Serves 6

Orange Blossom Croissants

6 croissants
1 (9-ounce) jar orange marmalade
6 tablespoons orange juice
6 slices shaved smoked ham
cream cheese, softened
1¼ cups half-and-half
6 eggs
1 teaspoon almond extract
fresh strawberries
fresh orange slices or mandarin orange sections

Cut each croissant horizontally into halves. Arrange the croissant bottom halves cut side up in a 9×9-inch baking dish. Combine the marmalade and orange juice in a bowl and mix well. Reserve several tablespoons of the mixture for later use. Spoon the remaining marmalade mixture over the croissant bottoms. Place 1 slice of the ham on each croissant bottom. Spread cream cheese over the cut side of the croissant tops and place over the ham.

Whisk the half-and-half, eggs and flavoring in a bowl until blended. Pour the egg mixture over the croissants and drizzle with the reserved marmalade mixture. Chill, covered, for 8 to 10 hours. Let stand at room temperature for 30 to 45 minutes. Bake at 350 degrees for 30 minutes. Serve hot, garnished with strawberries and orange slices.

Serves 6

Cream Caramel French Toast

21 slices cinnamon raisin bread
6 eggs
2 cups milk
2 cups light cream
1/3 cup sugar
1 tablespoon vanilla extract
1/2 teaspoon salt
sour cream
chopped walnuts, almonds or pecans

Turn a 9×13-inch baking dish with the long side toward you and arrange the cinnamon bread in 3 rows of 7 slices each crosswise in the pan. Combine the eggs, milk, cream, sugar, vanilla and salt in a bowl and beat until smooth. Pour gradually over the bread and cover with foil. Let stand in the refrigerator for 8 hours or longer.

Bake, covered, at 350 degrees for 15 minutes. Uncover and bake for 15 minutes longer. Cut into 9 to 12 squares. Invert the servings onto serving plates so the sauce is on the top. Top with a dollop of sour cream and chopped walnuts.

Serves 9 to 12

Mother's Day Waffles

2 cups flour
2 tablespoons sugar
1/2 teaspoon bourbon vanilla extract
1/2 teaspoon dry yeast
2 cups milk
1/2 cup (1 stick) unsalted butter, melted
3 egg yolks, lightly beaten
3 egg whites, stiffly beaten
confectioners' sugar (optional)
whipped cream (optional)
fresh mixed berries (optional)

Combine the flour, sugar, bourbon vanilla and yeast in a large bowl and mix well. Mix the milk and unsalted butter in a bowl. Whisk the milk mixture into the flour mixture. Let rise, covered with plastic wrap, at room temperature for 8 to 10 hours. Whisk in the egg yolks. Fold in the egg whites.

Pour 1/2 cup of the batter into each square section of the waffle iron and spread evenly so all the grids are covered with batter. Bake for 3 minutes. Serve hot with confectioners' sugar, whipped cream and fresh berries. You may freeze for future use. Reheat in the toaster on a low setting.

Makes 12 waffles

Berries à la 21 Club

Place 1 pint each fresh raspberries, blueberries and strawberries in separate decorative bowls. Pass the berries with 1 cup low-fat sour cream and ¼ cup light or dark brown sugar for guests to prepare as desired.

Chive Corn Muffins

1 cup flour
1 cup yellow cornmeal
1 tablespoon sugar
2 teaspoons baking powder
1 teaspoon salt
½ teaspoon baking soda
½ teaspoon cayenne pepper
¼ cup chopped fresh chives
1½ cups plain yogurt
2 eggs
3 tablespoons unsalted butter, melted

Position the oven rack in the center of the oven. Spray 10 standard muffin cups or 30 miniature muffin cups with nonstick cooking spray. Combine the flour, cornmeal, sugar, baking powder, salt, baking soda and cayenne pepper in a bowl and mix well. Stir in the chives.

Whisk the yogurt, eggs and unsalted butter in a bowl until blended. Add the yogurt mixture to the flour mixture and stir just until moistened. Spoon about ⅓ cup of the batter into each standard muffin cup or 1 heaping tablespoon of the batter into each miniature muffin cup.

Bake at 425 degrees for 20 minutes for standard muffins or 14 minutes for miniature muffins or until the muffins are puffed and golden brown and a wooden pick inserted in the center comes out clean. Cool in the pans on a wire rack. You may prepare up to 4 hours in advance. Let stand at room temperature in the muffin cups. Reheat at 350 degrees for 5 minutes or just until warm.

Makes 10 standard muffins or 30 miniature muffins

Blueberry Muffins

1³/₄ cups flour
2¹/₂ teaspoons baking powder
¹/₂ teaspoon salt
1 cup sugar
³/₄ cup (1¹/₂ sticks) butter
³/₄ cup buttermilk
1 egg, lightly beaten
1 cup fresh blueberries
1 tablespoon flour

Sift 1³/₄ cups flour, baking powder and salt together. Beat the sugar and butter in a mixing bowl until creamy. Stir in the buttermilk and egg. Add the flour mixture ¹/₂ at a time, mixing just until moistened after each addition.

Toss the blueberries with 1 tablespoon flour in a bowl. Fold the blueberries into the batter. Spoon the batter into paper-lined muffin cups. Bake at 400 degrees for 20 minutes.

Makes 1 dozen muffins

Key Lime Muffins

2 cups flour
1 cup sugar
1 tablespoon baking powder
¹/₂ teaspoon salt
¹/₃ cup milk
¹/₄ cup vegetable oil
¹/₄ cup Key lime juice
2 eggs, beaten
grated zest of 1 Key lime

Combine the flour, sugar, baking powder and salt in a bowl and mix well. Make a well in the center of the flour mixture. Whisk the milk, oil, lime juice, eggs and lime zest in a bowl.

Add the milk mixture to the well and stir just until moistened. Fill greased muffin cups ³/₄ full. Bake at 400 degrees for 18 minutes or until the muffins test done. Sprinkle with additional sugar if desired.

Makes 1 dozen muffins

Double Lemon Muffins

Lemon Syrup

3/4 cup water
1/2 cup sugar
1/4 cup fresh lemon juice
grated zest of 1 lemon
1/2 teaspoon lemon extract

Lemon Muffins

3 1/2 cups flour
1 1/2 cups sugar
1 tablespoon baking powder
1/2 teaspoon baking soda
1/2 teaspoon salt
1 cup milk
1/4 cup fresh lemon juice
2 eggs, lightly beaten
grated zest of 2 lemons
1 cup (2 sticks) butter, melted

For the syrup, combine the water, sugar, lemon juice, lemon zest and flavoring in a medium saucepan and mix well. Bring to a boil over medium heat, stirring constantly. Boil, covered, for 4 minutes, stirring occasionally. Remove from the heat. Let stand, uncovered, at room temperature.

For the muffins, mix the flour, sugar, baking powder, baking soda and salt in a bowl. Combine the milk, lemon juice, eggs and lemon zest in a bowl and mix well. Add the milk mixture and butter to the flour mixture and stir just until moistened. Fill greased muffin cups 2/3 full.

Bake at 375 degrees for 15 minutes or until the muffins test done. Pierce the top of the muffins with a fork or metal skewer. Brush with the syrup and sprinkle generously with additional sugar. Cool slightly before removing from the pan.

Makes 2 dozen muffins

Orange Blossom Muffins

Spice Topping

3 tablespoons sugar
1 tablespoon flour
1/2 teaspoon cinnamon
1/4 teaspoon nutmeg

Orange Muffins

4 cups baking mix
1/4 cup sugar
1/2 cup orange juice
2 tablespoons vegetable oil
1 egg
1/2 cup orange marmalade
1/2 cup chopped pecans (optional)

For the topping, mix the sugar, flour, cinnamon and nutmeg in a bowl.

For the muffins, combine the baking mix and sugar in a bowl and mix well. Make a well in the center of the baking mix mixture. Whisk the orange juice, oil and egg in a bowl until blended. Add the orange juice mixture to the well and stir just until moistened.

Fold the marmalade and pecans into the batter. Fill greased muffin cups 2/3 full. Sprinkle with the topping. Bake at 400 degrees for 18 minutes. Remove to a wire rack immediately.

Makes 1 dozen muffins

Raspberry Streusel Muffins

Streusel Topping

$1/4$ cup flour
$1/4$ cup chopped pecans
$1/4$ cup packed brown sugar
2 tablespoons butter, melted

Raspberry Muffins

$1^1/2$ cups flour
$1/2$ cup sugar
2 teaspoons baking powder
$1/2$ cup milk
$1/2$ cup (1 stick) butter, melted
1 egg, beaten
1 cup frozen raspberries

For the topping, combine the flour, pecans and brown sugar in a bowl and mix well. Stir in the butter.

For the muffins, combine the flour, sugar and baking powder in a bowl and mix well. Make a well in the center of the flour mixture. Whisk the milk, butter and egg in a bowl until blended. Add the milk mixture to the well and stir just until moistened. Fold in the raspberries.

Spoon the batter into greased muffin cups. Bake at 375 degrees for 20 to 25 minutes or until the muffins test done. Remove to a wire rack immediately.

Makes 1 dozen muffins

Flavored Butters

Each of these butters requires $1/2$ cup (1 stick) softened unsalted butter. Spoon the finished butter into a serving bowl or decorative molds and store, covered, in the refrigerator.

For Honey-Nut Butter, combine the butter with $1/4$ cup honey and $1/2$ cup chopped pecans in a bowl and mix until smooth.

For Orange Butter, pulse the butter in a food processor 14 times. Add 3 tablespoons confectioners' sugar, the grated zest of 1 orange and 2 tablespoons orange liqueur and pulse 10 to 12 times or until smooth.

For Strawberry Butter, cream the butter in a food processor until smooth. Add $3/4$ cup confectioners' sugar, 1 tablespoon lemon juice and 1 cup thawed frozen unsweetened strawberries. Pulse 10 to 12 times and scrape the side of the food processor. Pulse until smooth.

MENU

Bicycle Built for Two

"…but you'll look sweet upon the seat of a bicycle built for two." Pack your meal in an old basket and enjoy a ride to find the perfect spot to spread your blanket. Stop along the way and pick fresh flowers to take home and press to help you reminisce later about your perfect picnic. Make it a tradition.

Minted Orange Lemon Fizz

$1^{1}/_{4}$ cups water

$^{2}/_{3}$ cup sugar

$^{3}/_{4}$ cup orange juice

$^{3}/_{4}$ cup lemon juice

$^{1}/_{2}$ cup packed fresh mint leaves

1 tablespoon grated orange zest

2 cups lemon-flavor sparkling water

sprigs of fresh mint

Combine the water and sugar in a small heavy saucepan. Cook over medium heat until the sugar dissolves, stirring constantly. Remove from the heat. Let stand until cool. Stir in the orange juice, lemon juice, $^{1}/_{2}$ cup mint leaves and orange zest. Chill, covered, for 3 to 10 hours. Strain into a pitcher, discarding the solids. Stir in the sparkling water. Pour over ice in glasses. Garnish with sprigs of mint.

Serves 4 to 6

Carillon Beach

Carillon Beach is a community of unique beach homes and shops that represent the epitome of dream beach living. This location is the setting of this picnic because it's the perfect place for riding bicycles, beachcombing, and spreading a colorful blanket for a lazy afternoon picnic. The bells of Carillon are housed in a tower that sits in the center of the housing community, and concerts are played throughout most of the year.

In addition to these attractions, the beach community also offers a market and collection of restaurants, specialty shops, and one-of-a-kind collectible shops. The market area is reminiscent of days gone by and is complete with gaslights, cobblestone streets, and lush landscaping. To top it all off, the downtown area lines the shore of Lake Carillon, which offers spectacular views of both the lake and the Gulf of Mexico.

Buttermilk Sesame Crackers

$1^{2}/_{3}$ cups unbleached flour

$^{1}/_{2}$ cup sesame seeds, toasted

$^{1}/_{3}$ cup cornstarch

$^{3}/_{4}$ teaspoon salt

$^{3}/_{4}$ teaspoon baking powder

$^{1}/_{4}$ teaspoon baking soda

$^{1}/_{2}$ cup (1 stick) unsalted butter,
    chilled and cut into pieces

$^{1}/_{3}$ cup (or more) buttermilk

$1^{1}/_{2}$ teaspoons snipped fresh chives

$1^{1}/_{2}$ teaspoons minced fresh parsley

Process the first 6 ingredients in a food processor until combined. Add the unsalted butter. Pulse until crumbly. Combine the buttermilk, chives and parsley in a bowl and mix well. Add the buttermilk mixture to the crumb mixture gradually, processing constantly until a soft but slightly crumbly dough forms.

Divide the dough into 2 equal portions. Shape each portion into a disk. Chill, wrapped in plastic wrap, for 20 minutes or for up to 12 hours. Roll 1 dough portion $^{1}/_{8}$ inch thick on a lightly floured surface and cut into rounds with a 2-inch plain or scalloped cutter. Pierce the rounds with a fork. Arrange the rounds $^{1}/_{2}$ inch apart on a heavy baking sheet. Repeat the process with the remaining dough. Bake at 375 degrees for 12 minutes or until light brown. Remove to a wire rack to cool. Store in an airtight container for up to 1 week.

Makes 3 dozen crackers

Deli Roll-Ups Platter

Beef Roll-Ups

4 ounces cream cheese, softened
1/4 cup minced fresh basil or cilantro
2 to 3 tablespoons minced pepperoncini chiles or pickled
  jalapeño chiles
garlic clove, minced
8 ounces thinly sliced deli roast beef

Ham and Turkey Roll-Ups

12 ounces cream cheese, softened
1/2 cup shredded carrots
1/2 cup shredded zucchini
4 teaspoons dill weed
8 ounces thinly sliced deli ham
8 ounces thinly sliced deli turkey

For the Beef Roll-Ups, combine the cream cheese, basil, pepperoncini chiles and garlic in a bowl and mix well. Spread about 2 tablespoons of the mixture on each slice of beef and roll tightly to enclose the filling. Wrap individually in plastic wrap and store in the refrigerator. Slice into 1¹/₂-inch pieces to serve.

For the Ham and Turkey Roll-Ups, combine the cream cheese, carrots, zucchini and dill weed in a bowl and mix well. Spread about 2 tablespoons of the mixture on each slice of ham and turkey and roll tightly to enclose the filling. Wrap individually in plastic wrap and chill in the refrigerator for 8 hours or longer. Slice into 1¹/₂-inch pieces to serve.

To serve, arrange the roll-ups on a serving platter, alternating the beef, ham and turkey slices.

Makes 6 to 7 dozen roll-ups

Tomato and Basil Tart

Pastry

1¹/₄ cups flour
1/4 teaspoon salt
6 tablespoons butter, cut into pieces
2 tablespoons shortening
3 tablespoons ice water
1 tablespoon extra-virgin olive oil

Filling

1/3 cup extra-virgin olive oil
2 garlic cloves, thinly sliced
8 plum tomatoes, cut lengthwise into halves and seeded
salt and freshly ground pepper to taste
8 ounces goat cheese, crumbled
1/2 cup slivered fresh basil leaves

For the pastry, mix the flour and salt in a bowl. Cut in the butter and shortening until crumbly. Add the ice water 1 tablespoon at a time, mixing with a fork until the mixture adheres. Knead for a few seconds, shape into a ball and then dust with additional flour. Chill, wrapped in waxed paper, for 1 hour. Roll the dough to fit a 4×13-inch tart pan on a lightly floured surface. Fit into the tart pan, pressing to make the side thicker than the bottom. Trim the edge, allowing a ¹/₂-inch overhang. Fold the overhang over and crimp. Chill for 10 minutes. Brush the pastry with the olive oil.

For the filling, heat the olive oil in a nonstick saucepan over medium heat. Add the garlic and sauté for 1 minute. Add the tomatoes cut side down. Season with salt and pepper. Sauté for 4 to 5 minutes or until golden. Layer the goat cheese, basil leaves and tomatoes cut side down in the order listed in the prepared tart pan. Drizzle with the pan juices and sprinkle with salt and pepper. Bake at 400 degrees for 1 hour or until the crust is light brown.

Serves 4 to 6

Lemony Italian Salad

Lemon Dressing

1/3 cup cider vinegar
1/4 cup olive oil
2 tablespoons lemon juice
2 teaspoons chopped fresh rosemary
1/4 teaspoon salt
1/4 teaspoon pepper

Salad

2/3 cup dried lentils
1 1/3 cups water
8 ounces thinly sliced cooked ham
6 plum tomatoes, chopped
6 ounces Parmesan cheese, shredded
2 cups torn fresh spinach leaves

For the dressing, combine the vinegar, olive oil, lemon juice, rosemary, salt and pepper in a jar with a tight-fitting lid and seal tightly. Shake to mix.

For the salad, sort and rinse the lentils. Bring the lentils and water to a boil in a saucepan; reduce the heat. Simmer, covered, for 25 minutes or until tender; drain.

Combine the lentils, ham, tomatoes, cheese and spinach in a salad bowl and toss gently. Add the dressing and mix until coated. Serve warm or chilled.

Serves 4 to 6

Couscous and Chicken Salad

Orange Balsamic Dressing

3/4 cup orange juice
3 tablespoons balsamic vinegar
3 tablespoons freshly grated orange zest
1 tablespoon cumin or curry powder
1/2 cup olive oil

Salad

4 1/2 cups water
2 (10-ounce) packages couscous (3 cups)
1 cup dried currants
1 (3-pound) roasted chicken, skinned, boned, cut into bite-size pieces
1 1/2 cups drained chopped roasted red peppers
1 (15-ounce) can chick-peas, drained
1 cup chopped pitted kalamata olives
1 bunch green onions, chopped
1/2 cup chopped fresh cilantro
salt and pepper to taste
romaine leaves

For the dressing, mix the orange juice, balsamic vinegar, orange zest and cumin in a bowl. Add the olive oil gradually, whisking constantly until incorporated.

For the salad, bring the water to a boil in a saucepan. Stir in the couscous and currants. Remove from the heat. Let stand, covered, for 5 minutes. Fluff with a fork and remove the couscous mixture to a large bowl. Let stand until cool. Stir the chicken, roasted peppers, chick-peas, olives, green onions and cilantro into the cooled couscous. Add the dressing and toss to coat. Season with salt and pepper. Spoon the salad into a lettuce-lined bowl. You may prepare up to 1 day in advance and store, covered, in the refrigerator.

Serves 8

Curried Mango Chicken Salad

1 (8-ounce) jar mango chutney
1½ cups mayonnaise
1½ tablespoons curry powder
salt to taste
5 to 6 cups fresh broccoli florets
2 to 3 pounds boneless skinless chicken breasts,
    poached and chilled
1 large red bell pepper, finely chopped

Place the chutney in a food processor. Pulse for 15 to
20 seconds or until chopped. Combine the mayonnaise and
curry powder in a bowl and mix well. Stir in the chutney.
Chill, covered, in the refrigerator.

Bring a large saucepan of salted water to a boil. Add
the broccoli. Cook for 1 minute or until tender-crisp; drain.
Plunge the broccoli into a bowl of ice water to stop the
cooking process; drain.

Cut the chicken into bite-size pieces. Combine the
chicken, broccoli and bell pepper in a bowl and mix well.
Add the chutney mixture and stir until coated. Chill,
covered, until serving time.

Serves 10 to 12

Vegetable Finger Sandwiches

8 ounces tub-style cream cheese with onions and chives
8 ounces tub-style cream cheese with garden vegetables
1 (8-ounce) can crushed pineapple, drained
1 cup (4 ounces) shredded sharp Cheddar cheese
½ cup chopped pecans, toasted
2 carrots, shredded
½ medium red bell pepper, chopped
5 green onions, minced
2 garlic cloves, crushed
1 teaspoon Beau Monde seasoning
18 slices very thin whole wheat bread, crusts trimmed
18 slices very thin white bread, crusts trimmed

Combine the cream cheese, pineapple, Cheddar cheese,
pecans, carrots, bell pepper, green onions, garlic and Beau
Monde seasoning in a bowl and mix well. Spread the cream
cheese mixture on 1 side of each slice of the wheat bread.
Top with the white bread. Stack the sandwiches between
sheets of waxed paper and place in an airtight container.
Chill for up to 24 hours. Cut each sandwich into quarters.

Makes 6 dozen sandwiches

Flank Steak Sandwiches

2 teaspoons balsamic vinegar
1 teaspoon Dijon mustard
1/2 teaspoon chopped fresh tarragon
1/4 teaspoon thyme
1/4 teaspoon salt
1/8 teaspoon freshly ground pepper
1/3 cup plus 2 tablespoons olive oil
1 (12-ounce) flank steak
3 ounces Roquefort cheese, crumbled
2 ounces cream cheese, softened
2 teaspoons fresh lemon juice
salt and pepper to taste
1/4 cup walnuts, toasted and chopped
6 ounces snow peas, trimmed
2 Kaiser rolls, split

Whisk the balsamic vinegar, Dijon mustard, tarragon, thyme, 1/4 teaspoon salt and 1/8 teaspoon pepper in a bowl. Add 1/3 cup of the olive oil gradually, whisking constantly until incorporated. Reserve 2 tablespoons of the vinaigrette. Pour the remaining vinaigrette over the flank steak in a shallow dish, turning to coat. Marinate, covered, in the refrigerator for 1 to 10 hours, turning occasionally.

Process the Roquefort cheese, cream cheese and lemon juice in a food processor until smooth. Season with salt and pepper. Stir in the walnuts.

Heat 1 tablespoon of the remaining olive oil in a large skillet over high heat. Sauté the snow peas in the hot olive oil for 1 minute or until tender-crisp and bright green. Remove the snow peas to a bowl, reserving the pan drippings. Add the remaining 1 tablespoon olive oil to the reserved pan drippings; reduce the heat to medium-high. Add the steak.

Sauté for 4 to 6 minutes for medium-rare, turning once. Remove the steak to a cutting board. Slice diagonally into thin strips. Add the steak and reserved 2 tablespoons vinaigrette to the snow peas and toss to mix. Spread the Roquefort cheese mixture over the cut sides of each roll. Top evenly with the steak mixture. You may grill the steak over hot coals if desired.

Serves 2

Chilled Cantaloupe Soup

Peel a large cantaloupe and cut into chunks. Combine with 1 cup fresh orange juice, 1/2 cup plain yogurt, 1 tablespoon fresh lime juice and 2 to 3 tablespoons confectioners' sugar in a blender or food processor. Process until smooth. Chill, covered, in the refrigerator. Ladle into chilled soup bowls. Garnish each serving with 3 fresh raspberries.

Picnic Basket Basics

- *Tablecloth and/or blankets*
- *Paper or plastic plates and cups*
- *Plastic or stainless eating utensils*
- *Serving utensils*
- *Bottle opener and/or wine opener*
- *Salt and pepper*
- *Paper towels*
- *Thermoses of drinks and insulated cups*

Picnic Tips

- *Transport food in resealable plastic bags or tubs.*
- *Place the ice for the cooler in resealable plastic bags to place around the food and also to provide clean ice for drinks.*
- *Do not leave food out of the cooler or in the sun for a long time.*
- *Carry a clean-up size plastic bag to dispose of trash if receptacles are handy or to carry it home if not.*

Rocky Road Brownies

Brownies
2 cups flour
²/₃ cup baking cocoa
¹/₂ teaspoon baking powder
¹/₂ teaspoon salt
2 cups sugar
1 cup vegetable oil
2 teaspoons vanilla extract
4 eggs, lightly beaten
1 cup chopped pecans

Topping
2 to 3 cups miniature marshmallows
²/₃ cup chopped pecans
¹/₂ cup (1 stick) butter or margarine
5 tablespoons baking cocoa
6 tablespoons milk
1 (1-pound) package confectioners' sugar, sifted
¹/₃ cup chopped pecans

For the brownies, combine the flour, baking cocoa, baking powder and salt in a bowl and mix well. Beat the sugar, oil and vanilla in a mixing bowl until blended. Add the eggs and mix with a wooden spoon until smooth. Add the flour mixture gradually, stirring constantly just until blended; do not overmix. Stir in the pecans.

Spread the batter in a 9×13-inch baking pan sprayed with nonstick cooking spray. Bake at 350 degrees for 20 to 25 minutes or just until the brownies test done; do not overbake. Remove from the oven.

For the topping, sprinkle the marshmallows and ²/₃ cup pecans over the hot baked layer. Bake just until the marshmallows begin to puff and turn light brown. Remove from the oven.

Heat the butter in a 3-quart saucepan. Stir in the baking cocoa until blended. Add the milk and mix well. Bring to a gentle boil, stirring frequently. Remove from the heat. Stir in the confectioners' sugar. Spread the topping over the prepared layers, leaving the pecans and marshmallows exposed sporadically. Sprinkle with ¹/₃ cup pecans. Let stand until cool. Cut into bars.

Makes 3 to 4 dozen bars

Cherry Turnovers

3 pounds fresh or frozen Bing cherries, pitted
³/₄ cup granulated sugar
¹/₄ cup fresh lemon juice
¹/₄ cup plus 1 tablespoon cornstarch
¹/₂ cup water
¹/₂ teaspoon vanilla extract
2 pounds frozen puff pastry, thawed in the refrigerator
1 egg, lightly beaten
¹/₄ cup turbinado sugar

Cook the cherries in a saucepan over low heat for 10 minutes or until tender and most of the liquid has exuded, stirring occasionally. Press the cherries through a fine sieve and reserve the cherries. Add hot water if needed to the juice to measure 2 cups. Return the juice to the saucepan. Stir in the granulated sugar and lemon juice. Bring to a boil.

Mix the cornstarch and water in a bowl. Add to the cherry juice mixture, stirring constantly. Stir in the reserved cherries. Bring to a boil. Cook for 2 to 3 minutes or until thickened, stirring constantly. Stir in the vanilla. Pour into a bowl and chill. Roll the pastry ¹/₈ inch thick on a lightly floured surface. Using a 7-inch saucer as a guide, cut out 10 rounds. Chill the rounds until firm.

Line a baking sheet with foil or baking parchment. Brush the edge of 1 round with some of the egg. Spoon ¹/₂ cup of the cherry filling into the center of the round. Fold the dough over to form a half-moon. Press the edge to seal and crimp the seam with a fork. Arrange the turnover on the prepared baking sheet. Repeat the process with the remaining rounds, remaining egg and remaining cherry filling. Chill for 10 minutes or until firm.

Make 3 slits in the top of each turnover. Brush with the remaining egg and sprinkle with turbinado sugar. Bake at 375 degrees for 40 minutes or until golden brown.

Makes 10 turnovers

Double Cherry Streusel Bars

2 cups quick-cooking oats
1¹/₂ cups flour
1¹/₂ cups packed brown sugar
1 teaspoon baking powder
¹/₂ teaspoon baking soda
1 cup (2 sticks) butter
2 cups water
1 cup dried cherries
2 (12-ounce) jars cherry preserves (2 cups)
1 teaspoon finely grated lemon zest
¹/₂ cup coarsely chopped slivered almonds

Combine the oats, flour, brown sugar, baking powder and baking soda in a bowl and mix well. Cut in the butter with a pastry blender until crumbly. Reserve 1 cup of the crumb mixture. Press the remaining crumb mixture over the bottom of a 10×15-inch baking pan. Bake at 350 degrees for 12 minutes.

Bring the water to a boil in a saucepan. Remove from the heat. Stir in the cherries. Let stand for 10 minutes, drain. Combine the cherries, preserves and lemon zest in a bowl and mix well. Spread the cherry mixture over the baked layer. Sprinkle with a mixture of the reserved crumb mixture and almonds. Bake for 20 to 25 minutes or until golden brown. Cool in the pan on a wire rack. Cut into bars.

Makes 4 dozen bars

MENU

Pour l' Amour

We rarely slow down to embrace what we hold so dear, so take a long moment to indulge in a romantic evening. Hold hands across the table, look into each other's eyes, catch a glimmer in his smile, and enjoy the perfect meal. Whether along the shore or on the deck, make this an evening to remember.

Gulf Breeze

6 ounces cranberry juice
6 ounces orange juice
4 ounces vodka
¹/₂ ounce Grand Marnier
2 orange wedges, coated with sugar

Chill 2 highball glasses. Fill a cocktail shaker half full with ice cubes. Add the cranberry juice, orange juice, vodka and liqueur and shake vigorously.

Fill the chilled glasses half full of crushed ice. Strain the cocktail mixture equally into the glasses. Garnish the rim of each glass with 1 orange wedge.

Serves 2

White Chocolate Kiss Martini

Magic Shell dessert topping
baking cocoa
confectioners' sugar
4 ounces orange-flavor vodka
2 ounces amaretto
2 ounces white chocolate liqueur
2 chocolate kisses

Freeze 2 martini glasses for 5 to 10 minutes. Shake the Magic Shell and pour into a saucer. Spoon baking cocoa and confectioners' sugar in 2 separate saucers. Dip the rims of the chilled martini glasses in the Magic Shell, baking cocoa and confectioners' sugar. Return the glasses to the freezer.

Fill a cocktail shaker with ice. Add the vodka, amaretto and white chocolate liqueur and shake vigorously. Place 1 chocolate kiss in each prepared glass. Strain the cocktail mixture equally into the glasses.

Serves 2

Romantic Dinner on the Beach

You will find it easy to load up the right props, a wonderful meal, and your favorite person to make a romantic dinner just like ours—one that truly sizzles! Choose a beautiful outdoor spot that is as private as possible. Next, select the necessary table settings, such as a picnic blanket, tablecloth, or maybe a special centerpiece.

Always use candles, but make sure that they are not scented, since they could clash with the food. Pack everything for easy transport and set up in plenty of time to relax and enjoy. Make sure that dessert is just in time for viewing a spectacular sunset, providing a perfect ending to a perfect meal.

Garlic Tortilla Crisps

Cut four 8-inch tortillas into shapes with a cookie cutter or into quarters. Arrange in a single layer on an ungreased baking sheet. Melt 2 tablespoons butter in a saucepan. Stir in 1 teaspoon minced garlic. Brush the garlic butter over the tortillas.

Bake at 350 degrees for 12 to 15 minutes or until golden brown. Remove to a wire rack to cool. Store in an airtight container for up to 2 days.

Broiled Oysters with Curry Sauce

Oysters
2 cups sea salt or rock salt
12 to 18 fresh oysters, scrubbed

Curry Sauce
1 tablespoon unsalted butter
2 tablespoons minced shallots
1 teaspoon minced garlic
$1/4$ cup heavy cream
$3/4$ teaspoon curry powder
$1/2$ teaspoon cayenne pepper
$1/2$ teaspoon crushed saffron threads
1 tablespoon fresh lemon juice
$1/8$ teaspoon white pepper

For the oysters, spread the sea salt in a thick layer on a large baking sheet with sides to form a cushion for the oysters. Shuck the oysters, reserving the liquor and discarding the top half of the shells. Arrange the oysters on the half shells on the bed of salt. Strain the liquor.

For the sauce, heat the unsalted butter in a small saucepan. Cook the shallots and garlic in the butter over low heat for 3 to 4 minutes or until the shallots are tender, stirring frequently. Stir in the heavy cream, curry powder, cayenne pepper and saffron. Cook for 3 to 4 minutes or until thick and creamy, stirring frequently. Stir in about 1 tablespoon of the reserved oyster liquor, lemon juice and white pepper.

To serve, spoon the sauce over the oysters. Broil for 2 to 4 minutes or until the sauce begins to sizzle. Serve immediately.

Serves 2

Hearts of Palm Vinaigrette

Balsamic Vinaigrette

3 tablespoons balsamic vinegar

1 tablespoon red wine vinegar

salt and pepper to taste

$1/2$ cup plus 1 tablespoon olive oil

Salad

1 (5-ounce) package spring salad mix

1 (14-ounce) can hearts of palm, drained

1 (14-ounce) can whole artichoke hearts, drained

8 ounces fresh green beans, trimmed and steamed
     al dente

2 ripe tomatoes, cut into wedges

For the vinaigrette, combine the balsamic vinegar, wine vinegar, salt and pepper in a bowl and mix well. Add the olive oil gradually, whisking constantly until blended.

For the salad, place the salad mix on a large serving platter. Scatter the hearts of palm, artichoke hearts, green beans and tomato wedges over the salad greens. Serve with the vinaigrette.

Serves 4 to 6

Raspberry Spinach Salad

Raspberry Vinaigrette

2 tablespoons raspberry vinegar

2 tablespoons raspberry jam

$1/3$ cup vegetable oil

Spinach Salad

8 cups spinach, trimmed and torn

$3/4$ cup coarsely chopped macadamia nuts or toasted
     sliced almonds

1 cup fresh raspberries

3 kiwifruit, sliced

For the vinaigrette, process the vinegar and jam in a blender until blended. Add the oil gradually, processing constantly until incorporated.

For the salad, toss the spinach, $1/2$ of the macadamia nuts, $1/2$ of the raspberries, $1/2$ of the kiwifruit and the vinaigrette in a salad bowl until mixed. Sprinkle with the remaining macadamia nuts, remaining raspberries and remaining kiwifruit.

Serves 8

Recipe for this photograph on facing page.

Sirloin with Grilled Shrimp and Brie

2 (12-ounce) New York strip steaks
olive oil
salt and pepper to taste
2 long thin slices Brie cheese, at room temperature
4 slices avocado
4 large shrimp, butterflied, seasoned, grilled
Classic Madeira Sauce (this page)

Brush both sides of the steaks with olive oil and sprinkle with salt and pepper. Grill the steaks over hot coals to the desired degree of doneness. Remove the steaks from the grill and arrange on 2 serving plates. Top each steak immediately with 1 slice of the Brie, 2 slices of the avocado and 2 shrimp. Drizzle the Classic Madeira Sauce over and around the steaks. Serve immediately.

Serves 2

Classic Madeira Sauce

1/4 cup chopped carrots
1/4 cup chopped celery
1/4 cup chopped shallots
1/2 teaspoon chopped fresh thyme
2 tablespoons olive oil
1/2 cup Madeira
1 (10-ounce) can beef consommé
1 consommé can water

Sauté the carrots, celery, shallots and thyme in the olive oil in a skillet for 3 to 5 minutes or until the vegetables are tender. Stir in the wine. Cook for 2 minutes or until the liquid is reduced by 1/2. Process the wine mixture in a food processor or blender until puréed. Return the purée to the skillet.

Add the consommé and water to the purée and mix well. Cook over medium heat for 12 to 14 minutes or until the mixture is reduced and thickened, stirring frequently. Remove from the heat. Cover to keep warm. You may prepare in advance and store, covered, in the refrigerator or freezer. Reheat before serving.

Serves 2

New York Strips with Brandied Mushroom Sauce

Brandied Mushroom Sauce

1 cup chicken broth

1 ounce dried porcini mushrooms, rinsed and drained

3 tablespoons butter

1/4 cup minced shallots

8 ounces button mushrooms, cut into quarters

1 1/2 tablespoons flour

2 tablespoons brandy

Steaks

2 (12-ounce) New York strip steaks

salt and pepper to taste

2 tablespoons minced fresh flat-leaf parsley

For the sauce, bring the broth to a boil in a small saucepan. Remove from the heat. Stir in the porcini mushrooms. Let stand, covered, for 30 minutes or until softened. Strain the mushroom mixture through a fine sieve into a bowl, pressing the mushrooms to release additional liquid. Let the liquid stand to allow the sediment to separate from the liquid. Pour the liquid into another bowl, leaving the sediment behind. Chop the mushrooms coarsely.

Heat the butter in a heavy skillet over low heat. Stir in the porcini mushrooms and shallots. Cook for 10 minutes or until tender, stirring frequently. Stir in the button mushrooms. Cook, covered, for 8 minutes or until tender, stirring occasionally. Stir in the flour.

Cook for 2 minutes, stirring frequently. Add the reserved mushroom liquid and brandy gradually, stirring constantly. Bring to a simmer, stirring constantly. Remove from the heat. Let stand, covered, at room temperature for up to 3 hours in advance.

For the steaks, season the steaks with salt and pepper. Grill the steaks over hot coals to the desired degree of doneness. Bring the sauce to a boil over high heat. Boil for 1 minute or until thickened, stirring constantly. Drizzle the sauce over the steaks on serving plates. Sprinkle with the parsley. Serve immediately.

Serves 2

Valentine Food for Thought

Cabbage always has a heart; green beans string along.

You're such a cute tomato, will you peas to me belong?

You've been the apple of my eye, you know how much I care;

So lettuce get together, we'd make a perfect pear.

Now something's sure to turnip to prove you can't be beet;

So, if you carrot all for me, let's let our tulips meet.

Don't squash my hopes and dreams now, bee my honey, dear;

Or tears will fill potato's eyes, while sweet corn lends an ear.

I'll cauliflower shop and say your dreams are parsley mine.

I'll work and share my celery, so be my valentine.

—Jeanne Losey

Chicken Paillard with Tomato Salad

1 cup yellow cherry tomatoes, cut into halves
1 cup red grape tomatoes, cut into halves
1/4 teaspoon sea salt
2 ounces mild goat cheese, crumbled
2 tablespoons extra-virgin olive oil
freshly ground pepper to taste
4 boneless skinless chicken breasts
1 tablespoon extra-virgin olive oil

Place the tomatoes in a colander and set the colander over a bowl. Sprinkle the sea salt over the tomatoes and toss. Let stand for 15 minutes to release juices. Remove the colander. Add 1/2 of the goat cheese to the tomato juices and whisk until smooth. Whisk in 2 tablespoons olive oil and pepper. Fold the tomatoes and remaining goat cheese into the tomato juice mixture.

Pound the chicken 1/3 inch thick between sheets of waxed paper. Brush both sides of the chicken with 1 tablespoon olive oil. Grill the chicken over hot coals or in a grill pan over high heat for 5 minutes or until brown and almost cooked through; turn. Grill for 2 minutes longer or until the chicken is cooked through. Remove the chicken to dinner plates. Spoon the tomato and goat cheese salad equally over the chicken. Serve immediately.

Serves 4

Thai Curried Shrimp

1 cup chopped pecans
1 cup grated coconut
1 (10-ounce) can reduced-fat cream of mushroom soup
1 (10-ounce) can reduced-fat cream of celery soup
1 cup sliced fresh mushrooms
1/2 cup chopped green onions
1/3 cup chopped red bell pepper
1/4 cup nonfat milk or 2% milk
1 teaspoon (or more) curry powder
1 pound steamed seasoned shrimp, peeled and deveined
hot cooked white rice

Spread the pecans in a single layer on 1/2 of a baking sheet and the coconut on the remaining 1/2 of the baking sheet. Broil until the coconut is light brown, stirring frequently. Remove the coconut and pecans to separate plates to cool.

Combine the soups, mushrooms, green onions, bell pepper, nonfat milk and curry powder in a large deep skillet and mix well. Cook over medium-low heat until heated through, stirring occasionally. Stir in the shrimp. Simmer for 15 minutes, stirring occasionally. Spoon the shrimp mixture over rice on a serving platter. Allow your guests to sprinkle with pecans and coconut as desired.

Serves 4

Summer Succotash

4 ounces sliced bacon

1 pound fresh baby lima beans, or 1 cup frozen baby lima beans

salt to taste

4 ears sweet corn

1½ tablespoons olive oil

1 small sweet onion, chopped

1 large garlic clove, minced

12 ounces grape tomatoes, cut into halves (about 1½ pints)

1 tablespoon red wine vinegar

¼ cup fresh basil leaves

¼ cup arugula leaves

pepper to taste

Garlic Croutons (this page)

Fry the bacon in a skillet until brown and crisp. Drain, reserving 1 tablespoon of the bacon drippings. Crumble the bacon. Cook the lima beans in boiling salted water in a saucepan over medium heat for 10 minutes or just until tender. Drain in a colander and rinse with cold water to stop the cooking process; drain. Cut the tops of the corn kernels into a bowl using a sharp knife, reserving the juices.

Heat the olive oil with the reserved bacon drippings over medium heat. Cook the onion in the olive oil mixture until tender, stirring frequently. Stir in the garlic, Cook for 1 minute, stirring constantly. Add the corn and juices, tomatoes and vinegar and mix well.

Cook until the tomatoes begin to lose their shape, stirring constantly but gently. Remove from the heat. Stir in the beans and ½ of the bacon. Let stand until room temperature. Add the basil, arugula, salt and pepper and mix gently. Spoon the succotash over the Garlic Croutons on a serving platter. Sprinkle evenly with the remaining bacon.

Serves 6

Garlic Croutons

Cut six ½-inch slices from the middle of a round loaf of crusty bread. Brush both sides of the slices with olive oil. Heat a lightly oiled well-seasoned ridged grill pan over medium-high heat until hot but not smoking. Grill the bread in the hot pan until both sides are golden brown. Rub the cut sides of a garlic clove on 1 side of each slice and sprinkle with fine sea salt.

Broiled Herbed Tomatoes

3 medium tomatoes, cut lengthwise into halves
3 tablespoons mayonnaise
1 teaspoon Dijon mustard
1 tablespoon finely chopped fresh parsley
2 teaspoons finely chopped fresh chives
3 tablespoons freshly grated Parmesan cheese
salt and pepper to taste
1 tablespoon finely chopped fresh parsley

Arrange the tomatoes cut side up in a baking dish. Combine the mayonnaise, Dijon mustard, 1 tablespoon parsley, chives, 2 tablespoons of the cheese, salt and pepper in a bowl and mix well.

Spread 1 heaping tablespoon of the mayonnaise mixture over each tomato half. Sprinkle with the remaining 1 tablespoon cheese. Bake for 10 to 12 minutes or until heated through. Broil until brown and bubbly. Arrange the tomatoes on a serving patter and sprinkle with 1 tablespoon parsley. Serve immediately.

Serves 6

Orzo with Broccoli and Olives

1¹/₂ cups (about 9 ounces) uncooked orzo
salt to taste
florets of 1 bunch broccoli (about 1 pound)
3 tablespoons pine nuts
¹/₄ cup olive oil
¹/₂ teaspoon crushed red pepper
³/₄ cup crumbled feta cheese
¹/₂ cup (2 ounces) freshly grated Parmesan cheese
³/₄ cup brine-cured black olives, such as kalamata, cut
    into halves
¹/₄ cup chopped fresh basil
black pepper to taste

Cook the orzo in salted water using the package directions for 8 minutes or until al dente. Add the broccoli and cook for 2 minutes or until tender-crisp.

Sauté the pine nuts in the olive oil in a small heavy skillet for 3 minutes or until golden brown. Add the red pepper and sauté for 30 seconds or until aromatic. Remove from the heat.

Drain the orzo and broccoli and place in a large bowl. Add the undrained pine nuts and toss to coat well. Add the feta cheese, Parmesan cheese, olives and basil and toss to mix well. Season with salt and black pepper.

Serves 4

Citrus and Green Onion Couscous

6 cups chicken broth
3 cups couscous
1 cup chopped green onions
1 tablespoon grated orange zest
1 tablespoon grated lemon zest
salt and pepper to taste

Bring the broth to a boil in a saucepan. Stir in the couscous; reduce the heat. Simmer for 2 minutes. Let stand, covered, for 15 minutes. Stir in the green onions, orange zest and lemon zest. Season with salt and pepper. Spoon the couscous into a serving bowl.

Serves 6 to 8

Couscous with Cherry Tomatoes

1 1/2 pounds medium zucchini
1 cup chopped onion
1 1/2 teaspoons olive oil
1/4 cup water (optional)
1 large garlic clove, minced
2 1/2 cups canned reduced-sodium chicken broth
1 1/2 cups couscous
1 1/2 teaspoons butter
3 tablespoons chopped fresh thyme
salt and freshly ground pepper to taste
24 grape tomatoes or cherry tomatoes, cut into halves

Cut the zucchini crosswise into 3 pieces and cut each piece unto 6 wedges. Sauté the onion in the olive oil in a heavy saucepan over medium heat for 6 minutes or until tender and golden brown, adding 1/4 cup water if the onion becomes too dry before browning. Add the garlic and sauté for 1 minute. Stir in the broth and bring to a boil. Add the zucchini and cook for 3 minutes or until the zucchini is tender-crisp.

Stir in the couscous, butter, thyme, salt and pepper and remove from the heat. Let stand, covered, for 10 minutes or until the liquid is absorbed. Fluff with a fork and combine with the tomatoes in a serving bowl.

Serves 6

Chocolate Soufflés

6 teaspoons sugar
6 tablespoons unsalted butter
2 tablespoons heavy cream
8 ounces bittersweet chocolate or semisweet chocolate,
    finely chopped
4 egg yolks, lightly beaten
7 egg whites
1/4 teaspoon cream of tartar
1/8 teaspoon salt
1/4 cup sugar
Caramel Sauce (this page)

Butter six 1-cup ramekins and coat each with 1 teaspoon sugar. Tap the sides of the ramekins to remove any excess sugar. Heat 6 tablespoons unsalted butter in a small saucepan over low heat. Stir in the heavy cream. Bring just to a boil, stirring occasionally. Remove from the heat. Add the chocolate and stir until blended. Pour the chocolate mixture into a large bowl. Stir in the egg yolks.

Beat the egg whites, cream of tartar and salt in a mixing bowl just until stiff peaks form. Add 1/4 cup sugar gradually, beating constantly just until combined. Stir 1/4 of the egg whites into the chocolate mixture. Fold in the remaining egg whites gently but thoroughly.

Spoon the chocolate mixture into the prepared ramekins. Run the tip of a sharp knife around the edge of each soufflé. Arrange the ramekins on a baking sheet. Bake in the lower third of the oven at 375 degrees for 20 minutes or until the surfaces of the soufflés are cracked and puffed. Drizzle each soufflé with Caramel Sauce if desired. Serve immediately. The unbaked soufflés may be stored, covered with plastic wrap, in the refrigerator for 1 to 2 days before baking.

Serves 6

Caramel Sauce

3/4 cup sugar
6 tablespoons light corn syrup
1/4 cup water
1/8 teaspoon salt
1/2 cup heavy cream
1/2 teaspoon vanilla extract

Combine the sugar, corn syrup, water and salt in a heavy saucepan and mix well. Simmer until the sugar dissolves, stirring constantly. Bring to a boil. Boil until the mixture is golden caramel in color; do not stir. Remove from the heat. Add the heavy cream and vanilla and stir for 1 minute. Let stand until room temperature. You may prepare up to 3 to 4 weeks in advance and store, covered, in the refrigerator. Bring to room temperature before serving.

Serves 6

Apricot Tortoni

1/3 cup chopped almonds
3 tablespoons butter
1 1/3 cups graham cracker crumbs
1 teaspoon almond extract
3 pints vanilla ice cream, softened
1 (12-ounce) jar apricot preserves
1 cup whipping cream
1/4 cup sugar
1 teaspoon vanilla extract

Sauté the almonds in the butter in a skillet until light brown. Combine the almonds, graham cracker crumbs and flavoring in a bowl and mix well. Pat 1/3 of the crumb mixture over the bottom of a 9×9-inch dish. Spread with 1/2 of the ice cream and 1/2 of the preserves. Layer with 1/2 of the remaining crumb mixture, the remaining ice cream and the remaining preserves. Top with the remaining crumb mixture. Freeze, covered with plastic wrap, for several hours or until firm.

Beat the whipping cream in a mixing bowl until soft peaks form. Add the sugar and vanilla and beat until combined. Spread the whipped cream over the frozen layers. Freeze, covered with plastic wrap, until firm. Cut into squares and arrange the squares on doilies on individual dessert plates. Garnish with a sprig of fresh mint, strawberry or fruit of choice.

Serves 9

Chocolate-Covered Strawberries with Champagne

Chill your favorite Champagne. Wash and dry the strawberries, leaving the stems intact. Chill in the refrigerator so the chocolate will harden without dripping. Spoon 1 cup of Nutella or European chocolate-hazelnut spread in a double boiler or fondue pot and stir in 1 to 2 tablespoons heavy cream. Cook over low heat just until melted, stirring until smooth and adding additional cream if needed. Serve to your sweetheart.

Sunset Sweeps

Manhattan Martinis

Fiesta

Asian Expressions

MENU

Manhattan Martinis

Cold gin, an olive, and a whisper of vermouth— the classic martini will never go out of style. But the smart set is always open to something new and different. Present your guests with a panoply of new varieties to try, coupled with tasty hors d'oeuvre. Perhaps you and your friends will discover your own "classic."

Applejack Martini

2 ounces vodka
1 ounce sour apple schnapps
1/2 ounce cinnamon schnapps

ice cubes
1 cinnamon stick

Combine the vodka, schnapps and ice cubes in a cocktail shaker and shake vigorously. Strain into a chilled martini glass. Garnish with the cinnamon stick.
Serves 1

Blue Dolphin Martini

2 ounces vodka
1 ounce grapefruit juice
1/2 ounce blue curaçao

ice cubes
lemon zest

Combine the vodka, grapefruit juice, liqueur and ice cubes in a cocktail shaker and shake vigorously. Strain into a chilled martini glass. Garnish with lemon zest.
Serves 1

Chile Vodkatini

1 ounce chile vodka
ice cubes
1/4 ounce dry vermouth

cocktail olive
chile pepper

Shake the vodka and ice cubes in a cocktail shaker for 30 seconds. Swirl the vermouth inside a cocktail glass to coat, discarding the remaining vermouth. Pour the chilled vodka into the prepared glass. Thread the olive and chile pepper on a skewer for garnish.
Serves 1

Panama Country Club

The site of what is now the Panama Country Club was once called the community of Gay, which was located between two bayous on North Bay. The community was established in 1884 when Mr. A.J. Gay moved his family there from Georgia. The location was then a favorite of visitors who enjoyed the huge fruit trees and clear waters of the bay. Who would have imagined what the future would hold there?

In 1926, W.C. Sherman bought the land and opened an 18-hole golf course on the old Gay settlement. Since that time, green fairways and fabulous homes have been added to turn the land into a beautiful club setting amongst magnolias and blue-green waters. Since martinis and country clubs go hand in hand, this is the perfect location for a Martini Fete. Grab a golf cart and join us for a sunset toast to the good life!

Firefly Martini

2 ounces cranberry juice
1 ounce raspberry vodka
1 ounce orange curaçao
1/2 ounce lemon juice
ice cubes
orange twist

Combine the cranberry juice, vodka, liqueur, lemon juice and ice cubes in a cocktail shaker and shake vigorously. Strain into a chilled martini glass. Garnish the rim of the glass with an orange twist.
Serves 1

Chocolate Monkey Martini

3 ounces vodka
2 ounces brown crème de cacao
1 ounce crème de banana
ice cubes
sliced banana

Combine the vodka, liqueurs and ice cubes in a cocktail shaker and shake vigorously. Strain into a chilled martini glass. Garnish with sliced banana.
Serves 1

French Martini

2 ounces vodka
1 ounce pineapple juice
1/4 ounce Chambord
ice cubes
1 fresh red or black raspberry

Combine the vodka, pineapple juice, liqueur and ice cubes in a cocktail shaker and shake vigorously. Strain into a chilled martini glass. Garnish with the raspberry.
Serves 1

Key Lime Martini

lime wedge
graham cracker crumbs
1 ounce vodka
1/2 ounce coco reef rum
1/2 ounce lime juice
1/2 ounce cream
ice cubes

Rub the rim of a martini glass with the lime wedge. Dip the rim in the graham cracker crumbs. Combine the vodka, rum, lime juice, cream and ice cubes in a cocktail shaker and shake vigorously. Strain the martini into the prepared glass.
Serves 1

Purple Nurple Martini

2 ounces vodka
1 ounce blue curaçao
1 ounce cranberry juice
1/2 ounce grenadine
juice of 1/2 lime
ice cubes
1 lime wedge

Combine the vodka, liqueur, cranberry juice, grenadine, lime juice and ice cubes in a cocktail shaker and shake vigorously. Strain into a chilled martini glass. Garnish with the lime wedge.

Serves 1

Springtini

3 cups vodka
2 1/2 cups Champagne
1/2 cup bottled sweet-and-sour mix
2 tablespoons Chambord
6 teaspoons fresh lime juice
ice cubes

Combine the vodka, Champagne, sweet-and-sour mix, liqueur, lime juice and ice cubes in a large pitcher and mix well. Strain into chilled martini glasses. Dip the rims of the glasses in sugar if desired.

Serves 12

Martini Trends

The tendency to be more innovative and daring in the martini menu reflects two decades of change in the way we eat. Americans have gone from a meat and potatoes diet to the big borrowed flavors of Thai, Sichuan, Pacific Rim fusion, Mexican, Italian, and many more. This adventurous spirit has spilled over into the cocktail tradition with martinis that tempt the palette with flavors from different liqueurs, fresh fruit, spices, and herbs.

Shaken or Stirred

If all the ingredients in a martini are clear, it should be stirred with ice to maintain the clarity. If it contains milk, cream, or fruit, it should be shaken vigorously with ice. Either should be served in a chilled glass.

Parmesan Bacon Sticks

Cut 15 bacon slices into halves lengthwise. Wrap 1 bacon strip around each of 30 bread sticks and coat with ½ to ⅔ cup grated Parmesan cheese. Arrange in a single layer on a baking sheet. Bake at 250 degrees for 1 hour. Serve immediately.

Irish Shenanigan

ice cubes
3 ounces Irish whiskey
3 ounces lemon juice
1 ounce sloe gin
1 ounce light rum
1 ounce peach syrup
1 teaspoon superfine sugar
4 raspberries
2 strawberries
2 pitted fresh cherries

Chill 2 old-fashioned glasses. Fill a cocktail shaker half full of ice cubes. Add the whiskey, lemon juice, gin, rum, peach syrup and sugar to the cocktail shaker and shake vigorously. Fill the chilled glasses half full of ice cubes. Strain the cocktail mixture into the prepared glasses. Garnish each cocktail with 2 raspberries, 1 strawberry and 1 cherry.

Serves 2

Code Blue Dip

16 ounces cream cheese, softened
1 pound bacon, crisp-cooked and crumbled
1½ cups finely chopped green onions
1 cup sour cream
¾ cup (3 ounces) grated Parmesan cheese
½ teaspoon garlic powder
¼ to ½ teaspoon Tabasco sauce

Combine the cream cheese, bacon, green onions, sour cream, Parmesan cheese, garlic powder and Tabasco sauce in a bowl and mix well. Spoon the cream cheese mixture into a baking dish sprayed with nonstick cooking spray.

Bake at 350 degrees for 20 to 30 minutes or until brown and bubbly. Serve hot with wheat thins or assorted party crackers. You may prepare up to 8 hours in advance. Store, covered, in the refrigerator until time to bake.

Serves 16 to 20

Curried Cheese Dip

½ cup shredded coconut
8 ounces cream cheese, softened
1 cup (4 ounces) shredded Cheddar cheese
2 tablespoons dry sherry
¼ teaspoon curry powder
¼ teaspoon garlic salt
½ cup chutney
½ cup finely chopped green onions
½ cup chopped salted peanuts

Spread the coconut in a single layer on a baking sheet. Toast at 250 degrees until light brown, stirring frequently. Remove to a plate to cool. Combine the cream cheese, Cheddar cheese, sherry, curry powder and garlic salt in a bowl and mix well. Chill, covered, in the refrigerator until serving time.

Spread the cream cheese mixture on a serving platter, leaving a 1-inch border. Spread with the chutney. Sprinkle with the green onions, peanuts and coconut. Serve with assorted party crackers.

Serves 10 to 12

Pizza Pinwheels

1/2 cup (2 ounces) finely shredded Gruyère cheese
3/4 teaspoon sage
3/4 teaspoon oregano
1/4 teaspoon pepper
1 sheet frozen puff pastry, thawed
2 tablespoons honey mustard
2 ounces pepperoni, sliced
1 egg, lightly beaten

Combine the cheese, sage, oregano and pepper in a bowl and mix well. Lay the pastry on a lightly floured surface with the short side closest to you. Cut the pastry horizontally into halves.

Brush the honey mustard evenly on both halves, leaving a 1-inch border at the top. Layer evenly with the pepperoni and sprinkle with the cheese mixture. Brush the top edge with the egg. Roll the pastry tightly from the edge closest to you to the egg-coated top edge. Arrange the rolls seam side down on a baking sheet. Chill for 30 minutes or until firm.

Cut each roll into 1/4-inch slices. Arrange the slices cut side down 1 inch apart on a baking sheet lined with baking parchment. Bake at 400 degrees for 14 minutes or until golden brown. You may prepare the pastry rolls up to 1 day in advance and store, covered, in the refrigerator. Bake just before serving. Or freeze, tightly covered, for up to 2 weeks. Thaw in the refrigerator and bake as directed.

Makes 50 to 60 pinwheels

Bleu Cheese and Bacon Puffs

1 1/2 cups flour
1/2 teaspoon salt
1/4 teaspoon black pepper
1/4 teaspoon red pepper
1 1/2 cups water
1/2 cup (1 stick) butter
6 eggs
8 ounces bleu cheese, crumbled
8 slices bacon, crisp-cooked and crumbled
tops of 4 green onions, finely chopped

Mix the flour, salt, black pepper and red pepper together. Bring the water and butter to a boil in a saucepan, stirring occasionally. Stir in the flour mixture. Cook until the mixture adheres and forms a ball, stirring constantly with a wooden spoon. Remove from the heat. Let stand for 5 minutes.

Add the eggs 1 at a time, mixing well after each addition. Beat in the bleu cheese, bacon and green onion tops. Drop the dough by rounded teaspoonfuls 2 inches apart onto a lightly greased baking sheet.

Bake at 400 degrees for 20 to 25 minutes or until golden brown. The puffs will be moist in the center. Serve warm or at room temperature. You may prepare and store, covered, in the freezer for up to 3 months. Thaw in the refrigerator and reheat at 350 degrees for 5 minutes.

Makes 6 dozen puffs

Feta-Stuffed Baby Potatoes

12 small new potatoes uniform in size and shape
6 cups water
1½ teaspoons kosher salt
½ cup crumbled feta cheese
¼ cup pine nuts, toasted
2 tablespoons chopped green olives
1 tablespoon extra-virgin olive oil
1 tablespoon dried currants
½ teaspoon chopped lemon zest
¼ teaspoon oregano
¼ teaspoon pepper
24 fresh parsley leaves

Cut a thin slice from the top and bottom of each potato. Cut the potatoes crosswise into halves. Combine the potatoes and water in a saucepan. Add the salt. Bring to a boil over high heat; reduce the heat. Simmer for 10 to 15 minutes or until the potatoes are tender when pierced with a fork; drain. Let stand until cool.

Combine the feta cheese, pine nuts, olives, olive oil, currants, lemon zest, oregano and pepper in a bowl and mix well. Scoop out the center of each potato half with a spoon or melon baller. Fill the centers with 1 heaping teaspoon of the feta cheese mixture and top with a parsley leaf. Arrange the potatoes on a serving platter.

The feta cheese mixture may be prepared up to 2 days in advance and stored, covered, in the refrigerator, adding the pine nuts just before assembly. Let the mixture stand at room temperature for 1 hour. The potatoes may be cooked up to 4 hours in advance and stored, covered, at room temperature.

Makes 2 dozen

Tomato and Mozzarella Kabobs

Balsamic Vinaigrette
1 tablespoon balsamic vinegar
1 tablespoon olive oil
⅛ teaspoon salt
⅛ teaspoon freshly ground pepper

Kabobs
4 ounces mozzarella cheese, cut into twenty-four ½-inch
    cubes
1 teaspoon olive oil
⅛ teaspoon pepper
salt to taste
24 small cherry tomatoes (red and/or yellow)
24 (5-inch) wooden skewers
24 medium fresh basil leaves

For the vinaigrette, combine the vinegar, olive oil, salt and pepper in a jar with a tight-fitting lid and seal tightly. Shake to mix.

For the kabobs, toss the cheese with the olive oil, pepper and salt in a bowl. Thread 1 cherry tomato on a skewer. Fold 1 basil leaf into halves and slide onto the skewer. Add 1 piece of the mozzarella cheese. Repeat the process with the remaining skewers, remaining cherry tomatoes, remaining basil and remaining cheese mixture. Arrange the skewers on a serving platter and brush with the vinaigrette. Serve immediately. You may prepare up to 3 hours in advance and store, covered with plastic wrap, at room temperature.

Makes 24 kabobs

Crab and Mushroom Strudel

2 tablespoons butter
1 pound fresh mushrooms, chopped
2 tablespoons marsala
2 tablespoons chopped fresh parsley
lemon herbes de Provence to taste
salt and pepper to taste
8 sheets phyllo pastry
melted butter or butter-flavor nonstick cooking spray
bread crumbs
8 ounces fresh crab meat, shells and cartilage removed
3 ounces cream cheese, cut into pieces

Heat 2 tablespoons butter in a large skillet. Stir in the mushrooms and wine. Cook until the liquid evaporates, stirring occasionally. Remove from the heat. Stir in the parsley, lemon herbes de Provence, salt and pepper.

Stack the pastry sheets on a hard surface. Brush the top with melted butter and sprinkle with bread crumbs. Top with the crab meat and mushroom mixture and dot with the cream cheese. Roll as for a jelly roll and place seam side down on a baking sheet. Make several decorative slits in the top of the roll and brush with melted butter. Bake at 400 degrees for 25 minutes or until golden brown. Let stand for 5 minutes before serving.

Serves 4

Crab-Stuffed Mushrooms

1¹/₂ pounds fresh large mushrooms (12 to 16 mushrooms)
¹/₂ cup chopped onion
1 garlic clove, minced
3 tablespoons butter or margarine
¹/₂ cup soft bread crumbs
¹/₄ cup mayonnaise
¹/₄ cup chopped fresh parsley
2 to 3 tablespoons grated Parmesan cheese
2 tablespoons dry sherry
¹/₂ teaspoon Worcestershire sauce
¹/₄ teaspoon salt
¹/₄ teaspoon red pepper
8 ounces fresh lump crab meat, shells and cartilage removed
2 tablespoons butter, melted

Remove the stems from the mushrooms and chop, reserving the caps. Sauté the chopped mushroom stems, onion and garlic in 3 tablespoons butter in a large skillet for 3 to 5 minutes or until the mushrooms and onion are tender. Stir in the bread crumbs, mayonnaise, parsley, cheese, sherry, Worcestershire sauce, salt and red pepper gently. Fold in the crab meat.

Spoon the crab meat mixture evenly into the mushroom caps. Arrange the mushroom caps stuffing side up on a rack in a broiler pan. Drizzle with 2 tablespoons butter. Bake at 350 degrees for 20 to 30 minutes or until brown and heated through.

Makes 12 to 16 mushrooms

Champignon Surprise

24 slices thin bread

2 tablespoons butter, melted

3 tablespoons dried shallots

8 ounces mushrooms, finely chopped

$1/4$ cup ($1/2$ stick) butter

2 tablespoons flour

1 cup whipping cream

$1/2$ cup panko or fresh bread crumbs

3 tablespoons Worcestershire sauce

$1^1/2$ tablespoons Champagne mustard

1 teaspoon chopped fresh parsley

$1/2$ teaspoon herbes de Provence

$1/2$ teaspoon lemon juice

salt and pepper to taste

$1/3$ cup grated Asiago cheese

Cut a 3-inch round from the center of each bread slice with a biscuit cutter. Cover the rounds with a damp paper towel to prevent drying out. Brush miniature muffin cups with 2 tablespoons melted butter. Fit the rounds into the prepared muffin cups. Bake at 400 degrees for 10 minutes or until light brown.

Cook the shallots and mushrooms in $1/4$ cup butter in a sauté pan until all the liquid evaporates, stirring frequently. Remove from the heat. Stir in the flour. Add the whipping cream, panko, Worcestershire sauce, Champagne mustard, parsley, herbes de Provence, lemon juice, salt and pepper and mix well. Return the sauté pan to the heat.

Cook until very thick, stirring frequently. Let stand until cool. Chill, covered, in the refrigerator. Spoon the mushroom mixture into the prepared muffin cups. Sprinkle with the cheese. Bake at 350 degrees for 10 minutes. Broil just until brown. You may freeze the mushroom-filled baked cups for future use. Bake just before serving.

Makes 2 dozen appetizers

Colorful Caviars

Caviar is a term that technically refers only to the eggs, or roe, of various members of the sturgeon family. It is no longer restricted to the traditional varieties of beluga, osetra, and sevruga. Today, North American golden whitefish caviar is often served. Orange salmon roe and orange tobiko, or flying fish roe, are also popular. Tobiko is often colored with wasabi, a Japanese horseradish-like root.

MENU

Fiesta

Olé! Set the tone for a festive evening party with cool margaritas and hot spicy food. Decorate with food displayed on Mexican blankets or serapes. Scatter tropical fruits and flower petals for a colorful decor. Add lively Latin music and everyone will be dancing the mambo in no time.

Fresh Margaritas

1/2 cup fresh lime juice
1/2 cup fresh lemon juice
1/4 cup superfine sugar
4 teaspoons grated lime zest
4 teaspoons grated lemon zest
1/8 teaspoon salt

1 cup premium tequila (preferably 100% agave)
1 cup Triple Sec
2 cups crushed ice
lime slices or lime wedges (optional)

Combine the lime juice, lemon juice, sugar, lime zest, lemon zest and salt in a glass bowl and mix well. Chill, covered with plastic wrap, for 4 to 24 hours. The flavor is enhanced the longer the chilling time.

Strain the lime juice mixture into a pitcher or cocktail shaker, discarding the solids. Add the tequila, Triple Sec and 1 cup of the ice. Stir or shake to mix. Fill 4 margarita glasses evenly with the remaining 1 cup ice. Strain the margaritas into the ice-filled glasses and serve immediately. Rim the glasses with salt if desired and garnish the rims of the glasses with lime slices or lime wedges. The recipe will require 3 to 4 limes and 3 to 4 lemons.

Serves 4

Fresh Raspberry Margaritas

1 cup fresh raspberries
1/2 cup fresh lime juice
1/2 cup fresh lemon juice
1/4 cup superfine sugar
1/8 teaspoon salt

2 cups crushed ice
1 cup premium tequila
1/2 cup Chambord
1/2 cup Triple Sec
4 fresh raspberries or 4 orange twists

Purée 1 cup raspberries, lime juice, lemon juice, sugar and salt in a food processor. Strain the raspberry mixture into a pitcher or cocktail shaker, discarding the solids. Add 1 cup of the ice and the liqueurs. Stir or shake until mixed. Fill 4 margarita glasses equally with the remaining 1 cup ice. Strain the margaritas into the ice-filled glasses. Rim the glasses with sugar or raspberry sugar if desired. Garnish with a fresh raspberry or an orange twist.

Serves 4

Fiesta

Whether you're planning to celebrate Cinco de Mayo or just having friends over, everyone loves a fiesta! The mere word conjures up images of swirling vivid colors, music, food, and laughter.

Think about bright and bold decorations to enhance a Latin event. Pull out your colorful blankets, sombreros, dolls, and other souvenirs from trips south of the border. Add natural decorations such as cacti and chile peppers and incorporate them all into a festive atmosphere. Gather a variety of hot sauces to place around the table and purchase strands of chile lights to add a spicy glow to the party. Play traditional mariachi music to really set the tone for the fiesta.

Mango Batidas

1/4 cup sugar
1 lime wedge
1 ripe mango, cut into chunks (1 cup)
2 cups ice cubes
1 cup milk
5 tablespoons sugar
1/4 cup white rum
2 tablespoons fresh lime juice
1/8 teaspoon salt
4 lime slices

Spread 1/4 cup sugar on a saucer. Rub the rims of 4 cocktail glasses with the lime wedge. Dip the rim of each glass in the sugar and rotate gently to coat evenly.

Combine the mango, ice cubes, milk, 5 tablespoons sugar, rum, lime juice and salt in a blender. Process for 1 minute or until smooth and thick. Pour into the prepared glasses. Garnish the rim of each glass with a lime slice. Serve immediately.

Serves 4

Recipe for this photograph in sidebar on facing page.

Pineapple Tequila

1 large pineapple
4 cups white tequila
2 ounces dark brown sugar
1 vanilla bean, split

Rinse a large wide-neck ovenproof bottle. Heat the bottle at 225 degrees for 20 minutes to sterilize; cool.

Cut the top from the pineapple and discard. Peel, core and cut the pineapple into chunks small enough to fit through the neck of the sterilized bottle. Place the pineapple in the bottle. Whisk the tequila and brown sugar in a bowl until the brown sugar dissolves. Pour the tequila mixture over the pineapple. Add the vanilla bean to the bottle and shake gently. Let stand at room temperature for 1 week or longer before consuming, shaking gently several times each day. Serve straight up or shake with crushed ice and pour into a martini glass.

Serves 16 to 18

Corn Dip

3 (11-ounce) cans Mexicorn, drained
$^1/_4$ jar chopped jalapeño chiles, drained
2 cups (8 ounces) finely shredded extra-sharp Cheddar cheese
1 cup mayonnaise
2 teaspoons minced onion
1 teaspoon jalapeño chile seasoning

Combine the corn, jalapeño chiles, cheese, mayonnaise, onion and jalapeño chile seasoning in a bowl and mix well. Chill, covered, in the refrigerator. Bring to room temperature before serving. Serve with corn chip scoops.

Serves 8 to 10

Layered Shrimp Taco Dip

8 ounces reduced-fat cream cheese, softened
2 tablespoons whole milk or 2% milk
$^1/_2$ cup chili sauce
1 cup peeled cooked shrimp, sliced or chopped
4 scallions, chopped
$^3/_4$ cup chopped green bell pepper
1 (4-ounce) can sliced black olives, drained and patted dry
1 cup (4 ounces) shredded part-skim mozzarella cheese or
    shredded reduced-fat Monterey Jack cheese

Beat the cream cheese and milk in a mixing bowl until smooth. Spread the cream cheese mixture evenly on a small platter. Layer with the chili sauce, shrimp, scallions, bell pepper, olives and cheese. Chill, covered, for 1 hour or longer. Serve with tortilla chips.

Serves 8 to 12

Mango Cucumber Salsa

Chop 1 large mango, 1 cucumber, $^1/_2$ red onion, $^1/_2$ large tomato and 1 jalapeño chile and combine in a bowl. Add 1 tablespoon olive oil and 1 teaspoon grated lime zest and mix well. Season with lime juice, salt and pepper to taste. Serve with tortilla chips or as an accompaniment with seafood.

Mushrooms Stuffed with Guacamole

2 medium ripe tomatoes, seeded and chopped
1 small onion, chopped
2 fresh or pickled jalapeño chiles, seeded and
    finely chopped
1 teaspoon jalapeño hot sauce (optional)
1 teaspoon salt
1 ripe medium avocado
1/2 bunch fresh cilantro, stems removed and chopped
1 tablespoon white wine vinegar
2 tablespoons water
juice of 1 large lime or lemon (2 tablespoons)
freshly ground pepper
1 to 2 pounds fresh cremini mushrooms, stems removed

Combine the tomatoes, onion, jalapeño chiles, jalapeño hot sauce and salt in a bowl and mix well. Let stand at room temperature for 15 minutes.

Mash the avocado in a bowl with a fork until slightly lumpy. Stir in the cilantro, vinegar, water, lime juice and pepper. Fold the avocado mixture into the tomato mixture. Chill, covered, for 1 hour. Stuff the mushroom caps with the guacamole and arrange on a serving platter. Serve immediately.

Serves 8 to 10

Green Olive Cheese Puffs

1 cup flour
1/4 teaspoon red pepper flakes
3 egg yolks, lightly beaten
3/4 cup beer, at room temperature
2 tablespoons olive oil
1/2 teaspoon salt
1/8 teaspoon ground pepper
peanut oil for frying
10 ounces chorizo sausage, casings removed
3 egg whites, stiffly beaten
1/2 cup (2 ounces) grated Parmesan cheese
1/3 cup green olives, pitted and chopped
3 tablespoons chopped fresh parsley

Sift the flour into a bowl. Stir in the red pepper flakes. Make a well in the center of the flour mixture. Add the egg yolks, beer, olive oil, salt and pepper to the well and mix well; do not overmix. Let the batter stand, covered, at room temperature for 1 hour.

Heat peanut oil in a heavy saucepan to 375 degrees. Cook the chorizo in a skillet over medium heat for 3 to 4 minutes or until heated through, stirring with a wooden spoon to crumble; drain. Fold the chorizo, egg whites, cheese, olives and parsley into the batter. Drop the batter in batches by heaping tablespoonfuls into the hot peanut oil; do not crowd. Fry for 2 to 3 minutes or until golden brown, turning occasionally. Drain on paper towels. Serve warm.

Serves 10 to 12

Grilled Steak with Chimichurri Sauce

Chimichurri Sauce

1/4 cup fresh cilantro
6 garlic cloves
2 jalapeño chiles, stemmed and cut into halves
4 large bay leaves, crumbled
1 tablespoon oregano
1 teaspoon salt
1 cup flat-leaf parsley leaves
1/2 cup white vinegar
1/2 cup olive oil
1/4 cup fresh cilantro
pepper to taste

Skirt Steaks

6 (5- to 6-ounce) skirt steaks
salt and pepper to taste
tomato wedges (optional)

For the sauce, combine 1/4 cup cilantro, garlic, jalapeño chiles, bay leaves, oregano and salt in a food processor. Process until finely chopped, scraping the bowl occasionally. Add the parsley, vinegar, olive oil and 1/4 cup cilantro. Process until coarsely chopped. Season with pepper. Let stand, covered, at room temperature. You may prepare up to 8 hours in advance and store, covered, at room temperature.

For the steaks, season the steaks with salt and pepper. Grill the steaks over hot coals or broil for 3 minutes per side for medium-rare or to the desired degree of doneness. Arrange the steaks on individual dinner plates. Drizzle with some of the sauce and garnish with tomato wedges. Pass the remaining sauce.

Serves 6

Caramelized Carnitas

1 1/2 pounds boneless pork shoulder, cut into 1-inch cubes
2 tablespoons brown sugar
1 tablespoon tequila
1 tablespoon molasses
1/2 teaspoon salt
1/4 teaspoon pepper
2 garlic cloves, finely chopped
1/3 cup water
1 green onion with top, sliced

Arrange the pork cubes in a single layer in a skillet. Layer with the brown sugar, tequila, molasses, salt, pepper and garlic. Pour the water over the top. Bring to a boil; reduce the heat. Simmer for 35 minutes or until the water evaporates and the pork is slightly caramelized, stirring occasionally. Spoon the pork onto a serving platter and sprinkle with the green onion. Serve with wooden picks.

Serves 6 to 8

Stuffed Quesadillas

1¹/₃ cups (about) water
2 cups masa harina
Chorizo and Potato Stuffing (this page)
Beef Picadillo Stuffing (page 261)
Shredded Chicken Stuffing (page 261)

Add the water all at once to the masa harina in a bowl and mix just until moistened. Let rest for 10 minutes. Heat 1 or 2 heavy griddles over medium heat; a tortilla should sizzle when placed on the heated griddle.

Place a piece of plastic wrap on a tortilla press. Shape the tortilla dough into 1¹/₂-inch balls and place 1 at a time on the press, placing slightly closer to the hinge than the handle. Cover with a second piece of plastic wrap and press firmly. Peel off the top plastic and remove from the press; invert and peel off the bottom plastic. Place carefully on the heated griddle.

Cook each tortilla just until it begins to dry around the edge. Turn the tortilla and cook for a slightly longer time or just until it begins to brown. Turn again and cook until light brown; the entire process should take about 2 minutes. Remove and stack in a large plastic bag until all the tortillas are cooked.

Fill as desired with one of the stuffings suggested.
Makes about 16 (5-inch) tortillas

Chorizo and Potato Stuffing

6 small potatoes, peeled and cut into halves
salt to taste
*1 pound Mexican chorizo, casing removed and cut into
   ³/₄-inch pieces*
vegetable oil
¹/₄ cup chopped onion
pepper to taste

Boil the potatoes in salted water in a saucepan just until tender; drain. Cut into ³/₄-inch pieces. Blanch the potatoes in boiling water in a saucepan for several seconds. Drain and pat dry with a paper towel. Blanch the chorizo in boiling water in a saucepan for several seconds. Drain and pat dry with a paper towel.

Cook the chorizo in oil in a large skillet over medium-low heat for 10 minutes or until cooked through, stirring frequently to break up large clumps. Remove the chorizo to a bowl using a slotted spoon, reserving the pan drippings. Drain the reserved pan drippings, leaving just enough of the drippings to coat the bottom of the skillet.

Fry the potatoes and onion in the reserved pan drippings for 10 to 15 minutes or until brown, stirring frequently. Stir in the chorizo. Cook just until heated through, stirring frequently. Season with salt.
Stuffs about 16 quesadillas

Beef Picadillo Stuffing

2 garlic cloves, minced
2 tablespoons vegetable oil
1 pound ground beef
salt and pepper to taste
$1/2$ cup chopped onion
$1/2$ cup chopped tomato
$1/2$ cup tomato paste

Sauté the garlic in the oil in a skillet until golden brown. Add the ground beef, salt and pepper. Cook until the ground beef is almost cooked through, stirring frequently. Stir in the onion.

Cook until the onion is tender, stirring frequently. Add the tomato and tomato paste and mix well. Simmer for 10 to 15 minutes, stirring occasionally. Taste and adjust the seasonings.

Stuffs about 16 quesadillas

Shredded Chicken Stuffing

$1/2$ teaspoon minced garlic
2 tablespoons vegetable oil
1 cup chopped onion
$1/2$ cup julienned poblano chiles
1 cup julienned tomato
2 pounds shredded poached chicken
salt and pepper to taste

Sauté the garlic in the oil in a skillet until golden brown. Stir in the onion. Sauté for 1 minute. Add the poblano chiles and mix well. Sauté for several minutes. Stir in the tomato.

Cook for 2 minutes, stirring frequently. Stir in the chicken. Simmer for 2 to 4 minutes, stirring occasionally. Season with salt and pepper.

Stuffs about 16 quesadillas

Turkey Tortilla Roll-Ups

Mole Sour Cream Sauce

3/4 cup sour cream

3 tablespoons chopped fresh cilantro

2 teaspoons concentrated mole

1 1/2 teaspoons fresh lime juice

1/4 teaspoon kosher salt

Turkey Roll-Ups

6 (7-inch) fresh flour tortillas, at room temperature

1/2 cup finely chopped smoked turkey

1/4 cup canned diced green chiles

1 tablespoon concentrated mole

1 teaspoon minced garlic

1/2 teaspoon oregano

vegetable oil

For the sauce, combine the sour cream, cilantro, mole, lime juice and salt in a bowl and whisk until combined. Chill, covered, in the refrigerator.

For the roll-ups, cut each tortilla into four 2 1/2-inch rounds using a cookie cutter. Combine the turkey, green chiles, mole, garlic and oregano in a bowl and mix well. Arrange the tortilla rounds in batches of 6 on a work surface. Brush lightly with oil. Place 1 teaspoon of the turkey mixture on the lower third of each round. Roll tightly to enclose the filling and secure with wooden picks.

Arrange the roll-ups on a baking sheet lined with baking parchment. Brush each roll-up lightly with oil. Bake at 400 degrees for 10 to 15 minutes or until brown. Remove the wooden picks and serve with the sauce.

Makes 2 dozen roll-ups

Brazilian Rice and Beans

3 firm medium bananas

1 large onion, chopped

2 tablespoons minced fresh gingerroot

1 large garlic clove, crushed

vegetable oil

8 ounces ground beef

8 ounces pork sausage

1 teaspoon cumin

1/2 teaspoon cayenne pepper

1 (15-ounce) can kidney beans

1 (11-ounce) can black bean soup

1 (8-ounce) can stewed tomatoes

3 to 4 cups cooked rice

4 to 6 cups shredded lettuce

2 teaspoons minced cilantro

Cut the bananas into halves crosswise, then cut each half lengthwise. Sauté the onion, gingerroot and garlic in a small amount of oil in a large skillet until tender; push to 1 side of the skillet and add the bananas. Sauté for 30 to 45 seconds. Remove the bananas to a plate and add the ground beef, sausage, cumin and cayenne pepper to the skillet. Cook until brown and crumbly, stirring constantly. Add the undrained beans, soup and tomatoes. Simmer, covered, for 30 minutes, stirring occasionally.

Spoon the rice onto serving plates and top with the bean mixture. Sprinkle with the lettuce and cilantro. Serve with the sautéed bananas.

Serves 6

Margarita Pie

Pretzel Crust

$1/2$ cup (1 stick) butter or margarine

$1^1/4$ cups finely crushed pretzels

$1/4$ cup sugar

Pie

1 (14-ounce) can sweetened condensed milk

$1/3$ cup lime juice

2 to 4 tablespoons tequila

2 tablespoons Triple Sec or other orange-flavor liqueur

1 cup whipping cream, whipped

For the crust, heat the butter in a saucepan until melted. Remove from the heat. Stir in the pretzel crumbs and sugar. Pat the crumb mixture over the bottom and up the side of a buttered 9-inch pie plate. Chill in the refrigerator.

For the pie, combine the condensed milk, lime juice, tequila and liqueur in a bowl and mix well. Fold in the whipped cream. Spoon the filling into the prepared pie plate. Freeze, covered, for 2 hours or chill for 4 hours. Garnish with additional whipped cream, orange twists, fresh mint leaves or additional pretzels crumbs if desired.

Serves 6 to 8

Mocha Bundt Cake

Cake

1 (2-layer) package yellow cake mix without pudding

1 (6-ounce) package chocolate instant pudding mix

1 cup vegetable oil

$3/4$ cup water

$1/2$ cup sugar

$1/4$ cup vodka

$1/4$ cup coffee-flavor liqueur

4 eggs

Coffee Glaze

$1/2$ cup confectioners' sugar

$1/4$ cup coffee-flavor liqueur

confectioners' sugar to taste

For the cake, combine the cake mix, pudding mix, oil, water, sugar, vodka, liqueur and eggs in a mixing bowl. Beat at low speed for 1 minute. Beat at medium speed for 4 minutes, scraping the bowl occasionally.

Spoon the batter into a nonstick bundt pan. Bake at 350 degrees for 60 to 70 minutes or until a wooden pick inserted in the cake comes out clean. Cool in pan for 10 minutes. Invert onto a wire rack. Pierce the top of the cake with a fork.

For the glaze, mix $1/2$ cup confectioners' sugar and liqueur in a bowl until a glaze consistency. Spoon the glaze over the warm cake. Let stand until cool. Dust with confectioners' sugar to taste.

Serves 16

MENU

Asian Expressions

Twinkling lights, shiny black lacquer dishes, and silky kimonos are required. Your guests will feel like they've boarded the Orient Express when they walk across your lawn. Grab some chopsticks and a fruity cocktail...and enjoy the trip.

Bangkok Punch

Ginger Infusion

2 quarts water

1 cup sugar

12 ounces fresh gingerroot, peeled
    and chopped

1 stalk lemon grass, cut into thirds

1 Thai chile, stemmed and seeded

Punch

$1^1/_2$ ounces dark rum

$1^1/_2$ ounces papaya juice or pineapple
    juice

$^1/_2$ ounce lemon juice or lime juice

$^1/_8$ teaspoon cayenne pepper

1 pineapple wedge

For the infusion, combine the water and sugar in a stockpot and stir until the sugar dissolves. Combine the gingerroot, lemon grass and Thai chile in a food processor. Pulse until the mixture is coarsely chopped. Add the gingerroot mixture to the sugar mixture and mix well. Bring to a boil.
Boil until the mixture is reduced by $^1/_2$. Let stand until cool. Strain the gingerroot mixture through a fine sieve into a bowl, discarding the solids. You may store, covered, in the refrigerator for up to 2 weeks.

For the punch, combine 3 tablespoons of the infusion, rum, papaya juice and lemon juice in a cocktail shaker and shake vigorously. Pour over ice in a glass. Top with the cayenne pepper and pineapple wedge.

Serves 1

Midori Cocktail

ice cubes

$1^1/_2$ ounces Midori

$1^1/_2$ ounces vodka

$^1/_3$ cup strained fresh orange juice

3 melon balls

Fill a long-stemmed glass with ice cubes. Add the liqueur, vodka and orange juice and stir to mix. Garnish with a skewer threaded with the melon balls.

Serves 1

Asian Influences

Because of its location as a coastal town and its military installation, Panama City has had influences from a variety of countries and cultures. Many people of Asian descent have moved to the area and in turn have left their mark on many things, especially the cuisine. Asian restaurants and food shops are scattered throughout Bay County, and locals have grown very fond of their delicious styles of cooking. Our Asian Fete has brought together these various styles of cooking and features delightful ideas for entertaining guests.

The shores of North Bay and the sweeping lawn of a country club estate provide the backdrop for our party. Asian statues were collected along with silk screens, kimonos, and other objects d'art to use as decorations. Food is displayed on shelves, vases, and rattan mats, with sushi in its own special dishes.

Sake Martini

Peel an English cucumber and cut into halves lengthwise. Combine with 1 pint vodka in a sealable glass jar and seal tightly. Let stand at room temperature for 6 days.

Chill 4 to 6 martini glasses. Remove the cucumber halves from the vodka and discard. Fill a cocktail pitcher half full of ice cubes. Add the vodka and 4 ounces dry sake and stir 50 times. Strain into the chilled glasses. Garnish with a thin fresh cucumber slice.

Blue Moon Sake Cocktail

ice cubes
¼ cup sake, chilled
¼ cup vodka
4 teaspoons peach nectar

4 teaspoons blue curaçao
1 teaspoon lime juice
2 lime twists

Chill 2 martini glasses. Fill a cocktail shaker with ice cubes. Add the sake, vodka, peach nectar, liqueur and lime juice. Shake vigorously and strain the cocktail mixture into the chilled glasses. Garnish the rim of each glass with a lime twist.
Serves 2

Gingered Sake Spritzers

1 (28-ounce) bottle ginger ale, chilled
12 ounces sake

2 teaspoons angostura bitters
6 lime slices

Combine the ginger ale, sake and bitters in a pitcher and mix well. Add the lime slices. Pour the spritzer over ice in glasses.
Serves 6

Shanghai Cocktail

1 ounce lemon juice
1 ounce Jamaican rum

¼ ounce Pernod
¼ teaspoon grenadine

Combine the lemon juice, rum, liqueur and grenadine in a cocktail shaker. Shake vigorously and strain into a cocktail glass.
Serves 1

Sweet and Spicy Gingered Almonds

1/4 cup sugar
1/4 cup sesame seeds
2 teaspoons ginger
1/2 teaspoon cumin
2 teaspoons salt
1 1/2 teaspoons crushed red pepper flakes
2 tablespoons vegetable oil
2 cups blanched whole almonds
1/2 cup sugar

Mix 1/4 cup sugar, sesame seeds, ginger, cumin, salt and red pepper flakes in a bowl and reserve.

Heat the vegetable oil in a heavy skillet over medium heat. Add the almonds and sauté for 2 minutes. Sprinkle with 1/2 cup sugar and continue to cook for 10 to 15 minutes or until the sugar starts to melt and caramelize, shaking the skillet rather than stirring to prevent burning. Stir the almonds and cook until dark golden brown and beginning to smoke.

Combine the hot almond mixture with the sesame seed mixture in a bowl and toss to coat well. Spread the almond mixture on a nonstick baking sheet and separate quickly with 2 forks. Cool to room temperature. Store in an airtight container for up to 3 weeks.

Makes 2 cups

Grilled Marinated Beef with Vegetables

2 tablespoons sugar
3/4 teaspoon cornstarch
1 tablespoon chopped lemon grass
1 tablespoon minced garlic
1 tablespoon soy sauce
1 tablespoon vegetable oil
1 pound flank steak, cut diagonally into thin slices
salt and pepper to taste
16 (6-inch) rice paper rounds (bahn trang)
1/2 cup grated carrots
1/2 cup watercress leaves
1 red bell pepper, julienned
1 cucumber, peeled, seeded and julienned

Combine the sugar and cornstarch in a bowl and mix well. Stir in the lemon grass, garlic, soy sauce and oil. Add the steak and turn to coat. Marinate, covered, in the refrigerator for 8 to 10 hours, turning occasionally; drain. Sprinkle the steak with salt and pepper. Grill over medium-high heat for 2 minutes per side or to the desired degree of doneness. Let stand until cool.

Dip the rice paper rounds into warm water just until softened. Pat dry with paper towels. Place the rice papers on a hard surface. Arrange the steak, carrots, watercress, bell pepper and cucumber down the center of the rice papers, dividing the ingredients equally. Roll to enclose the filling and arrange seam side down on a platter. Whisk the fish sauce, vinegar and chopped green onions in a bowl and serve with the rice paper rolls if desired.

Serves 8

How to Make
Sushi Rolls

Nori are thin sheets of dried seaweed used to wrap sushi; they can be purchased at a Japanese market or many large supermarkets. Place a sheet of nori shiny side down on a slightly larger square of foil or a bamboo mat designed for the purpose. Place 1 to 3 tablespoons of sushi rice on the nori sheet and spread evenly with moistened fingers, leaving a one-inch edge at the top and building up the sides to form edges. Spread a small amount of wasabi across the center and add the desired fillings. Roll the foil or bamboo mat around the nori to enclose the filling and hold for 30 seconds to secure the shape. Moisten the edge and press to seal tightly before unrolling the foil or mat.

Sushi Rolls

Sushi Rice

1³/₄ cups Japanese short-grain rice

2 cups water

3 tablespoons rice wine vinegar

2¹/₂ tablespoons sugar

2 teaspoons sea salt

Sushi Rolls

nori seawood

bamboo mat

wasabi

pickled ginger (optional)

smoked salmon (optional)

caviar (optional)

flaked crab meat (optional)

chopped steamed shrimp (optional)

flaked cooked tuna (optional)

chopped cooked squid (optional)

sliced cucumbers, carrots, mushrooms, avocado (optional)

For the rice, rinse the rice in a bowl, changing the water as many times as needed until the water runs clear. Let stand for 10 minutes; drain. Combine the rice and 2 cups water in a 2-quart saucepan. Bring to a boil over high heat. Boil for 5 minutes, stirring frequently. Remove from the heat. Let stand, covered, for 10 to 15 minutes. Spoon the rice into a bowl.

Combine the vinegar, sugar and salt in a bowl and stir until the sugar and salt dissolve. Fold the vinegar mixture into the rice; do not stir. Let stand until body temperature. You may prepare several days in advance and store, covered with plastic wrap, in the refrigerator. Bring to room temperature before serving.

For the rolls, place a sheet of nori seaweed on a bamboo mat. Shape a small handful of the sushi rice into a log with moistened hands and place the rice log in the center of the seaweed. Spread the rice evenly over the seaweed to within ¹/₂ inch of the edges. Spread a streak of wasabi across the middle, and then layer with the optional ingredients as desired over the wasabi. Make sure the seaweed sheet with rice and fillings are pulled down towards you on the sushi mat. Roll the sushi mat with seaweed and filling into a cylinder. Press the mat around the roll for about 30 seconds to shape it, then moisten the margin of seaweed and seal the roll as tightly as possible. Chill, wrapped tightly in plastic wrap, until serving time. Cut each roll into halves and then each half into thirds. Arrange the sushi on a serving platter and serve with wasabi paste, pickled ginger and soy sauce.

Makes variable servings

Leafy Sushi Rolls

4 varieties of small lettuce leaves
Sushi Rice (page 268)
sliced smoked salmon (optional)
caviar (optional)
capers (optional)
lemon zest (optional)
flaked crab meat (optional)
lemon juice (optional)
pickled ginger (optional)
wasabi (optional)

Tear small portions of the lettuce leaves and shape into cups in the palm of your hand. Shape the rice into balls to fit the lettuce cups with moistened hands. Arrange the rice balls in the lettuce cups. Top with salmon, caviar or capers or just caviar and lemon zest. Or, top with crab meat, lemon juice, pickled ginger, caviar or capers. A dollop of wasabi can be added to the top of the rice with other toppings. Use your imagination and taste to create your toppings.

Makes variable servings

Smoked Salmon Sushi

6 ounces sliced smoked salmon
1 cup prepared Sushi Rice (page 268)
lemon zest
capers
pickled ginger
soy sauce
wasabi

Arrange the smoked salmon on a square wooden mold, covering evenly. Shape the rice into a square on the salmon and cover with plastic wrap. Cut a square of cardboard the size of the mold and place on the plastic wrap covering the rice. Wrap in plastic wrap and chill for 30 minutes or longer. Invert onto a work surface and remove the plastic wrap and mold carefully. Cut into small squares. Garnish with lemon zest and capers. Serve with pickled ginger, soy sauce and wasabi.

Serves 6

Orange Cilantro Cream

Combine 3 tablespoons marinade reserved from the Pork Tenderloin Brochettes (this page), ¹/₂ cup sour cream, 2 tablespoons finely chopped fresh cilantro, the finely chopped zest of 1 orange, and hot pepper oil to taste in a saucepan and mix well. Bring to a boil. Taste and adjust the seasonings. Spoon into a bowl and chill, covered, in the refrigerator for up to 1 day.

Pork Tenderloin Brochettes

bamboo skewers
¹/₂ cup fresh orange juice
2 tablespoons fresh lime juice
2 tablespoons vegetable oil
1 teaspoon chopped fresh oregano
1 teaspoon chopped fresh cilantro
1 teaspoon chopped fresh marjoram

¹/₄ teaspoon cumin
salt and freshly ground pepper to taste
1 (1-pound) pork tenderloin, cut into 1-inch cubes
fresh cilantro leaves
Orange Cilantro Cream (this page)

Soak bamboo skewers in cold water in a bowl for 30 minutes or longer. Whisk the orange juice, lime juice, oil, oregano, cilantro, marjoram, cumin, salt and pepper in a bowl. Reserve 3 tablespoons of the marinade for the Orange Cilantro Cream. You may prepare the marinade up to 1 day in advance and store, covered, in the refrigerator.

Thread the pork on the soaked skewers and arrange in a nonreactive dish. Pour the remaining marinade over the skewers and turn to coat. Marinate, covered, in the refrigerator for 6 to 12 hours, turning occasionally; drain.

Grill the pork 3 inches from the heat source over medium heat for 4 to 8 minutes per side or just until cooked through, turning once. Arrange the skewers on a large serving platter. Garnish with fresh cilantro leaves. Serve with Orange Cilantro Cream.

Serves 4 to 6

Sweet-and-Sour Chicken Tartlets

Chicken Filling

¾ cup chopped cooked chicken

½ cup shredded carrots

⅓ cup chopped unsalted peanuts

3 tablespoons sliced green onions (white and green parts)

2 tablespoons soy sauce

1 tablespoon chopped fresh parsley

1 teaspoon grated fresh gingerroot

1 teaspoon sesame oil

1 garlic clove, minced

Tartlets

8 ounces cream cheese, softened

1 tablespoon milk

45 miniature phyllo shells

Sweet-and-Sour Sauce (this page)

For the filling, combine the chicken, carrots, peanuts, green onions, soy sauce, parsley, gingerroot, sesame oil and garlic in a bowl and mix well. Chill, covered, for several hours to allow the flavors to blend.

For the tartlets, beat the cream cheese and milk in a mixing bowl until light and fluffy. Coat the bottoms and sides of the phyllo shells evenly with the cream cheese mixture. Spoon the filling into the shells and drizzle with Sweet-and-Sour Sauce.

Makes 45 tartlets

Sweet-and-Sour Sauce

¼ cup packed dark brown sugar

2 teaspoons cornstarch

1 cup water

¼ cup ketchup

2 tablespoons vinegar

1 tablespoon Worcestershire sauce

3 drops of Tabasco sauce

Combine the brown sugar and cornstarch in a small saucepan and mix well. Add the water, ketchup, vinegar, Worcestershire sauce and Tabasco sauce gradually, stirring constantly.

Cook over medium heat for 5 minutes or until slightly thickened, stirring frequently. Let stand until cool. Chill, covered, in the refrigerator.

Makes 2½ cups

Sesame Chicken Skewers

2 large boneless skinless chicken breasts
2 tablespoons rice wine vinegar
2 tablespoons dark Asian sesame oil
2 tablespoons soy sauce
1 tablespoon finely chopped garlic
¼ cup each white and black sesame seeds
3 tablespoons flour
2 teaspoons cornstarch
peanut oil
48 snow peas, ends and strings removed
1 red bell pepper
Ginger Chile Dip (this page)
red leaf lettuce

Cut the chicken into 48 bite-size chunks. Whisk the vinegar, sesame oil, soy sauce and garlic in a bowl. Add the chicken and toss to coat. Marinate, covered, in the refrigerator for 8 to 10 hours, turning occasionally; drain.

Combine the sesame seeds, flour and cornstarch in a shallow dish and mix well. Coat the chicken with the sesame seed mixture. Arrange the chicken in a single layer on a tray. Let stand for 10 minutes. Heat enough peanut oil in a sauté pan to measure ¼ inch. Brown the chicken on all sides in batches in the peanut oil; drain.

Blanch the snow peas in boiling water in a saucepan for 1 minute. Drain in a colander and rinse with cold water to stop the cooking process. Pat dry with paper towels. Wrap each snow pea around a piece of chicken and thread on wooden skewers.

Cut the top from the bell pepper and discard. Remove the seeds and membranes. Fill the bell pepper with Ginger Chile Dip. Line a serving platter with red leaf lettuce. Arrange the bell pepper upright in the center of the platter and surround with the chicken skewers.

Serves 12

Ginger Chile Dip

¾ cup mayonnaise
2 tablespoons chile paste with garlic
1 tablespoon minced fresh gingerroot
1 tablespoon rice wine vinegar
1 tablespoon soy sauce
1 tablespoon sugar
1 teaspoon sesame oil
⅛ teaspoon Tabasco sauce

Combine the mayonnaise, chili paste, gingerroot, vinegar, soy sauce, sugar, sesame oil and Tabasco sauce in a bowl and mix well.

Makes 1 cup

Chicken Satay with Cucumber Relish

Chicken

1 pound boneless skinless chicken breasts
1/2 cup lime juice
1 tablespoon honey
1 tablespoon grated lime zest
1 teaspoon minced garlic

Cucumber Relish

1 cup finely chopped seeded peeled cucumber
1/2 cup finely chopped seeded tomato
2 tablespoons minced fresh cilantro
2 tablespoons rice vinegar
1 teaspoon minced garlic

For the chicken, cut the chicken into 1-inch pieces. Arrange the chicken in a large shallow dish. Whisk the lime juice, honey, lime zest and garlic in a bowl. Pour the lime juice mixture over the chicken, turning to coat. Marinate at room temperature for 30 minutes, turning frequently.

Thread the chicken on short skewers. Broil or grill for 5 to 10 minutes or until the chicken is brown and cooked through, turning frequently.

For the relish, combine the cucumber, tomato, cilantro, vinegar and garlic in a bowl and mix well. Let stand at room temperature for 15 minutes. Serve with the chicken.

Serves 4

Sichuan Shrimp in Lettuce Leaves

Sichuan Sauce

2 teaspoons each cornstarch and cold water
1 tablespoon ketchup
1 tablespoon Shao-Hsing wine or dry sherry
2 teaspoons oyster sauce
3/4 teaspoon sugar
salt and freshly ground white pepper to taste

Shrimp

2 teaspoons each shallot oil and minced fresh gingerroot
1 1/2 teaspoons bean sauce
12 ounces shrimp, peeled, deveined and cut into 1/2-inch pieces
1 small red bell pepper, cut into 1/4-inch pieces
1 small green bell pepper, cut into 1/4-inch pieces
1/4 cup finely chopped water chestnuts
1 jalapeño chile, minced
3 tablespoons chopped crisp shallots
12 iceberg lettuce leaves

For the sauce, dissolve the cornstarch in the cold water in a bowl. Add the ketchup, wine, oyster sauce, sugar, salt and white pepper to the cornstarch mixture and mix well.

For the shrimp, heat a wok over high heat for 30 seconds. Add the shallot oil and tilt the wok to ensure even coverage. Add the gingerroot and bean sauce when a wisp of white smoke appears. Stir in the shrimp. Add the bell peppers, water chestnuts and jalapeño chile and mix well. Stir-fry for 3 minutes or until the vegetables are tender-crisp and the shrimp turn pink. Make a well in the center of the wok, pushing all the ingredients slightly up the side of the wok. Stir the sauce and add to the well. Stir the shrimp and vegetables into the sauce. Stir-fry for 2 minutes or until heated through. Stir in the shallots. Serve in the lettuce leaves.

Serves 2

Apricot Dipping Sauce

*Combine ¹/₂ cup apricot preserves,
1 tablespoon water, 2 teaspoons fresh lime
juice, 2 teaspoons soy sauce, 1 teaspoon
Dijon mustard and ¹/₄ teaspoon minced
gingerroot in a food processor. Process until
smooth. Chill, covered, in the refrigerator for
up to 1 week.*

Shrimp and Sesame Sticks

Shrimp Filling

1¹/₃ pounds shrimp, peeled and
    deveined
¹/₄ cup sesame seeds, toasted
3 scallions, chopped
1 tablespoon sesame oil
1 tablespoon soy sauce
1 tablespoon cornstarch
1¹/₂ teaspoons minced fresh
    gingerroot
1 teaspoon minced garlic

Sesame Sticks and Assembly

12 (12×17-inch) frozen phyllo pastry
    sheets, thawed
¹/₂ cup (1 stick) plus 2 tablespoons
    unsalted butter, melted
1 egg, lightly beaten
2 tablespoons sesame seeds, toasted
kosher salt to taste
Apricot Dipping Sauce (this page)

For the filling, combine the shrimp, sesame seeds, scallions, sesame oil, soy sauce, cornstarch, gingerroot and garlic in a food processor. Pulse until the consistency of a paste.

For the sticks, cover the pastry with 2 overlapping sheets of plastic wrap and a dampened tea towel. Remove 1 pastry sheet at a time, keeping the remainder covered to prevent drying out. Brush generously with unsalted butter. Stack 2 more pastry sheets on top, generously brushing each sheet with butter. Cut the stack lengthwise into halves. Arrange ¹/₂ of the stack with the long side nearest you. Shape 3 tablespoons of the filling into a narrow rope with dampened fingers. Place the rope on the edge nearest you and roll tightly to form a long thin roll. Repeat the process with the remaining ¹/₂ stack. Brush the tops of the rolls with the egg and sprinkle with sesame seeds and salt. Cut each roll crosswise into 4 sticks. Arrange seam side down 1 inch apart on 2 large baking sheets.

Repeat this process with the remaining pastry sheets, remaining filling, remaining egg, remaining sesame seeds and salt. Bake in the upper and lower third of the oven at 450 degrees for 15 minutes or until golden brown, switching the baking sheets halfway through the baking process. Remove to a wire rack to cool slightly. Serve warm with Apricot Dipping Sauce.

Makes 8 shrimp and sesame sticks

Curried Mango Shrimp Salad

12 won ton wrappers
vegetable oil
1/2 cup mayonnaise
2 tablespoons chopped fresh cilantro
5 teaspoons fresh lime juice
2 teaspoons mango chutney
3/4 teaspoon Thai green curry paste
12 ounces peeled cooked medium shrimp,
    coarsely chopped
salt and pepper to taste
fresh cilantro leaves

Cut each won ton wrapper into 4 squares. Brush 1 side of each square lightly with oil. Press each square oil side down into a miniature muffin cup. Bake at 325 degrees for 10 minutes or until golden brown. Cool in cups on a wire rack. Store in an airtight container at room temperature.

Whisk the mayonnaise, chopped cilantro, lime juice, chutney and curry paste in a bowl until combined. Stir in the shrimp. Season with salt and pepper. You may prepare up to 1 day in advance and store, covered, in the refrigerator.

To serve, spoon 1 teaspoon of the shrimp salad into each won ton cup. Garnish with cilantro leaves.

Makes 4 dozen

Ginger-Glazed Shrimp

Ginger Glaze
1/3 cup water
1/4 cup seasoned rice vinegar
2 teaspoons chopped lemon grass bulb
2 teaspoons minced fresh gingerroot
1 teaspoon lime zest
1/4 teaspoon crushed red pepper
1 1/2 teaspoons cornstarch
1 tablespoon water

Shrimp
12 cups water
1 tablespoon kosher salt
24 medium to large shrimp
24 fresh cilantro sprigs

For the glaze, combine 1/3 cup water, vinegar, lemon grass, gingerroot, lime zest and red pepper in a small saucepan. Dissolve the cornstarch in 1 tablespoon water in a small bowl and whisk into the saucepan. Bring to a boil over medium heat and cook for 1 minute or until thickened, whisking constantly. Spoon into a bowl and chill in the refrigerator.

For the shrimp, bring the water and kosher salt to a boil in a large saucepan over medium heat. Add the shrimp and cook for 3 minutes or until opaque; drain. Arrange on a tray and chill in the refrigerator.

Peel the shrimp leaving the tail intact. Cut a 1/2-inch slit down the back of each shrimp and rinse in cold water to remove the vein; pat dry. Place a cilantro sprig in each slit and serve with the glaze.

Makes 2 dozen

Vietnamese Spring Rolls

8 ounces rice vermicelli
2 pounds medium shrimp, peeled and deveined
25 spring roll wrappers or rice papers
2 bunches watercress, large stems removed
5 large carrots, finely shredded
2 red bell peppers, julienned
5 Hass avocados, cut into lengthwise slices
Nuoc Cham Sauce (this page)

Pour cool water over the vermicelli in a bowl. Let stand for 20 minutes or until pliable. Cook the shrimp in boiling water in a saucepan for 1 to 2 minutes or until bright pink. Remove the shrimp to a colander with a slotted spoon, reserving the cooking liquid. Rinse the shrimp with cold water and pat dry. Cut the shrimp lengthwise into halves. Chill, covered, in the refrigerator.

Bring the reserved cooking liquid to a boil. Add the vermicelli. Cook for 1 minute or until al dente, stirring frequently. Drain in a colander and rinse until cool. Let stand for 20 minutes or until dry, tossing occasionally.

Cover the spring roll wrappers with a damp tea towel. Remove 1 wrapper at a time to prevent drying out. Place 1 wrapper on a hard surface. On the lower $1/3$ of the wrapper, arrange 4 shrimp halves in a line. Top with 3 sprigs of watercress, a large pinch of carrot, 2 bell pepper strips and some of the vermicelli. Press to flatten and top with 1 avocado slice. Roll tightly to enclose the filling, folding in sides as you roll. Repeat with the remaining wrappers, remaining shrimp, remaining watercress, remaining carrots, remaining bell peppers, remaining vermicelli and remaining avocado. Arrange the rolls seam side down on a serving platter. Cut crosswise into halves to serve. Serve with Nuoc Cham Sauce.

Makes 25 whole spring rolls

Nuoc Cham Sauce

6 tablespoons light brown sugar
2 large garlic cloves, cut into halves
2 jalapeño chiles, seeded and coarsely chopped
$1/4$ cup fresh lime juice
$1/4$ cup water
$1/4$ cup finely chopped fresh cilantro
$1/4$ cup finely chopped spearmint
2 tablespoons Vietnamese fish sauce

Combine the brown sugar, garlic and jalapeño chiles in a food processor. Pulse until the mixture forms a paste. Spoon the brown sugar mixture into a bowl. Stir in the lime juice, water, cilantro, spearmint and fish sauce.

Makes $1^1/_2$ cups

Cookbook Committee

Vicki Mergenthal, *Chairman*
Joree Hamm, *Co-Chairman and Recipe Chairman*
Cindy Reimers, *Finance Chairman*

Recipes

Joree Hamm, *Chairman*
Michelle Holland, *Co-Chairman*
Pam McElreath, *Co-Chairman*
Melanie Walters, *Co-Chairman*
Amy Counts
Susan Dantzler
Cathie Hanson
Sandy Hundley
Kristy McKinney
Rhonda Stopka

Non-Recipe Text

Kelly Roberson, *Chairman*
Kara Davis
Tina Nichols
Kim Syfrett

Marketing

Cille Boyd, *Chairman*
Kelly Forehand
Terry Kinsey
Patty Vaught

Art and Design

Rachelle Youd, *Chairman*
Susan Harrison
Jenny Lewis

Supper Club Leaders

Joy Coker
Lisa Downey
Carla Drummond
Kristi Fisher
Scotti Haney
Mara Harrison
Diana Hundley
Kay Judah
Mary Kiehn
Sealy Ledman
Ashlie Overman
Julie Prevost

Recipe Contributors and Testers

Barbara Abbott
Maria Abrams
Barbara Almond
Linda Arnold
Laura Baker
Jill Bauer
Agatha Bennett
Liz Bennett
Debbie Bernstein
Shari Beshear
Diane Biano
Brianne Biddle
Mary Bonham
Cille Boyd
Jim Boyd
Kathy Bradford
Beth Branham
Lori Brites
Beth Brock
Deb Brown
Sandy Brown
Callie Bryant
Eva Bryant
Terra Burgreen
Dorothy Burton
Angie Buttram
Bill Cappleman
Jennifer Cappleman
Carolyn Carroll
Holly Carter
Brian Chambless
Kelli Chapman
Pamm Chapman
Sandra Chisholm
Marian Clark
Sue Clark
Louise Clements
Mary Marie
    Chapman-Clemo
Pat Clemons

Joy Coker
Carol Collins
Clay Collins
Marion McElvey Collins
Melonie Corbin
Rae Cotton
Salie Cotton
Amy Counts
Steve Counts
Christy Courthand
Kay Cox
Suzanne Crumble
Susan Dantzler
Kara Davis
Annabel Deramo
Stella Deramo
Laura Dobbins
Lisa Downey
Carla Drummond
Tiffany DuBose
Debbie Earnest
Darlene Fensom
Jan Fensom
Joe Ferary
Cynthia Fields
Louise Fishel
Kristi Fisher
Todd Fisher
Peggy Fleitman
Kelly Forehand
Marcia Forehand
Stephanie Frimet
Julie Fulcher
Judy Gaal
Leah Gaal
Anda Gagnet
Lee Gagnet
Sandy Gallati
Bunny Garr
Carol Garrison

Judy Garrison
Sara Gibbs
Nina Godwin
Gloria Goodreau
Leslie Gortemoller
Kim Goslin
Barbara Grabowski
JoAn Gramling
Lisa Gramling
Linda Grantham
Laura Griffitts
Brandy Haiman
Bonnie Hale
Karen Hale
Lesley Hall
John Hamlin
Lisa Hamlin
John Hamm
Joree Hamm
Elizabeth Hamrick
Sarah Haney
Scotti Haney
Cathie Hanson
Jean Hanson
Kim Harders
Marion Harrington
Cathy Harrison
Linda Harrison
Mara Harrison
Susan Harrison
Denis Healey
Lora Healey
Cliff Higby
Susan Higby
Helen Hindsman
Nanette Hitchcock
Annie Holcombe
Hannelore Holland
Michelle Holland
Day Ann Hopes

Martha Ann Horn
Angela Howell
Joanne Howell
Haley Hughes
Kristy Hughes
Mary Hulgan
Diana Hundley
Hollie Hundley
Sandy Hundley
Ashby Hunnicutt
Candi Hutchison
Mary Catherine Jinks
Cathy Johnson
Nellie Johnson
Patti Johnson
Kay Judah
Kenny Keltner
Mary Ann Keltner
Mary Kiehn
Michelle Kinard
Terri Kinsey
Barbara Knowles
Lynn Koehnemann
Tina Kovaleski
Helen Kruse
Rose Marie LaBarre
Elsie Cel Labasan
Ashley Lark
Chrissy Lark
Doedy Lark
Melissa Lawley
Judy Lawrence
Sealy Ledman
Jenny Lewis
Shandra Limcangco
Fred Lindholm
Jayne Lindholm
Judy Lindholm
Lisa Lindholm
Mayra Lindholm

Bobbi Lindsey
Jane Little
Eugenia Lloyd
Jennifer Lloyd
Ann Logue
Shannon Lord
Dick Lovejoy
Reba Lovejoy
Jack Lundgard
Michelle Maginnis
Annette Maro
Cathie Matthe
Jane Mayberry
Peggy Mayheu
Lisa McClendon
Martha McCormick
Patty McDaniel
Pam McElreath
Bill McKeithen
Blanford Dixon McKenzie
Rob McKenzie
Fran McKinney
Joanne McKinney
Kristy McKinney
Cande McNeil
Bettina Mead
Georgia Mergenthal
Vicki Mergenthal
Cassie Meyer
Kendall Middlemas
Martha Middlemas
Vicki Middlemas
Shay Miles
Kerri Miller
Mary Millett
Ellen Millour
Carol Mizell
Nicole Mockler
Raymond Mockler

Trish Molvig
Cindy Montgomery
Nikki Morrow
Julie Mullins
Alex Murphy
Helen Myers
Marilyn Nations
Tina Nichols
Allyson Noland
Barri Noll
David Noll
Barbara O'Connell
Ashlie Overman
Sarah Palmer
Jennifer Parsons
Jean Pasley
Gethyn Phillpott
Heather Pike
Jean Pitts
Betty Powell
Teresa Powell
Kim Powers
Mikki Prescott
Susan Prescott
Frances Prevost
Julie Prevost
Dottie Ralston
Jackie Rampietti
Shelia Ray
Billy Redd
Ben Redding
Dee Redding
Judy Reece
Michelle Reece
Pam Reece
Ann Reese
Mary Louise Reese
Cindy Reimers
Donna Rendlen

Phyllis Rhodes
Kelly Roberson
Carla Roche
Cindy Ropa
Joe Rudolph
Marianne Rudolph
Kim Ryan
Tina Sain
Melissa Sale
Vicky Sanborn
Jane Sapoznikoff
John Sapoznikoff
Lauri Schafer
Virginia Seal
Kimberly Segler
Patty Segler
Cindy Seltzer
Tammy Shannahan
Suzanne Sheffield
Elizabeth Shelley
Bettina Sheppard
Claire Sherman
Jane Sinclair
June Smith
Lyn Smith
Carol Southerland
Stacey Southerland
Rebecca Spann
Katherine Sparks
Rob Spencer
Boots Spivey
Ellie Spivey
Martha Spivey
Dot Springer
Barbara Stein
Paul Stellato
Rhonda Stopka
Lisa Strickland
Barbara Summers

Chris Sunderman
Ann Syfrett
Clayton Syfrett
Kim Syfrett
Patricia Tannehill
Kelly Tessitore
Bernice Thiele
Carolella Trappe
E. Troncale
Tammy Trumbull
Kirby Trunzo
Ellen McKenzie Tutte
Susie Underhill
Patty Vaught
Suzanne Vickers
Carol Vickery
Cumi Walsingham
Pam Wasingham
Melanie Walters
Virginia Ware
Kerry Warner
Liz Warren
Trish Warriner
Daphne Watts
Suzanne Way
Pam Weathersby
Kathy Weitekamp
Molly Ann West
Margaret Whitford
Jana Wibberly
Elsie Williams
Marti Willis
Sandra Wilson
Sandy Wing
Kevin Youd
Rachelle Youd

Index

Beverages, Alcoholic

Absent Husband Cocktail, 81
American Beauty Cocktail, 99
American Cocktail, 13
Applejack Martini, 245
Bangkok Punch, 265
Bloody Mary, 55
Blue Dolphin Martini, 245
Blue Moon Sake Cocktail, 266
Buttered Bourbon and
    Cider, 81
Champagne Cups, 15
Chile Vodkatini, 245
Chocolate Martini, 246
Classic Eggnog, 72
Cosmopolitan, 37
Electric Lemonade, 165
Firefly Martini, 246
Florida Citrus Fizz, 213
Floridian Cocktail, 13
French Martini, 246
Fresh Margaritas, 255
Fresh Raspberry Margaritas, 255
Frozen Peacharitas, 187
Fruit Slush, 187
Gingered Sake Spritzers, 266
Gulf Breeze, 231
Hawaiian Lady, 197
Hot Scandinavian Christmas
    Punch, 71
Hurricane Cocktail, 99
Irish Shenanigan, 248
Islander Cocktail, 197
Key Lime Martini, 246
Kir Royale, 13
Lemon Drop Martini, 29
Mango Batidas, 256
Manhattan, 43
Midori Cocktail, 265
Mimosa, 55
Missionary's Downfall, 175
Peach Bellini, 213
Peppermint Hot Chocolate, 64
Pineapple Tequila, 256
Purple Nurple Martini, 247
Raspberry Champagne
    Punch, 143
Red-Headed Mermaid, 198
Red-White-Blue Hawaiian, 175
Sake Martini, 266
Sazerac Cocktail, 103
Sea Horse, 198
Shanghai Cocktail, 266
Ship Ahoy, 198
Springini, 247
St. Charles Cocktail, 103

Strawberry Champagne
    Punch, 71
White Chocolate Kiss
    Martini, 231
White Sangria, 115

Beverages, Nonalcoholic

Apricot Tea, 135
Banana Punch, 165
Cranberry Mulled Cider, 61
Festive Punch, 61
Fresh Raspberry Lemonade, 175
Hot Cocoa for a Crowd, 64
Kiddie Sangria, 115
Minted Orange Lemon Fizz, 223
Orange Dreamsicle Punch, 135
Snowdrift, 58
Sunny Day Punch, 151
Tropical Fruit Sun Tea, 153

Biscuits

Buttermilk Cheddar
    Biscuits, 110
Famous Cheese Biscuits, 194
Fluffy Angel Biscuits, 93
Miniature Cheese
    Biscuits, 159

Blueberry

Blueberry Muffins, 219
Fourth of July Blueberry Pie, 185
Lemon Blueberry Cake with
    White Chocolate
    Frosting, 184

Breads. *See also* Biscuits; Corn
    Bread; French Toast;
    Muffins; Waffles

Anadama Rolls, 147
Bacon and Onion Spiral
    Bread, 66
Cheesy Artichoke Bread, 128
Christmas Stollen, 58
Cranberry Yam Bread, 66
Garlic Bread, 119
Glazed Orange Bread, 59
Herb and Buttermilk
    Breadsticks, 148
Herbed Sesame Twist Bread, 171
Lemon Cranberry Loaf, 59
Muffuletta Bread, 104
Muffuletta Twist, 104
Parmesan Bacon Sticks, 248
Pesto and Pine Nut Bread, 128
Quick Yeast Rolls, 65
Scones, 137

Sweet Bow Tie Rolls, 159
Tuscan French Bread, 179

Broccoli

Broccoli and Olives
    Vinaigrette, 33
Curried Mango Chicken
    Salad, 226
Orzo with Broccoli and
    Olives, 238

Butters

Honey-Nut Butter, 221
Mustard Butter, 65
Orange Butter, 221
Orange Zest Butter, 147
Strawberry Butter, 221

Cakes

Chocolate Doberge Cake, 111
Coconut Layer Cake, 48
Coconut Macadamia Pound
    Cake, 209
Fresh Apple Cake, 96
Frosted Red Velvet Cake, 75
Fudge Yule Log, 74
Glazed Key Lime Cake, 195
Lemon Blueberry Cake with
    White Chocolate
    Frosting, 184
Milk Chocolate Candy Bar
    Cake, 150
Mocha Bundt Cake, 263
Petits Fours, 138
Pumpkin Pound Cake, 95
Raspberry Pound Cake, 185
Spice Cake, 97
White Chocolate Raspberry
    Cake, 22

Candy

Dainty Rose Macaroons, 139
Easy Pecan Pralines, 113
Key Lime Fudge, 76
Old-Fashioned Divinity, 67
Peppermint and Pecan
    Chocolate Bark, 73
Perfect Peppermint Patties, 73
Pulled Mints, 141
Toffee, 76

Cantaloupe

Cantaloupe Vinaigrette, 118
Chilled Cantaloupe Soup, 227
Luau Shrimp and Fruit
    Salad, 205

Carrots

Balsamic-Glazed Carrots, 47
Carrots with Black Olives
    Provençal, 47
Glazed Julienne of Root
    Vegetables, 91

Cheese. *See also* Cheesecakes,
    Dessert; Cheesecakes, Savory

Artichoke and Smoked Ham
    Strata, 53
Asparagus and Cheese Pie, 155
Cheesy Artichoke Bread, 128
Christmas Torta, 55
Curried Cheese Dip, 249
Garlic Gruyère Mashed
    Potatoes, 46
Green Chile Casserole, 193
Hash Brown Casserole, 214
Layered Shrimp Taco Dip, 257
Mascarpone Ice Cream, 129
Muffuletta Twist, 104
Nutty Pinecones, 82
Salpicon Salad, 204
Spinach Soufflé with Gouda
    Cheese, 21
Stuffed French Toast, 57
Stuffed Pork Tenderloin, 85
Tiramisu Ice Cream, 129
Wine and Cheese
    Omelet, 145

Cheese, Blue-Veined

Asparagus Bleu Cheese Rolls, 14
Bleu Cheese and Bacon
    Puffs, 250
Bleu Cheese and Spiced Pecan
    Terrine, 15
Bleu Cheese Shortbread with
    Walnuts and Chutney, 38
Caesar Salad with Bleu
    Cheese, 42
Flank Steak Sandwiches, 227
Pecan and Stilton Napoleons, 37
Roast Pork Tenderloin with Port
    and Bleu Cheese Sauce, 43
Romaine Salad with
    Grapefruit, 28
Roquefort Fondue, 63
Spinach Salad with Gorgonzola
    Dressing, 18
Timberland Pizza, 126

Cheese, Brie

Baked Brie with Caramelized
    Onions, 72

284

Bay Publications
P.O. Box 743
Panama City, Florida 32402
(850) 785-7870
www.bayfetes.com

Bay Fêtes

Please send _____ copies of *Bay Fêtes* at $34.95 each $ _____

Florida residents add 8% sales tax $ _____

Postage and handling at $3.50 each $ _____

Total $ _____

Name _____

Address _____

City _____ State _____ Zip _____

Telephone _____ Email _____

Method of Payment: [   ] MasterCard   [   ] VISA

[   ] Check payable to Bay Publications

Account Number _____ Expiration Date _____

Cardholder Name _____

Signature _____

Photocopies will be accepted.